The Student's Research Companion

The Student's Research Companion

The Purpose-driven Journey of Scientific Entrepreneurs

Omid Aschari
and
Benjamin Berghaus

OXFORD
UNIVERSITY PRESS

OXFORD
UNIVERSITY PRESS

Great Clarendon Street, Oxford, OX2 6DP,
United Kingdom

Oxford University Press is a department of the University of Oxford.
It furthers the University's objective of excellence in research, scholarship,
and education by publishing worldwide. Oxford is a registered trademark of
Oxford University Press in the UK and in certain other countries.

© Omid Aschari and Benjamin Berghaus 2023

The moral rights of the authors have been asserted

Published in the United States of America by Oxford University Press
198 Madison Avenue, New York, NY 10016, United States of America

British Library Cataloguing in Publication Data
Data available

Library of Congress Control Number: 2022945462

ISBN 978–0–19–285531–2

DOI: 10.1093/oso/9780192855312.001.0001

Printed and bound in the UK by
Clays Ltd, Elcograf S.p.A.

To those who commit to grow into purposeful academic research

and

to those who inspire, encourage, and empower them.

Foreword

I am honoured by the opportunity to write this foreword for this wonderful book by Omid Aschari and Benjamin Berghaus. *The Students' Research Companion: The Purpose-driven Journey of Scientific Entrepreneurs* relies on input from over a dozen top scientific mentors worldwide to analyse how to gain better value from research-focused Bachelor's and Master's theses, which are now the norm in many academic institutions. Such theses can help students develop a scientific mindset they can later apply in their careers, whether they pursue a research-focused profession or not. However, students do not always understand how thesis writing can serve their professional development, and as a result, do not appropriate all value from this long-term and valuable process.

To tackle this challenge, Omid and Benjamin came up with this book project, aiming to help students view their thesis not as the culmination of their scientific career, but rather as an opportunity to understand how the scientific method offers a valuable problem-solving approach when facing future challenges.

I think my personal story helps illustrate the value of this book. As a first-generation university student, I initially saw my Master's thesis as something I had to finish to receive my Master's degree, and I thought I needed a high grade to receive *cum laude* (the highest distinction at my home university) and start my career. During the process, however, I was able to find a topic I was passionate about: the fact that a critical phase in the ownership of any publicly listed firm involves the initial public offering (IPO) of its shares. A well-documented phenomenon in the literature is the underpricing of IPOs—that is, the fact that IPO shares tend to be sold at a price lower than the market price, which is realized once shares are freely traded. Underpricing also results in firms receiving less money for selling securities to the market, which significantly raises their cost of capital. In my Master's thesis, I argued that the quality of legal protections in a country would negatively affect IPO underpricing. I tested my model, using quantitative methods on my own hand-collected dataset of 2,920 IPOs in 21 countries with different institutional and legal frameworks, and found broad support for my predictions. Later I published this work in the *Journal of Banking and Finance* (2010), and this was the start of my academic career.

Up to now, I have supervised more than 150 Bachelor's and Master's theses at different universities in the Netherlands, France, Germany, Switzerland, and the US, and have witnessed first-hand the struggles experienced by many students as they pursue their degrees. I observed that, while many struggle while trying to finish their theses, for others, writing a thesis turns out to be a life-changing experience, while some just finish it to check a box on their path to getting an academic degree.

I will use this book as a guiding tool to instil in my students a passion for the process of developing a thesis. The book sets out to improve the effectiveness of the thesis as a learning tool, enhance the quality of student research, and invigorate graduates' inclination to apply a scientific mindset in their careers. I believe it will be a great asset for me and all those who are mentoring young students before they finish their academic careers. I am confident that this book has the potential to impact society by transforming future leaders' academic journeys. Life is too short to just check a box, and the important problems addressed by our students are too big to be heedlessly tackled.

Marc van Essen

Preface

Writing is discovering. This book is no exception. When we went into this project, we were not yet aware of how much distinctly cultural shape and texture there was to our thinking about useful mindsets to engage your final academic project. Merely conducting the project allowed us to structure our thoughts, nudged us to review the literature, to gather and mull over colleagues' perspectives, to formulate, refine, and revise our perspective on the subject. A perspective that only came to be through preparing a treatment on the matter, synthesizing the trajectories of our colleagues' contributions with what we personally found useful.

The mission of research is to validly, reliably, and objectively help illuminate the answers to a question. Countless methodology courses and intricate guidelines on rigour attest to that mission. There are whole summer schools on research methodology. What remains eerily confined to a lecturer's rhetorical asides, context study seminars, and extracurricular activities is discussion of the purpose of research. Often, we learn and teach minute details about what we do and how we do it, but little energy goes into learning and teaching why we do research. Merely looking at today's academic landscape, you would often be forgiven for thinking that we do research merely to build research careers, build programmes, and foster institutions.

The purpose of research, consequently, moves to the centre of our attention. Why do we teach? Why should anyone learn? Why not just 'play the game' and off you go? Why should we be curious (beyond what matters for the exam)? Even the most engaging and cutting-edge institutions find it hard to explain the answers to that in a way that does not sound disappointingly shallow, inflationary, grandiose, repetitive, voguish, or utterly romantic. Part of the problem is that the question of purpose is often only allotted the smallest share of consideration in order not to take away precious time from discussing topical news, going into detail, or discussing a new methodology. What seems to come more easily, and to promote academic training more convincingly, is the easily presented impact on graduate career advancement and salaries (information that also greatly influences rankings). But, of course, that is not everything: there is always the highlighted commitment to academic excellence, creating the perfect circle of providing the subject with itself as its purpose.

The solution to this seemingly all-encompassing critique is simpler than meets the eye: show, don't tell. The purpose of an academic training is much more immersive, personal, and transformational than what can be explained without sounding like advertising copy. The purpose of an academic training is much more impressively experienced than explained. Any personal experience of the value and purpose of an academic training put to good use brings to life the investment (often at least partially publicly) in a person's development. The final academic project inhabits the crucial plot of educational career real estate: it is our final academic opportunity to enable the next generation to understand how academic research can unfold its specific power and make an important contribution to a rational, progressive, and democratic society.

If we—students and teachers, collaboratively—fail to generate a lasting impression of the potential of academic training as a tool, there will not be much evidence to encourage the future application of what graduates have been taught over many years. If the final opportunity to galvanize academic training fails more often than not, we have already lost our grip on the claim to the fame of academic excellence.

If we—students and teachers, collaboratively—shy away too frequently from identifying and pursuing the challenges that stand between today's society and its better future, academia will not have earned its funding. This means encouraging ourselves to be more normative, more opinionated, more imaginative, and more driven than simply investigating objectively, avoiding mistakes, and eradicating biases. None of this suggests a betrayal of our standards. All of it means we must enable our standards to help lead the discussion of what the future ought to look like, what needs to be done to get there, and how to motivate that change. Academia must find its place not only in explaining the world, but in consciously informing and leading ways towards its own progress. When and where academia fails to raise the societal bar, populists will always be there to lower it.

Academic excellence, in our view, is not won or lost with many millions in grants, third-party funding, or published papers. It is not conferred by governmental administrations or even scientific associations. And it cannot be made real simply by putting the words into a brochure or an institution's vision statement website.

Instead, academic excellence is reached or missed silently in each impressive or unconvincing learning experience. As a learning experience, the final academic project has many critical characteristics: it is among the most demanding, the most independent, and the closest to generating evidence on whether academic training reaches fruition in a student's mind and hands.

With its unique and often overlooked role in providing this academic proof of concept to millions of students around the world, each year, and its particular position as the culmination point of learning and research, we have come to consider reaching a continuously positive learning experience, and the success of the final academic project, as the backbone of academic excellence. The final project is, indeed, an exam—for the students, but possibly even more so for the learning institutions themselves.

Academic excellence should not only be defined by amount of papers published, grants won, or external funding secured—or the degree of external validation an organisation can secure. It should be defined by students' and teachers' ability to co-create meaningful and lasting experiences of research for their graduates - the degree of internal validation the organization can create for itself.

This book is an attempt to popularize and illustrate this perspective, encourage like-minded colleagues to connect and collaborate, and to help educators and their students discover ways toward encouraging and enabling each final academic project to become a convincing experience of academic excellence.

Omid Aschari and Benjamin Berghaus

Contents

CONDUCT

COMPLETE

The authors

Professor Omid Aschari (omid.aschari@unisg.ch) is an Associate Professor of Strategic Management and Managing Director of the Master's in Strategy and International Management (SIM-HSG) at the University of St Gallen since its inception in 2003. Today, SIM-HSG is widely respected for educational excellence, innovation and for generating exceptional value for students, employers, and society at large. It has been ranked number 1 in the world for a record-setting twelfth consecutive year by the *Financial Times* Global Masters in Management Ranking.

Omid is an experienced international executive coach and leadership developer with his own practice. His mission is to help individuals and teams grow, generate meaningful impact for their organizations, and live happy lives. His expertise encompasses leader effectiveness, strategic management and culture transformation. Omid's 25 years of experience include positions as board member, manager, entrepreneur, management consultant, and trainer. His views are frequently picked up by media. In public appearances, he addresses topics of high significance for leaders and organizations. In 2022, he was Visiting Professor at the Chair for Sustainability VIVA Idea Schmidheiny at INCAE Business School, Costa Rica. In 2021, he received the prestigious Mentor Award of the SHSG University of St. Gallen, and he was twice nominated for the CS Award for Best Teaching. In 2007, he was awarded a Master of Arts HSG Honoris Causa by the SIM Alumni Association. He is a member of the Beta Sigma Honor Society and honorary member of the Sigma Squared Society.

Omid studied Business Administration at Johannes Kepler Universität Linz, Austria, and graduated with an MBA from the Peter F. Drucker and Masatoshi Ito Graduate School of Management, California, USA. He received a PhD in the field of organizational learning and systemic transformation from Johannes Kepler Universität Linz, Austria. He holds several professional certifications in the field of training, coaching, and leadership development.

Omid was born in Linz, Austria, into a Bahá'í family. He lives in St Gallen, Switzerland, is married, and the father of three children. He has a culturally diverse background and views himself as a committed world citizen. In addition to sports and music, his interests include philosophy, comparative world faiths, astrophysics, and the arts.

Dr Benjamin Berghaus (HSG) (benjamin@brghs.de) is a scientific entrepreneur at the intersection of research, education, and practice in his field. Since 2018, Benjamin has established himself with a broad portfolio of self- and co-initiated projects geared towards fostering young people at the transition from the academic to the professional phase of their lives.

Benjamin has co-founded and leads the development and analysis of the Career Profiler project. This project enables 25 Swiss universities to better counsel their students on suitable career paths, and to generate insight into the prevailing career-related attitudes and goals of students. He is in the process of founding Research Stride, a digital contextual offer to this book which strengthens students' self-leadership skills, makes exchange among students and supervisors more efficient, and enables universities to generate transparency over the countless ongoing projects and other ways in which each institution contributes to its constituencies. Benjamin is a former core faculty member of the Master's in Strategy and International Management (SIM-HSG) at the University of St Gallen. He teaches regularly at the MBA programme at the University of St Gallen, and bases his practice on international teaching experiences with leading schools such as ESMT Berlin, EM Lyon, Hanken SSE, Rotterdam School of Management, as well as his formal university teaching qualification from the University of St. Gallen.

Benjamin received his PhD from the University of St. Gallen for his research on prestigious employer preference among jobseekers, and was awarded his master's degree by the University of Hildesheim, Germany, for his research on entry-level vocabulary modules in multilingual information retrieval systems. During his PhD programme, he initiated and co-founded a Competence Center on Luxury Management which he led for five years. He is an established researcher, teacher, and speaker on the subject of managing prestigious brands. Before his PhD, he worked as a manager in the German automotive industry.

Benjamin was born in Frankfurt am Main, Germany. Today, he lives with his wife in Munich, Germany. An information scientist by original training, marketeer by career fortune, management researcher and educator by stroke of luck, and academic mentor and scientific entrepreneur by conviction, Benjamin pursues his career as an exploration rather than being guided by a strict itinerary. He is a tech nerd, loves to bake his bread, and cherishes long walks and talks with those dear to him.

INTRODUCTION

This book can help you reflect upon, think differently about, and make more of your final academic project. Here, we have framed your final academic project as a type of intellectual journey. This perspective suggests that this book to be a sort of printed travel companion. This introduction will help you navigate the book and use it in a way that generates most benefit to you. Let everything you find in this book be a starting point for your own critical reflections, your own ideas, and your way to enjoy your journey.

Our motivation

Most academic programmes require student-led, more or less research-oriented projects as a demonstration of academic proficiency. Sandwiched between demanding coursework and the promised land of employment, many students experience their final project as a burdensome final chore on their academic bucket list. From this perspective, in many cases the final project merely extends the transactional learning experience of a tertiary education. Consequently, a sizeable share of students do not experience their final projects (in particular, more research-oriented projects) as a particularly purposeful or worthwhile, let alone enjoyable, learning opportunity. Each year, roughly 50 million of the best-educated minds around the world[1] spend the final several months of their academic programme on a mandated project that appears to many to be less than it could be.

The idea behind this book and all related activities is to help unlock some of the vast potential that we currently appear to lose. The overarching goal of our initiative is to foster students' adoption of a positive attitude, useful mindsets, and confidence about their own academic proficiency. Considering the range of current and emerging future societal, political, technological, and environmental challenges, we need those best educated to be not only well-versed in their scientific capacities but also motivated to apply them. We depend on our alumni to build on their acquired capabilities to help solve these challenges when they advance into positions of responsibility. Given our students' talent and education, many of them will reach positions where this inclination will make a difference.

Consequently, we do not want a student's thesis, dissertation, or keystone project to be their final academic project. We need it to be the first of many future well-designed solutions to critical problems. This book project is the centrepiece of our initiative.

Our three objectives are to help increase the effectiveness of the final academic project as a learning tool, to strengthen the quality of student research,

---

[1] Estimate based on latest figures (2013–15: 44.2 million tertiary graduates in 142 listed countries worldwide) by UNdata, 'Graduates from tertiary education: both sexes', at https://bit.ly/3s7Apt3, checked Nov 2022.

The Student's Research Companion. Omid Aschari and Benjamin Berghaus, Oxford University Press.
© Omid Aschari and Benjamin Berghaus (2023). DOI: 10.1093/oso/9780192855312.003.0001

and to fortify the inclination of alumni to apply their scientific mindset when they advance into responsible positions. The strategy for reaching these objectives revolves around illustrating a final academic project's full scope of potential purpose, and explaining how students can design their project to reach this goal and thus draw meaning and motivation from it.

Our key proposal is to reconsider the final academic project from its perception as an obligatory examination and rather rediscover it as a multifaceted opportunity for students, academics, and the institutions in which they collaborate. It is not a toll to be paid in order to graduate, but rather an opportunity to invest in a future trajectory. Above all else, we look for ways to remap the final academic project, from treating it as a mere administrative transaction to recognizing it for what it can be: an educational transformation.

It may seem strangely fixated that we draw so much inspiration from one specific academic experience, and indeed the last such experience that most students may go through. However, if there ever was a make-or-break situation designed into an educational programme, then this is it: equipped with nothing but their still freshly acquired skills, a sense of pursuit, and the motivation to make a difference, the examination in truth focuses not on our students, but on us who taught them, on what we taught them, and on the attitudes we bestowed on them. This is where academy ultimately makes or breaks it. This is where we win, this is where we lose. We are convinced that every day, we can only measure our academic excellence by the number of minds won for those standards we see as central to our way of creating insight: students are central to academia.

This is also the place where a young apprentice counts on a more advanced peers' interest, encouragement, patience, and empowerment. This is where trust in academic peership is built or withers away. The difference between not only relying on the methodologies, standards, and qualities of academia, but also on its people. By logical conclusion, we ought to carefully develop and prepare those who will academically mentor our students not only in the wholesale teaching of lectures, but especially in the individual accompaniment during their most challenging projects. We remain convinced that the younger, more relatable, well-developed peer easily creates more benefits for both parties than the less balanced and more dependency-inducing lopsidedness of involving the most experienced but also far removed educators in mentoring processes. Similar in priority is the revision of the professionalization of young academic working positions and developmental support.

Whether this assessment turns out favourably or unfavourably depends, to a large degree, on the attitudinal structure that students adopt from their learning environments. If that structure has been cultivated to grow toward curiosity, the desire to make a contribution, and self-leadership skills that enable a sustainable and responsible conduct under much stress, there will be little standing in between our graduates and solving societal challenges with the means of academic cultivation. If that structure has been cultivated to grow toward jobs and transactional rewards, then all we do is to produce employees. Universities of tomorrow cannot be thoroughly content with that role of a career placeholder and certification institution. University leadership teams play a crucial role in picking those difficult battles that enable their organisations to grow as much as we demand from our students and ourselves.

In this highly complex and risky instance of challenge, everything comes together that may convey and fortify the perception of a unique value and societal place of academia in a young mind—or might call just that into question by suggesting academic work to be indistinguishable of complicated busywork.

Let us now look at this nucleus of the academic experience, let us find out how we can make the final academic project become the starting point of tomorrow's university.

About this book

This book resembles a broad collection of invitations to review your own position, discuss, and add your own thoughts on some of the key experiences and challenges you might encounter when working on your final academic project or mentoring those who are working on their own.

We intend to provide you with ample opportunity to strike up a conversation about the role of an academic education, the critical incident of the final academic project, and how to turn today's often lacklustre experience of student research into an experience that provides evidence that all those years invested in training and self-development yield reliable, effective results. The critical evidence it takes to redeem the investment into young minds by seeing them trust what they learned to be actionable solution strategies and not just examination contents.

The nature and tone of this book is close to those contributions we as academic mentors might make in a discussion with our students or other supervisors during one of the many challenges encountered when conducting a research project. We source our thoughts from our own experiences and contextualize them with those of our contributors.

There is one distinct assumption that encouraged us to adopt this style: researchers and supervisors are, above anything else, people. They are not purely rational agents who seek to implement methodology. When we look around ourselves, we see many academic settings that pride themselves in training and measuring the success of turning people into para-algorithmic agents or memory machines. We do not believe that any tertiary academy should have that goal.

Instead, we understand researchers to be purposefully, entrepreneurially, and responsibly acting people who seek to make a meaningful contribution to an audience and thus help progress come to be. There are people at the heart of our assumption. People who can be lost or won for the particularities of the problem-solving approach involved in academic conduct. People who seek to speak to others in order to make sense of the challenges they face. People who find another person's subjective perspective useful in order to find out how

The Student's Research Companion. Omid Aschari and Benjamin Berghaus, Oxford University Press.
© Omid Aschari and Benjamin Berghaus (2023). DOI: 10.1093/oso/9780192855312.003.0002

they might formulate their own—and not just receive regulations and paper recommendations.

The idea of trying to speak with each other about the academic experience entails addressing topics that otherwise might remain inaccessible. All those responses that emerge from facing and mastering challenging and self-imposed projects, from picking out the guiding stars by which to navigate through the myriad decisions, from fearing to write 'the wrong text', to being overwhelmed by the amount of personal development choice after having graduated from ever more scholastic academic programmes that do their best to limit the amount of choice experienced—and many more. None of these topics are academic in terms of their subject. Instead, they are widespread, personal responses to the academic experience; to us, they resemble the greatest untapped potential in the modern academic landscape. In this light, codes of conduct, ethics boards, and strategy initiatives appear to function as not much more than figleaves. Likewise, campus counselling services provide valuable support but often concern themselves predominantly with providing band-aids to those who hurt themselves by getting caught in the university machine. The academic experience needs addressing—not from the perspective of administration, politics, professors, benefactors, or anyone else but from the perspectives of students. They are, in our eyes, the academy's primary reason for being, no matter where modern political or funding necessities may have shifted them. The university works well if it excels at conveying, and providing evidence for, the usefulness of academic standards and conduct to its students. In other words: the university works well if it makes sense to students. Even though this may read as less than a demanding goal, we find too many graduates wondering whether the university really does make sense to them. While the final academic project is just one sliver of the overall academic experience, it is the most standardized and established shared experience of students, right at the end of their academic careers. It is the perfect place to focus a discussion on how to make this the most convincing, sensible, and purposeful academic experience possible. With some luck, and some time leading the discussion that this book might stir up, we may find discover experiential textures, patterns, and sensations that we might then not only involve in the final academic experience but also increasingly sprinkle throughout.

Thus, this book is intended to be much more of an overture than a final movement. The piece we play—and in which we wholeheartedly encourage you to join in—seeks to collect and curate helpful mindsets for students who are beginning their final academic project—material for students, supervisors, and ourselves to learn, share, and commonly benefit from. The motivation behind this curation is to help students experience a more inspiring involvement with research, to help young academics to discover valuable mindsets to share with their mentees, and to encourage university leadership to rediscover the value of the many hundreds of academic final projects which often do not receive the amount of attention they deserve.

To our two central audiences, students and young academic supervisors, this book can provide the role of a counterpart, a perspective to contemplate but also to sharpen their claws on. This book does not pretend to define or capture the truth on the subject of academic mentoring, but it sets out to help others to find their own truth. Writing the book, we have instead discovered how distinct and imprinted our culture of thinking had become. This distinctness warrants awareness, the need to remain critical, and the need to seek greater diversity in thought. We present our beliefs so that you can have a peer's view on topics you may find difficult (or rather exciting?) to discuss with others.

If you are reading this as a student and you try to make sense of your upcoming or ongoing final academic project, this book is intended to be one of your more easy-to-reach-for companions on your journey. It provides at least two and in many cases several perspectives on fifty common challenges when working through a thesis, dissertation, or research-oriented capstone project. As such, it can serve as a good starting point for you to reflect on the specifics of the individual challenge you face, and on how to discuss and solve your individual questions with friends, colleagues, your supervisor, or outside counsellors.

If you are reading this as a young academic who is trying to settle into your new role as a future research mentor, this book intends to provide you with food for thought when considering how you might go about helping your students succeed. We have not yet heard of universities that provide a systematic training for research mentoring. Strangely, it remains the norm that most junior academics remain apparently unsupported on the path to growing into their research mentoring role. Given that scientific mentoring is a demanding skill to acquire, we believe that lending a helping hand and providing the opportunity to mull over some of the more tricky situations you can find yourself in is not only useful but necessary to help academic mentors to develop. To be frank, one of the reasons we wrote this book, and are working toward complementing it with appropriate tools to grow into a useful initiative, is so that we may become better research mentors ourselves.

What this book is not

This book is not the result of a research project. Instead, it is a reflection on personal experiences, observations, and propositions as well as a curated collection of thoughts from our contributors about the potential of student research and the many ways in which useful mindsets can help or damage the experience. One reason for this approach was our initial review of published research focusing on the academic final project. This review yielded many interesting, highly focused contributions but little broad, integrative reflection, and synthesis about not only individual parts but instead something closer to the comprehensive academic research experience of students. We hypothesized that mature fields like research on higher education would follow the same conventional reward systems as our own: to encourage exploring the details with more and more intricate methodologies than try and foster integration and cross-disciplinary synthesis.

This book does not provide simple answers. Rather, consider its remarks as nudges towards a direction in which your answers lie. We have tried to avoid presenting you with a guide that explains most facets step by step or drafts your options to act so that you merely need to colour them in. The mindsets in this book should be a nudge in a helpful direction to make the most of your final academic project, an encouragement if you feel that our thoughts ring true to you, and a suggestion to reconsider if they do not. The trajectory to try and make your final academic project more than a mere final examination to be checked off might not be useful to everyone—scenarios are imaginable in which you simply cannot afford the luxury—but it tries to illustrate what we believe is a productive way of approaching research as a graduating student.

This is not a theory or methodology book. We do not dive into specific fields. Instead, we try to be as agnostic as possible and are open to broadening our horizon in relation to what research means in a broad variety of academic fields. We do not speak to specific methodologies, since we feel that others have done this extensively. Instead, we are trying to help bridge a divide that seems to grow with the share of young people attending universities as part of their education: as a tertiary academic education is reaching an ever broader demographic and is reaching majority shares in developed countries, there are many more people studying today to continue onto a job outside instead of inside academia. To many, academia is not a destination, but a rite of passage. When academia still was a place to receive training for an academic career destination, future academics saw intrinsic purpose in adopting the teachings of academia—this would be the future basis of their careers. Since there are now plenty of people who are perfectly convinced that they will not work in academia, there is much less intrinsic purpose and implicit attractiveness to an academic culture—an academic culture that, to make matters worse, has morphed from the manufacture of intellect to a training industry. In our view, to make this expensive academic rite of passage effective in contributing to the development of young talent, it seems that there needs to be a better 'human–research interface'. Merely conveying research as an activity that requires a researcher as flawlessly algorithmic as possible does not generate much traction with talents who will not work in academia. We are instead trying to explore the idea of a researcher as a purposefully acting human being who employs research to the best of their abilities to contribute to solving one of the challenges felt in the communities they empathize with. To our minds, this is a more contemporary, complete, and responsible way of thinking about what research is all about.

Chapter structure and features

This book is structured to follow five stages of working on a final academic project: approaching the project, beginning it, being stuck right in the middle of it, completing your project, and continuing afterwards.

Each of the stages is divided into ten mindsets that follow a mixture of 'frequently asked questions' and 'would have been useful to have been considered questions' from experience. These mindsets are laid out in several ways in order to offer you a good chance to catch the idea we are on about, and to be able to object, criticize, see and think of the questions differently. This is our key goal: to have made you think about a subject that seems to be important to you. Our aim is that, after having read one of the mindsets, you have a second (sometimes more) opinion(s) to work with to further your own position. In a way, it is a discussion. Our part in this discussion is usually structured in the following way:

The idea in a nutshell—You need to know where things are headed. That is why each chapter's essence is captured in its leading two-line abstract.

Metaphorically speaking—Doing research is akin to undertaking a journey. In each chapter, we try to convey the idea in terms of a metaphor. Our goal is to present a memorable impression and inspire you to think freely about the subject.

Rough coordinates—It helps to provide some waypoints if you want others to follow a path. Each chapter draws from key ideas that warrant revisiting.

We have turned to the *Oxford English Dictionary* to the most apt definitions. We are grateful to Oxford University Press for permission to reprint definitions from the Oxford English Dictionary.

Train of thought—This segment in each chapter elaborates our perspective on the subject at hand. This is our subjective take, based on the experience we have with the chapter's subject. It provides one plausible way of thinking about the topic.

In essence—These are the three key takeaways from our train of thought …

To reflect—and three questions to ask and reflect upon yourself.

Two travellers' tales—Every traveller has their story. To apply the ideas which have been presented, each chapter includes two scenarios related to the chapter's topic. These are intended to help you consider what might be your best path of action.

Devil's advocate—This segment discusses at least one instance in which our train of thought loses its traction or where even the opposite might be true. This is another segment that encourages you to use your critical thinking reflexes.

How to tackle—There are multiple ways to cross the river, and this would be our suggestion. Most chapters will provide a way of approaching the challenge involved. Reads sensibly to you? Excellent! Needs adjustment? Feel free!

Experienced peers' two cents—After collecting our thoughts, we interviewed a panel of ten friendly academic mentors and put their perspectives next to ours, side by side. We were happy to find a great deal of overlap in terms of topics, but also an interesting diversity in views and ways of phrasing perspectives. We have aggregated the thoughts of our panellists in each chapter. The idea here is to show that there is no one right or wrong way of thinking about each topic; instead, for each researcher there is a multitude of ways to think about challenges and solutions.

Key terms

This book deals with a ubiquitous subject in the academic world—albeit a subject that is interpreted in countless ways across countless disciplines, cultures, schools, institutes, and programmes. Consequently, it seems prudent to define terms as we use them in this book.

Final academic project—The mandatory self-study exam at the end of most bachelor's and master's level programmes and, with some adjustments, doctoral programmes. In more traditional universities of Central Europe, the prevalent form will be a research project that culminates in a thesis or dissertation text. In more applied or thoroughly practice-oriented schools, this may be a capstone project with or without an external organization acting as a topic sponsor, or even an embedded and documented internship. This book is written from experience on mentoring applied research projects that result in a thesis document: inspired by a practical problem but research-based in the nature of its methodology to contribute to a solution. Thoroughly research-oriented work can benefit from many of the mindsets presented in this book. Only thoroughly practice-oriented final academic projects like internships or corporate projects may yield less benefit from considering the insights presented in this book. The mandate to involve oneself with academic methodology and standards fades away under this condition.

Thesis—While we adopted the term 'final academic project' as thoroughly as possible throughout the book, we reverted to speaking of a thesis as the produced text in which the final academic project would be documented. This is the type of document our thoughts and ideas most readily speak to.

Student—In our book, we consider all those who are tasked to conduct their final academic project as students, no matter the previous amount of academic training. Students may be undergraduates, postgraduates, or doctoral candidates. We encountered an interesting sentiment in some of our discussions that extends this definition: some of our most experienced contributors wondered about how much difference there truly was between professors and students. Both operate under the same assumptions when they seek to learn more about a subject, set up their projects, or face challenges. Thus, while the narrower definition seems more intuitive, the broader definition might include all those who seek to learn—and it would be a pity to exclude those with more experience from that definition. We decided against speaking of 'scholars', since we felt there was too much unintended connotation in that term for it not to mislead and distract from our thoughts.

Scientific entrepreneur—In our reflections on the subject and on what we would consider as a useful mental model to draw inspiration from when designing and conducting a research project, we developed the idea of exploring the role of an entrepreneur who invests their time and effort into producing a contribution to help an audience solve their challenges. Since we do not intend to suggest commercial profitability as the central aim of this person, we steered our thinking instead towards the profile of a social entrepreneur who uses academic aptitude to create a contribution predominantly for the purpose of helping to solve a challenge while keeping resources in mind mostly as a means of sustaining their intended activities. This led us to our conceptual understanding of a scientific entrepreneur. This profile is not yet fully fleshed out, but we believe that it provides an interesting foundation on which to explore and explain to young academics how academic work can be contribution-centric, audience-focused, and thus steered towards academic work as a more purposeful experience—our overarching goal. We look forward to exploring this idea further and further, encouraging others to point out the potentials and pitfalls of this early prototypical development.

Supervisor—The reality of final academic projects suggest that most institutions agree to call those academics accompanying students on their final academic project 'supervisors'. We are not happy with that term, since a useful interpretation of the role encompasses much more than the administrative, hierarchical, almost corporate, and rather disempowering sense of supervision. We have decided to stick with the term, however, to remain comprehensible in our development and to illustrate a path forward.

Academic mentor—Throughout the book you will come across the term 'academic mentor' every once in a while. In our minds, this term fits much more with our understanding of a useful role to adopt when accompanying students on their projects. However, our observations suggest a need to provide thoughts on how to work with today's predominant and limited model of the supervisor and its many rather pragmatic interpretations.

Beyond the book

While we are proud and excited to find our ideas published in such an admirable format, and with such an esteemed company of contributors and a stellar publishing partner, we have always felt that what we are trying to craft goes beyond a book and instead attempts to build a stage on which a discussion on the future of the final academic project can take place. Our goal is to try and inspire an initiative of rediscovery, change, and progress in critical learning experiences such as the final academic project.

This book and its content is not set in stone—it is subject to revision, extension, and continuous improvement. In particular, this first edition merely sets the tone and takes inventory of the experiences and beliefs we hold at the outset of the project.

We welcome criticism, feedback, suggestions, and ideas for developing the material further or extending it purposefully.

While the book will remain semi-static in nature even with regular revisions and editions, we extend our thoughts presented in the book digitally on the web at www.studentsresearchcompanion.org. Here, we provide an opportunity to comment on mindsets, ask questions, propose ideas, and use contextual digital offers.

The contributors

We have been fortunate to have spoken to and learned from these academic mentors from around the world.

Samer Atallah

We encountered Samer through his work at The American University in Cairo (AUC), a CEMS partner university. Samer works as Associate Professor and Associate Dean for Graduate Studies and Research at the AUC, as well as being a non-resident scholar at the Middle East Institute. Previously, he worked as Assistant Professor at AUC. He obtained his PhD at McGill University.

Samer illustrates a clear link between the positioning of a university and the consequential role of academic thesis writing in the system of value generation. In terms of a transforming academic landscape, he observes the role of academic theses chiefly in the context of those programmes that have higher shares of graduates that go on to work in research. Particularly memorable impressions from our discussion include the quality of curiosity necessary to do research, the function of curiosity as the central motivator and enabler in overcoming challenges, and his perspective on the role of supervisors.

Kim Beasy

We are fortunate to have become aware of Kim's work and won her support for this book project through her co-authorship of the insightful and thought-provoking article 'Drowning in the Shallows: An Australian study of the PhD Experience of Wellbeing'.[1] Today, Kim works as a Research Fellow at Swinburne University of Technology. Previously, she was Lecturer in Pedagogy and the Curriculum, focusing on equity and diversity, at the

---

[1] Beasy, K., Emery, S., & Crawford, J. (2021). Drowning in the shallows: An Australian study of the PhD experience of wellbeing. Teaching in Higher Education, 26(4), 602–618.

The Student's Research Companion. Omid Aschari and Benjamin Berghaus, Oxford University Press.
© Omid Aschari and Benjamin Berghaus (2023). DOI: 10.1093/oso/9780192855312.003.0003

University of Tasmania, where she was also awarded her PhD and worked as a Sustainability (Project) Officer and Unit Coordinator.

While discussing students' experience of the final academic project, and useful mindsets for it, Kim reminded us of a perspective of critical importance: any student's experience of their project hinges to a large degree on the performance and appropriateness of the academic and administrative system they are subjected to. Any useful shared mindset cannot and should not hide the fact that the greatest potential for improvement is in revising and optimizing this final academic project system. While a mindset can help individual students cope with being subjected to a system in need of optimization, it cannot and should not help systematically offload onto students the duty to cope with a non-optimal system. Particularly striking and memorable ideas include transferring insight from social care research into the academic domain by rethinking and systematically increasing the number of social and academic supports during the final project. Other thoughts circled around the observations of and solutions to time-poverty among students and supervisors alike.

Gundula Bosch

We are fortunate to have won Gundula's cooperation after we learned of her work as Director of the R3 Center for Innovation in Science Education (R3ISE) at Johns Hopkins Bloomberg School of Public Health. The R3ISE centre produces doctoral, master's, and certificate programmes aiming to bring more critical thinking, interdisciplinary collaboration, and practical ethics considerations into graduate student training in biomedicine, health, engineering, and technology. The R3ISE team strives to educate broadly interested scientists who are not only technically proficient but particularly open-minded, reflective, creative, and skilled in scientific reasoning, problem-solving, and innovative research design.

Several distinct themes became salient in our discussion with Gundula: we spoke the role of curiosity in applying academic skills, and of how transferring conceptual insights across topical borders seemed critical in fortifying an open and engaging academic mind. We discussed the role of imagination in unlocking and comprehending why things are the way they are. How much and what kind of a perspective shift does it take to finally understand the most challenging questions and start working towards an answer? Finally, we explored the interconnection between rigour, reproducibility, and responsibility.

Matthew Farmer

We became aware of Matt and his work through his co-authorship of the critically important and valuable article 'Marketing Ideas: How to Write Research Articles that Readers Understand and Cite'.[2] Matt completed his PhD at the University of Arizona in 2021, and begins teaching as an Assistant Professor at Utah Valley University in autumn 2022. His previous academic steps include his BA at Lambuth University and his MBA at University of Memphis.

Matt provided valuable and encouraging perspectives on students' ability to make an impact with their final academic project work. This goal does not require the work to become widely known and highly regarded, but it may already be reached if it has helped the student to reach a new perspective, a new insight into the matter being investigated. Helping students reach their project goals means to him, as a supervisor, to leave an impression on those students. Matt shared many helpful and practical approaches to getting started in academic writing, and to thinking usefully about the individual steps on the common ladder of academic writing.

Steven Floyd

We are fortunate to know Steve as one of our colleagues at the University of St Gallen, where he, until recently,acted as permanent Guest Professor. Steve was part of the core faculty of the SIM programme in St Gallen, where he also supervised final academic projects. Omid vividly remembers his refined qualities as an exceptional scholar and mentor to young researchers. In his central role, he was Emeritus Professor of Innovation and Entrepreneurship at the University of Massachusetts at Amherst. His academic writing seminar in 2014 made a significant impact on Benjamin Berghaus, who was attending as a PhD student at the time. Steve's seminar thus certainly contributed to the early roots of this book through his role-modelling as one of the many experienced and inspiring peers you may be fortunate to meet and to learn from at university.

In our discussions, Steve raised a key idea that immediately resonated with many impressions we captured in our book, but which we found it hard to find a term for: the paradoxes of good conduct in research. Encouraged by this congruence, we chose to frame the chapter epilogues along the idea of navigating these paradoxes. Beyond paradoxes, Steve reminded us of the

---

[2] Warren, N. L., Farmer, M., Gu, T., & Warren, C. (2021). Marketing ideas: How to write research articles that readers understand and cite. Journal of Marketing, 85(5), 42–57.

nature of the challenge embodied in working on your research project, the importance and characteristics of the supervisee–supervisor relationship, and the necessity of integrating both theoretical and practical thought.

With great sadness, we have learned of Steve's passing just a few months before the release of this book. He has achieved what many aspire to: to be thoroughly missed as an exceptional teacher, a generous colleague, a thoughtful and kind person whose company and guidance one sought and cherished.

Urs Jäger

We are fortunate to know Urs as Chair for Sustainability VIVA Idea Schmidheiny and as Associate Professor at INCAE Business School. His work focuses on the area of general management and strategic change in emerging countries, particularly social inclusion in formal and informal markets, and creating concepts based on process philosophy, to generate a sustainable economic and social impact. He also serves as Executive Director of the organization VIVA Idea, where he generates new teaching methods to create and disseminate knowledge about collective impact strategies. Previously, he was part of the core faculty of the SIM programme in St Gallen, where he also supervises final academic projects to this day.

During our conversations on the subject, Urs shared with us several particularly noteworthy observations from his experience as a supervisor. Central among those, we found the notion of students' intellectual attitudes particularly valuable for supervisors when considering candidates. This attentiveness to students' conceptions of science's key terms is just one of many characteristics, including skills, capacity, adaptiveness, energy, and many more, that can help careful supervisors to decide whether and how to best support students seeking research mentorship.

Timo Korkeamäki

We were fortunate to gain Timo's cooperation and insight through the link in the CEMS university network between Aalto University and the University of St Gallen. Timo is the Dean of the School of Business at Aalto. Before joining Aalto, he was Professor of Finance and head of the Department of Finance and Economics at Hanken School of Economics in Helsinki.

Through our exchanges on the subject, Timo set out a wonderfully open and continuously growing perspective on the functions and objectives of academia. Part of our discussions circulated around whether universities should place greater emphasis on teaching the 'how' or the 'why' of phenomena. Beyond these broader ideas, he also shared very specific recommendations, such as his thoughts on the value of a focused research question or on the necessity sometimes to leave a question be for a few days. Some of his most memorable thoughts relate to the seminar he found most valuable while being a PhD student, and which type of help he is still most grateful for to his PhD supervisor.

Günter Müller-Stewens

Günter's work as a scientific mentor is among the original inspirations for this book project. It is our particular pleasure to have captured his thoughts on the matter after having worked with him for many years. He has been a long-term colleague of Omid Aschari and Benjamin Berghaus' secondary PhD supervisor. From 1991 until February 2017, he was a Chair holder and Professor of Strategic Management, and from 1997 until 2016 he was executive director of the Institute of Management and Strategy at the University of St Gallen. From 2005 until 2007, he was Dean of the School of Management. Also, from 2002 until end of 2015 he was co-founder and Academic Director of the Master's in Strategy and International Management (SIM), as well as co-founder and academic director of the Master's in Business Management (MUG) from 2011 until 2016. He is currently working at the University of St Gallen on a freelance basis, and lectures there.

When speaking in the context of this project, Günter shared his conviction about the necessity to keep research within the context of practical problems and their solutions. Through his career, he has gained the impression that the purpose of (at least applied) research is to serve its application and not predominantly itself. He watches the modern academic publication system with considerable doubt about how much it helps research to achieve this goal. Another key perspective he shared relates to the inner spirit of a project and one's self. He suggests trying to identify that spirit, and following where it may lead you.

Madhu Neupane Bastola

We invited Madhu to join our panel of associated academic mentors and the interview series after having been impressed by her work on the positive and negative impact of phrasing feedback in supervisor–student relationships[3]. Madhu is a lecturer at Tribhuvan University in Nepal. She received her Master of Education (TESOL) degree from the University of Sydney, Australia, and her PhD from Hong Kong Polytechnic University, where she is currently working as a Postdoctoral Fellow researching graduate research and supervision.

In our discussions, Madhu shared deeply compassionate and optimistic perspectives on the experience of student researchers and the leverage inherent in a supervisor's role. In her research, she has found evidence for the detrimental and supportive power that a harsh or kind word in feedback can have on student motivations, sense of self-worth, and advancement. One key perspective she shared is that every academic supervisor can choose to look upon their students' work and be either interested or not. Another of her thoughts which made a lasting impression was her reminder that we as supervisors cannot give what we do not have. From her perspective, (we) supervisors need to be continuous learners. Madhu is convinced we can make a difference if we take the responsibility of supervision seriously.

Ansgar Richter

We were fortunate to win Ansgar for the panel of academic mentors through our link in the CEMS university network between Rotterdam School of Management and the University of St Gallen. Ansgar is Dean of Rotterdam School of Management, Erasmus University (RSM), where he is a Professor of Corporate Strategy, Organisation and Governance. His research interests are at the interface of strategy, organization, and governance: dynamic capabilities, organizational design, incentives, ownership and justice in organizations, and the strategy and structure of professional service firms. Ansgar received his PhD from the London School of Economics (LSE). His list of former employers include McKinsey & Company, the EBS Business School, the Liverpool Management School, and the Surrey Business School.

While discussing the experience of the final academic project, Ansgar shared perspectives of encouragement and empowerment with us. One of the many insightful ideas he illustrated was the likeness of students and supervisors—despite all differences, 'both are, in fact, students'. This resonated particularly well with our take on the supervisor as an advanced peer. Ansgar pointed to the opportunities of rediscovering and leveraging

---

[3] Neupane Bastola, M., & Hu, G. (2021). Supervisory feedback across disciplines: does it meet students' expectations?. Assessment & Evaluation in Higher Education, 46(3), 407–423.

the potential of the final project for students, but also to the contribution that universities can make through actively fostering student research output. Many further notable thoughts deal with the value of working with primary data, finding a topic that feels purposeful, and knowing the audience for your project.

Marc van Essen

We are excited to have won Marc as the contributor of this book's foreword. Marc is Associate Dean of International Programs and Partnerships, Department Chair, and Professor for International Business at Darla Moore School of Business. *U.S. News & World Report* has ranked Darla Moore School of Business 1st for its Undergraduate International Business Degree consecutively for 24 years and among the top 3 for its International MBA programme for 33 consecutive years. Marc was awarded his PhD in Management from Rotterdam School of Management. Among several other assignments, he is a former colleague who worked as a professor of entrepreneurship and innovation and taught in the Strategy and International Management programme at the University of St Gallen between 2015 and 2019.

In his foreword to our book, Marc describes a very personal connection with the book's subject: from setting up and succeeding with his own student research project to progressing from the experience; from maturing and growing as a researcher to becoming a mindful and empowering supervisor himself. Reading his text enabled us to see another reality of research: fields may have their 'seminal papers', but (possibly even more importantly) people have them too. Both kinds of seminal papers generate an impulse—one for a whole community of people, the other first and foremost for a single person. While writing the 'seminal paper' for one's field may seem more impressive, writing the 'seminal paper' for one's own significant phase of advancement is the necessary precursor for a community to emerge. Enabling more smart and driven people to achieve their 'seminal paper', to mature their own ideas to fruition in their final academic project, is our common mission.

We are proud to share the thoughts of every one of our colleagues listed above alongside our own perspectives in this first edition of the book. We are convinced that great academic mentoring converges just as much on several great ideas as it is a matter of diversity of thought and the necessity of hearing a range of opinions to form your own.

Our academic contributors were not able to read the main text of this book before it was published. Thus, their contribution merely implies their willingness and ability to help develop student research further. Their contribution does not imply their approval of or support for our or any other view outlined in this book. This project brings together different views for the sake of a more complete understanding of the subject.

We are convinced that improving student's academic experiences benefits from sharing perspectives in a debate about the topic. This debate will make identifying both the convergence points and the necessary range in diversity of opinions palpable. If you would like to join this debate, visit us at www.studentsresearchcompanion.org

APPROACH

Any experienced traveller will likely tell you that your journey begins with preparation. Certainly, undertaking a journey requires a well-packed bag, some sturdy shoes, and above all a reliable map. But beyond anything else, you shall pack a useful state of mind. Because a useful state of mind will enable you to make up for what you did not pack, maybe never owned, but will need to learn on the spot.

Skills and the will to grow

Do not expect to approach your project fully prepared. Rather bring a set of foundational skills and the will to grow yourself through the challenge.

Metaphorically speaking

Research means exploring. As an explorer, you don't embark on a journey that solely takes you places you already know. Being an explorer means that you go where you have not (and maybe no one has) been before. This entails that you will encounter challenges you will not have met or mastered before. The central question is whether you are up to growing to meet the challenge.

On the other hand, any responsible explorer will only undertake excursions that they consider as balanced in risk and return. The sense of an exploration is to return from it to tell the tale. There is no use in setting up explorations that will certainly overburden the explorer, leave them exhausted, and the journey's destination unvisited.

Rough coordinates

Learning—'To acquire knowledge of (a subject) or skill in (an art, etc.) as a result of study, experience, or teaching.'[1]

Growth—'The action, process, or manner of growing; both in material and immaterial senses; vegetative development; increase. The process of causing or assisting to grow; production by cultivation.'

Challenge—'A difficult or demanding task, esp. one seen as a test of one's abilities or character.'

Maturing—'To cause to develop fully (the mind, a faculty, etc.); to perfect the development of (a person) mentally and physically.'

[1] Authors' selection of definitions in the *Oxford English Dictionary* suitable to the chapter's trajectory.

The Student's Research Companion. Omid Aschari and Benjamin Berghaus, Oxford University Press.
© Omid Aschari and Benjamin Berghaus (2023). DOI: 10.1093/oso/9780192855312.003.0004

Train of thought

When you start to consider your final research project, your early premonitions may point to confusion rather than clarity. Among many practical things, you wonder how big of a challenge the project is going to become for you, personally. How much time and effort is this going to take? Are you well-enough equipped with regard to your methodology and subject experience?

Since you are quickly approaching the end of a demanding academic programme spanning many years, you will, at least to some degree, have adopted strategies to balance your workload and be efficient. After all, many of your academic experiences until now will likely have been revolving around a sense of synthetic production of results for exercise or examination purposes. And that is what frequently happens among exercises and examination assignments: your mind discovers the underlying reward logic and optimizes for the game, not the purpose of the game. The name of the game is university and you begin to optimize for that.

For your final academic project, however, our aim is to win you for an alternative strategy: to try to abandon the sense of your project merely being another synthetic demonstration of your abilities. Instead, we encourage you to adopt the sincere, earnest, and sometimes radical idea of committing your time and skill to making a non-synthetic, a purposeful contribution. We want to encourage you to emancipate yourself from the institution that educated you. This is no exercise—we want to you graduate in the holistic sense of the word.

If this sounds like an interesting perspective, chances are that those strategies that served you well during your cross-country run of school and academic programmes might not hold true on the last wind-swept plain you have to cross before reaching the finish line. You've heard of thunderstorms and hail on that plateau, you've heard of both sunny victory strides from some colleagues and arduous limping from others. The only insight that appears constant across all others' tales is that everyone seems to fare slightly differently.

When you see the research project that will conclude your academic programme on the horizon, much of your performance and much of the benefit you generate depends on the state of mind with which you approach the project. Above all possible alternatives, we would like to encourage you to approach, design, and engage the project with one clear conviction: research is an exercise in purposeful thinking. The degree to which you trust yourself to think your way out of a challenge will determine whether you will experience the project positively or negatively. Completing your final academic project is not about being tested for knowledge. It is not an intelligence test. It is also not a test of your determination, general creativity, or specific writing skills. It is all of the above, and even more. While that may sound stressful, this mindset holds the keys to mastering the challenge:

It is unlikely that you will bring all capabilities to the project in advance. Rather, the point of a final academic project is to bring with yourself a good share of the requirements for successful completion, and think, learn, and build those capabilities you did not have before. If a final project was merely an examination of your previously held capabilities, you'd be short-handed in the most important learning opportunity your programme may have to offer: the experience of growing into your goals.

Certainly, working on your own implies that you bring necessary requirements to the project. But if you plan to work on a reasonably challenging project, you will need to be able to build some requirements while on the project. You will need to be able to learn and grow yourself out of the challenge and towards the ability of creating a solution. This will be the basis for that particular sense of achievement on graduation day: the lasting impression that you have never thought so hard, learned so much, and matured your mind so noticeably as you did during this project. This is a particularly impressive sense of accomplishment, beyond any grade or other laurels. If you are free to make this choice, consider aiming for this sensation.

The most important implication of this perspective is to try and shift your mind away from any form of 'merely playing the game well' that you may have adopted during your studies, and towards putting your capabilities to sustainable, constructive, and impact-oriented use. Until now, many parts of your programme were exercises mandated by your programme. Now, it is time to consciously change course and find that heading which will lead you to an interesting and purposeful place after university—the place where challenges are not exercises to attain grades, but factual hurdles in the way of progress. Your research project does not have to be the final piece of busy work you ought to deflect or manage away as well as possible; you have it in your hands to make it that much more.

Rather, consider your project to be a unique opportunity to create a meaningful positioning on a topic that you either already enjoy or can become friends with. Above anything else, do not fear that you might come ill-prepared. Rest assured that you will. Everybody does. You do research to contribute and to grow. If you go through your final academic project without learning a thing, you may have missed a considerable part of the benefit your academic programme can provide you with: not only enabling you to think for yourself, but providing you with evidence that what you have learned comes to fruition in your own hands.

Adjust your expectations of what your final academic project can represent for you. Try not to discard it as that final chore. Rather, consider it an opportunity to illustrate your proficiency, (more or less) supported by a research mentor provided to you by your university. You need not fear too much that your proficiency will be not good enough if you respect some fundamental skills of the trade, such as demonstrating some insight into the field you chose to contribute to, citing appropriately, and using a spell-checker. None of these fundamental skills are mysterious or secret—you will have met all of them during your studies in one form or another.

Rest assured that most mediocre or even weak work in research is not caused by simplicity or straightforwardness, but rather by being overwhelmed by self-inflicted complexity. The most elegant and robust work is often impressive because of its simplicity and resulting clarity. However, one of the many paradoxes of research is that most people need ample knowhow to arrive at a beautifully straightforward project, and that unmitigated complexity commonly is a sign of lack of experience. You will succeed if you realize the potential of the opportunity of a final academic project, and approach it knowing that you will have to think your way through this one.

In essence

- Conceptualize your project as a learning experience and not just an examination of your capabilities.
- Be prepared not to know everything in advance, but instead to think yourself out of inevitable challenges.
- Think and act beyond generating a grade and a certificate with your final academic project—make your months with the project matter.

To reflect

- What do you bring to the thesis?
- What do you want your final academic project to bring to you?
- What do you want to contribute through your work?

Two travellers' tales

Max sees his BA thesis as an opportunity to demonstrate what he has learned. He picks a topic he knows, methodologies he feels comfortable with. He performs well, does not learn much from the experience, but manages to reach a good grade. That is his return. He has used six months to demonstrate what he can do, based on what he already knew.

Jenny sees her BA thesis as an opportunity to challenge herself, within reason. She picks a topic interesting but still somewhat new to her, and realizes that she will have to invest in mastering the methodologies best suited for the field. She experiences a greater struggle than Max, learns more during her thesis, and manages to reach a good grade. She has used six months not only to demonstrate to others what she is capable of, but also to teach herself and to go beyond her original capabilities, and has worked on something that mattered to her and others. Jenny has gone beyond her status quo and stretched for personal growth—and that is what she has got.

Devil's advocate

There is no way around it: the final academic project is an examination mandated by your university to test your research aptitude. Since this is the externally mandated role of a thesis, there is no changing this most fundamental role. However, many people are not particularly keen on merely jumping through an examination hoop. This mindset presents a purposeful way of interpreting the final academic project in a way that may yield more return than just a grade.

Especially for those who try to make their final academic project a particularly worthwhile project, it is important to balance their enthusiasm with the ability to properly scale the importance of their project within their lives. It is essential to remember, 'it's just a thesis', 'it's just another project', and to train to consciously and appropriately ascribe the importance of this one project in the context of all the other things that demand your attention. Nothing is won by enthusiasm that overloads your capabilities. Keep in mind that the greatest elegance is in rather simple projects and in ideas beautifully and robustly implemented.

Try to keep this thought in your first aid kit for the more critical phases of your project. Until then, why not try to design a project that has higher potential than merely granting you the right to own your degree? When approaching the project, try to see the opportunity for what it can be worth. 'Reality'—insurmountable limitations encountered along the way which will cut back on your ideal outcome—will set in sooner or later, anyway. If your start with already strictly limited ambition, you risk ending up with a result that provides you with too little opportunity to grow. Instead, you set yourself up for only marginal potential to get rewarded for your months of work with a great sense of accomplishment.

How to tackle

To successfully complete a thesis, you need to contribute two qualities: first, skill, and second, the will to grow. You can operate on 100% skill and no intent to grow, but this will cut you short on the return on your invested time because you will not have given yourself much opportunity to grow.

Consequently, think about where you want to grow and how much growth you are willing to invest into the project (remember that growth requires effort and risk).

For your final academic project to come together, you need subject insight as well as skills in positioning your topic, data acquisition and analysis, synthesis, and writing. Consider in which areas you see the need or your personal interest to grow.

Balance your skill and growth portfolio—don't select a project that will overburden you with too much requirement for growth. A project that allows for some growth might consciously plan growing into one or two skills you do not have developed at the necessary level yet. A very demanding project in terms of growth might ask of you to grow in three or four skills in which you feel the need or wish to grow. Consider illustration 1 to plan your balance of contributions and growth areas.

Experienced peers' two cents

'Thesis writing is developing a way of thinking about the world, of focusing on a particular question, of identifying relevant problems, building basic knowledge around that problem, conceptualizing that knowledge base, trying to push that knowledge further by getting new data or theorizing. The way the process rolls and into a thesis should reflect the way of thinking. This way of thinking can be applied throughout your career.' (Steven Floyd)

'Most important is to have the curiosity of a researcher. That is critical. If the learner does not have the curiosity and the eagerness to continue with every

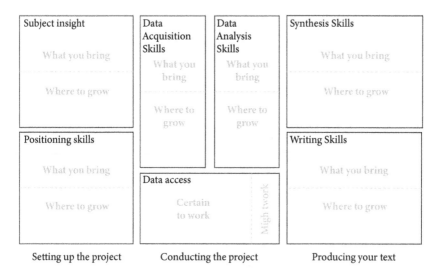

Illustration 1: Balance what you bring and where you want to grow. Careful of data access!

single challenge, then they are just "checking a box" when completing their thesis. Those who really have the curiosity of a researcher tend to overcome the challenges they meet. The best students that I have are always the ones that don't come back to me. They tell me: I faced the problem, I looked it up and this is my suggested solution. That is a signal to me of a researcher/a scholar that will go far.' (Samer Atallah)

'A good way to go is to answer: what makes me curious? What we always try to do, when we collaborate with organizations, is to discover something that is surprising us. Suddenly, you have the feeling: bingo! That's something I have never noticed before and that I would like to generate a better understanding of. Something that makes me curious. I am curious, but my assumption is that other practitioners are also curious to get a better idea of what's happening and what's going on here.' (Günter Müller-Stewens)

'It's a student's chance to think critically about a specific topic, project, or area. It's a chance for them to take everything that they have learned and all the skills that they have acquired and try to channel that into the mark they want to leave. Into what they want to contribute to this conversation. It's them leaving their mark on the world, them getting a chance to essentially participate.' (Matt Farmer)

'So do I have to know everything to succeed? No. You need to know the requirements, but then you need to be willing and eager to grow into a position in which you can answer the question.' (Samer Atallah)

'There are a number of criteria that help to make the motive of a student more transparent, e.g. the attitude a student has concerning what knowledge and thinking mean; how open and radical the person is; how extreme or less extreme and how adaptive or non-adaptive the student is. The student's readiness to invest time, resources, and knowledge into writing such a thesis is decisive. After that comes the student's capacity to learn, his/her receptivity, ability to criticize or to be criticized, and a general open-mindedness when embarking on such a learning process. Then come cognitive abilities—the extent to which the student is able to understand and formulate arguments. Finally, it is the student's flexibility to go way beyond their comfort zone and to test new limits (whether these be the limits in a field study in the slums or limits concerning data usage and/or processing).' (Urs Jäger)

'The most useful mindset to bring appears to be a growth mindset. I also like to call that having a clear motive or motivation—your motivation for doing the research. The way you understand the purpose of writing the thesis: "Why are you doing that?" The most important mindset for succeeding in a thesis project is to consider it as a learning opportunity. It is not just a component in graduation. There is a secondary purpose: it's a great learning opportunity! In the end, working on your thesis is the best opportunity for receiving one-on-one mentoring—a mode of teaching and learning that universities do not offer in most other situations. If you have a learning motive, it encourages you to invest time and effort without getting too tired. If you do not identify with the project, the outcome will not be good. If you know why you are doing it, if you take it as a learning opportunity, thus learning to make informed decisions, that will be a lifelong skill adopted.' (Madhu Neupane Bastola)

Relevance follows audience

Relevance is the life-blood of your project. It entails that you not only can explain that your topic is important, but also to whom and why.

Metaphorically speaking

Research means purposefully exploring an intriguing idea. But intriguing to whom? Certainly, intriguing to you—but only to you? If you are the only one interested in reaching your destination, your path might become pretty long and lonely. In simple terms, no one would care much about what you might find.

Instead, consider first identifying an audience that you would like to contribute to. You might share their values, be able to get behind their mission, or simply deem their objectives worthy of your support. What are their questions? What challenges are they trying to overcome? Once you know your audience, it becomes easier to identify questions that are relevant independently of your individual preference. But there is more about relevance than simply checking a box—it can be a source of energy for you to keep going. When in doubt whether your motivation is strong enough for the big journey, consider borrowing some motivation from those who would love to see you succeed.

Rough coordinates

Interest—'To affect with a feeling of concern; to stimulate to sympathetic feeling; to excite the curiosity or attention of. / To cause (any one) to take a personal interest, share, or part in (a scheme, business, etc.); to induce to participate in; to engage in. reflexive. To take active part in.'

Relevance—'Connection with the subject or point at issue; relation to the matter in hand.'

Audience—'The action of hearing or listening; attention to what is spoken; (also) the opportunity to be heard, or an instance of this; (a) hearing.'

The Student's Research Companion. Omid Aschari and Benjamin Berghaus, Oxford University Press.
© Omid Aschari and Benjamin Berghaus (2023). DOI: 10.1093/oso/9780192855312.003.0005

Associate—'To join (persons, or one person with [*to* archaic] another), in [*to* obsolete] common purpose, action, or condition; to link together, unite, combine, ally, confederate.'

Train of thought

Approaching your final academic project is almost always equivalent to finding a topic to work on. There is a widely held belief that you can only work on a topic that you personally care for, a topic you can stand behind. While the sentiment is understandable, it is one of the great myths of student research. Indeed, this has the potential to be the beginning of many rather depressing moments.

The assumption can be misleadingly because it is thoroughly egocentric. The consequence of only or predominantly taking into consideration what you care about will likely lead you sooner or later to feel that no one really cares about what you research besides yourself—but you risk also being painfully correct in your assessment, too. An alternative path to a motivating research project, consequently, is not to jump down the beautiful waterfalls of egocentricity but rather explore a path down the side of the cliff that others will appreciate your finding and sharing insight on.

Consider your research project as an imaginary friend. A friend that grows stronger and healthier and funnier and more content, the more people care for her. Your friend will be a source of good spirits, encouragement, motivation, and pride if they know that people are interested, if your audience loves to learn more, if experts stay after a presentation because they want to be introduced to her by you. Conversely, consider your research project a friend that grows weaker and weaker, more pessimistic, and agitated the less others care for her. A research topic without any resonance can be a dismal affair to anyone who is not the most enduring, resourceful, and independent soul.

Consider the degree to which you will likely identify yourself with your project. This is going to be the focus of your personal and professional work for several months. If you are at least a somewhat empathetic person, your will likely experience personal identification with your research project. You will be happy if it runs well, you will be sad if it does not, and you might panic when you get stuck for too long. Only very few have such robust mental bulkheads that their personal emotional balance remains untouched by any dark clouds over their research project. In these cases, when for brief moments you cannot really explain why you work on what you work on, it is an enormous relief to borrow the interest of your audience as a stand-in for your own motivation. A seemingly detached and irrelevant project (and most projects feel like that from time to time) is much easier to walk away from than an audience that you planned to contribute to.

There is a pragmatic solution to this issue. Before considering your own preferences, allow your topic choice to be driven by the preferences of an audience that you would like to associate yourself with in future. This implies two consequences. First, you need to build empathy with your academic or practice audience, and identify those challenges and tasks that truly mean something to many in this audience. Be reasonably certain that you can stand behind the reasons why these people find interest in the subject. Here, it is great to listen to your inner voice: you might be driven to help people who are motivated to do things responsibly, performance-minded, progressively, internationally or any other way—that is your choice. Try to find the audience that tends to speak the same emotional language as yourself.

Second, make sure that you understand the challenge that your audience is trying to meet. This includes the mechanics of the challenge, the motives behind the wish to solve the question, and the tools available or realistically imaginable to help solve the question. It is incredibly easy to get any (or even many) parts of this incorrect. Speak to your audience and get an understanding of the landscape of challenges they face. Many of these challenges will be too large in scope for you to tackle. A heterogeneous audience will most likely have several challenges in mind. Sometimes, these challenges are interrelated. At other times, these challenges really are (or hinge on) the same thing; they just look different due to inconsistent use of language. Try to identify the key challenges at stake, and address them in an orchestrated effort within your capabilities. Beware the pitfall of trying to cover all issues—focus is key. After some deliberation with your audience, some thinking, and some discussion with your supervisor, you will have shaped a meaningfully founded topic.

While this might read like a wholehearted advertisement for applied research, it is not. Building on identifying an interesting and 'worthy' audience is as helpful for applied research as it is for basic research. The only difference is that for basic research, your audience will predominantly be researchers and not practitioners. The recommendation to align your positioning with the interests and challenges of a known audience remains just as useful.

In essence

- If you choose your topic predominantly according what you like, don't be surprised if you are the only person who likes your project. That is the only person you optimized for.
- Instead, consider who you would like to associate with and which problems these people are faced with. Pick a topic that may help them solve their challenges.
- Draw motivation from the fact that you know other people who are interested in what you research when you feel pressure during the final academic project process.

To reflect

- Which group of people would you like to associate yourself with in future?
- Which problems are these people faced with?
- How would a research project be positioned to help your audience solve a challenge?

Two travellers' tales

Julie sees her BA thesis as an opportunity to finally work herself into her favourite topic. She starts with high hopes and finds herself working through the same ups and downs that most junior researchers appear to experience. Every time, she pulls herself up by her bootstraps, and finally hands in her project and makes her next step. She succeeds and completes her thesis.

James sees his BA thesis as an opportunity to identify the current challenges of the field that he would like to contribute to and maybe work at in future. He speaks to a few practitioners and researchers in the field, and finds a handful of currently salient challenges in the field that he is interested in. He starts with high hopes and finds himself working through the same ups and downs that most junior researchers appear to experience. Every time he feels down, he still knows that he is not only completing his thesis but also making his best effort to contribute to a field that he wants to work in. This motivates him to complete and finally hand in his project, in order to make his next step. He succeeds and completes his thesis.

Devil's advocate

There are cases in which a traditional topic or field can benefit from an entirely atypical approach. In this case, you work on a project that is so far ahead of the curve that either no one will spend much time trying to understand what you are aiming to do or some people may even actively work against you, since they see their own solutions threatened. It goes without saying that this is risk and should not be attempted on a hunch but be based on a well-calculated plan. In this case, you may find it difficult to position your project in alignment with an audience.

Even in this case, however, you are aligning your efforts with the challenges of an identifiable group. There might simply be no community of researchers yet trying to find a solution akin to the one you have in mind. In this specific case, headwinds might even indicate you are onto something.

How to tackle

To make the most of your thesis, it is useful to position your project in relation to an audience. For this, you need to first understand the audience, its motives and challenges—and above anything else, the structure of its challenges. Here is where you can look for those missing bits and pieces that can help solve a problem.

In applied sciences, the audience will likely be practitioners but this does not necessarily have to be the case—the audience could be other researchers or, most likely, a mix of both. Conversely, in fundamental sciences, the audience will likely be other academics, but this will not necessarily be the case—the same alternatives apply as above.

This is the place where you have the greatest freedom to personally decide what you want to work on, maybe only limited by the confines of the programme within which you plan to conduct your project. Many of the design decisions you'll be faced with will be determined much more by this choice and its consequences than by your choice of topic.

Coming back to the key idea: externally validated relevance of your project will be a key component to your motivation during the challenging bits of your thesis. Thus, be sure not to place all your bets on the broadly perpetuated 'it's key that you are interested in your subject'—that's often not enough to pull you through rough patches. Try to find a topic that is interesting to an audience that you can define, would like to learn more about, and that you would like to make a contribution to. Consider multiple possible audiences, the reason why they are fascinating to you, their challenges, and your initial ideas to approach their challenges (see illustration 2).

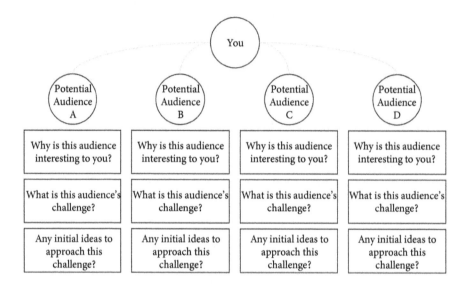

Illustration 2: Consider the perspectives of different audiences to position your project.

Experienced peers' two cents

'I always encourage the students to think about who the audience for the thesis is. I encourage them to (to some extent) work with that audience. That audience may be a company or some kind of organization. The student should seek opportunities to present his/her findings to them. I encourage students to express and explain their thesis to people close to them, e.g. family or friends. They should have an audience beyond themselves and the supervisor.' (Ansgar Richter)

'My most important recommendation is to clearly understand and alignment with the problem you would like to help solve. To know precisely which practical problem you would like to tackle. This means not only to theoretically understand the problem, but to also, in the back of your mind, to develop an idea of how your research can help solve the problem. This means not just the almost ritualistic managerial implications of most published articles, but a deep inner grappling with what you intend to improve by suggesting a redesign. While setting up your research, you can help this by speaking to those who experience the problem first-hand in order to review your set-up for plausibility that this set-up will actually generate something helpful. They can provide feedback and often provide suggestions.

'To avoid allowing your project to drift away from what matters to your audience, it is critical to keep in touch with the subject, the individual case you research. Of course, this can be more challenging if you are working on a quantitative project with large case numbers. But even there you can always pick individual cases to reflect about, consider what your observations can trigger within that particular case, and review whether your ideas to meet the challenge are actually helpful. Time and again, check for plausibility, ideally with your research's target group. Of course, that can be cumbersome. You have to persuade practitioners to review your thoughts with you, and it might be that your project's contribution is not always seen as such. But it is critical to keep an open, careful, and critical mind here.

'Another way of looking at it is this. Your research might be functional and purposeful, not for every one of your originally intended audience, but for only a some of them. The goal is to reach a more differentiated understanding of where your idea manifests itself, what your recommendations might be, where these recommendations might generate most benefit, and which requirements must be met for your insights to yield benefit.

'In both cases, keeping in close contact with those who encounter the problem you aim to help provide a solution for is necessary and valuable.' (Günter Müller-Stewens)

'We need to be connected to practice. We cannot be philosophers who learn about real life while they are taking a walk. It is important to listen to the environment to keep our offerings up to date. At the same time, there is extra value in going through the why-question.' (Timo Korkeamäki)

'Years ago, with some colleagues, we collected a random sample of 120 papers in top journals. We found that only about 20 of those articles actually achieved a significant contribution to both practice and the academy, measured by citations and judgments of practitioners. Something we always debated in St Gallen on the subject of the ultimate accomplishment is whether we should hold the thesis to the standard of whether it is accepted for publication or for conference presentation—whether it is communicated to the narrower scientific or broader scientific and practitioner community.' (Steven Floyd)

Rigour suggests approach

Rigour is the opposite of making things so complicated and occult that you as a researcher cannot handle them any more.

Metaphorically speaking

Research means knowing how you can advance. Advancing means not walking in circles, not exploring a field that others have explored before you, constantly stumbling and falling, or not thinking you have made progress. It means knowing how to operate your mode of progress.

Consequently, if you choose to put some distance between where you were and where you want to get, you will choose the vehicle that you can operate. If you have a pilot's licence, you can fly—if you do not, you might decide to sail your boat. If you cannot operate either, maybe you drive a car, a motorbike, or a bicycle. At the very least, you will likely be able to hike. But you would not expect yourself to land a plane at your destination without any opportunity to have learned how to fly.

Rigorous, reliable, and valid application of methodology, just like modes of travel, are here to help. They can turn you into an impressively efficient traveller. But to ensure you reach your destination, you need to be (or grow into being) able to operate them appropriately—rigorously. This suggests: do what you can.

Rough coordinates

Guideline—'A rule, principle, or general statement which may be regarded as a guide to procedure, policy, interpretation, etc., or (especially) as giving authoritative guidance. In later use often in plural: a set of such rules, statements, etc.'

Capable—'Able to take in with the mind or senses; able to perceive or comprehend.'

The Student's Research Companion. Omid Aschari and Benjamin Berghaus, Oxford University Press.
© Omid Aschari and Benjamin Berghaus (2023). DOI: 10.1093/oso/9780192855312.003.0006

Expertise—'(a) Expert opinion or knowledge, often obtained through the action of submitting a matter to, and its consideration by, experts; an expert's appraisal, valuation, or report. (b) The quality or state of being expert; skill or expertness in a particular branch of study or sport.'

Requirement—'Something called for or demanded; a condition which must be complied with.'

Train of thought

Scientific work thrives on relevance, but differentiates itself through rigour. Indeed, the rigorous application of scientific methodology is the most distinct delineation between the work of practitioners and the work of scientists. Each group adheres to the procedural guidelines they set for themselves. There are advantages (countless detailed and freely available instructions on how to implement most methodologies) and challenges (countless niche and sometimes even slightly mysterious specializations) here, but in the end, rigour is here to help you reach your goal.

Suppose you enter a regatta. You have sailed before, but you are by no means a professional skipper. At the regatta, there are multiple classes you might subscribe to. Will you pick the hardest, most demanding, and most technical class of boats? Surely not—you will pick a class of boats with which you are comfortable and at least somewhat experienced. One in which you can see yourself actually completing the race, not hurting yourself or anyone else. The idea of being a responsible sailor automatically directs you to pick a challenge that suits you. This idea of being a responsible sailor is somewhat related to working rigorously—both are attitudes towards how valid and reliable your process is going to be.

With regard to rigour, the work of a Bachelor, a Master, a PhD candidate, or a professor can be comparable. As long as the bachelor remains within the scope of their abilities and experience, they will be in a position to produce work that can be as rigorous as that of a professor, who will have a wider scope of abilities and experience and whose methodology may be more extensive and complex. Rigorous application of methodology does not necessarily speak to complexity, innovativeness, or any other impressive quality of methodology other than the reliability, validity, and objectivity of its implementation. Of course, this has a lot to do with how much the research of a less experienced scholar can promise to deliver: if you do not have a pilot's licence and only a vague idea of how flying works, don't promise others to fly them around in your plane.

There should not automatically be more or less rigour involved if everyone, from a Bachelor to a professor, attempts to work scientifically. Scopes of contributions are different, promised deliveries will be different, but what is being delivered ideally achieves the same robustness. Every sailor is expected to act responsibly within their own capabilities—from those who sail a skiff to those who command a frigate. Certainly, the complexity of involved methodology will vary with the size, the team involved, the amount of responsibility, and the degree of innovation. However, with regard to the fundamental understanding and general mindset in adhering to scientific process, the aims to generate knowledge and to subject your own work to substantial criticism will need to be compatible.

While this may seem ambitious, it can be a great relief: if a younger scientist is being asked to give rigour priority when designing her project, the resulting design will be much less flamboyant and far-reaching than if she is asked to reach for the methodological stars. Giving priority to rigour means to scale the research objective down to a size that will be actually attainable, and not predominantly designed to sound impressive.

The most concrete outcome of giving rigour the priority in your project will have to do with whether the methodology you employ will reliably provide a valid insight into the solution to your research question. Giving rigour priority means putting the validity and reliability of your contribution above the potential outlandishness of your research question.

In many cases, this implies either asking more humble questions or configuring your methodology better—in many cases, it means both. Rigour does not aim to obfuscate your results by employing particularly convoluted analyses and massaging your data until it fits your story. Rigour goes hand in hand with manageable methodology, diligent implementation, and transparent analysis. When in doubt, opt either for the methodology that you feel familiar with or the one that you would like to acquire. Consider the unwavering requirement of rigour in your project to allow you to pick what you know how to implement, rather than planning what sounds flashy but about which you have no idea, and which might not even fit your project.

In essence

- Rigour is a large part of what qualifies your work as a product of academic processes. It is a decoration or an appendage—for academic research, it should be the starting point.

- The aim of working rigorously is not to demonstrate a particularly high degree of ability to endure a senseless chore. It is to ensure that your work will generate the return you desire—valid, reliable, and objective.
- The often overlooked benefit of working rigorously is that you can finally delegate some design decisions. While your whole project will seem to you like an endless chain of design decisions, you do not have to design your methodology from the ground up. Here, you are invited to follow others and adopt their tools. This is the central component of the idea behind the saying that research means 'standing on the shoulders of giants'.

To reflect

- What is the methodology that is most suited to help solve my research question? Do I feel comfortable in applying this methodology?
- If you don't feel comfortable: which quality of results can you generate rigorously given your methodological skill set, and how would you need to adjust your research question in order not to over-promise? Is this still interesting enough?
- If it does not seem interesting enough: do you need to reconsider your audience/the issue you would like to help solve?

Two travellers' tales

Mike sees the methodology involved in his thesis as the ultimate antagonist in his thesis: 'I simply don't have enough experience and insight into all of these semi-occult research methods.' He tries to pick the topic and approach that seems easiest to him, and simply get it over and done with. In the end, this is an examination—rather safe than sorry. He manages to pull through.

Dana sees the methodology involved in her thesis as something she still needs and wants to learn more about and build some experience with. She recognizes that any methodology will have its gurus, but also its entry- and intermediate-level areas where she can still get on board and hone her skills. She picks a topic and approach that feels in balance with what she can and wants to reach while working on her thesis. Dana considers the demand for working rigorously quite pragmatically: 'So they have this set of manuals explaining proven-to-work methodology and they want me to adhere to that—seems like the efficient path to take. I don't want to make up my own methodology just to find out that I delivered kind of a hack-job in the end. No one expects me to perform at guru-level and understand every single specialization of the methodology I apply—just that I'll try as far as I can to achieve a robust result.' She completes a well-balanced and carefully developed thesis.

Devil's advocate

Perfect rigour is a North Star. It provides you with a direction, but it does not take into account how much effort can be invested in your specific project so that it still produces an efficient result. In the end, you will need to sensibly balance costly investments into extensive methodology with a plausible return. Conduct a project of appropriately limited contribution within the realm of what is possible.

How to tackle

Scientific rigour is what differentiates scientific research from other forms of work. There is no way around informing yourself about the most appropriate methodology and its application for your project if you want to generate a result that will be recognizable as scientific work.

Sadly, a sizeable share of older and even some contemporary literature on methodology does a disservice to its understanding and application. It is interesting to speculate why that is. Maybe academics try to construct a moat around their knowledge; great methodologists may not always also be great teachers, or it may simply be difficult for many specialists to explain fundamentals and intermediate material in comprehensible form. If you find yourself looking at a close-to-incomprehensible book on methodology, rest assured that it might not be your fault, but an inaccessible presentation of the material.

That said: excellent literature and explanations of methodology are available. Some of this can be found in printed form, but most is accessible online as web pages or videos. These online resources are often extremely granular, and explain what you need in pragmatic terms. It seems that the motives of these authors are tied to the quality of their explanation and less to sticking to the orthodoxy of the field. Even though this sounds both obvious and overly pragmatic, it is still true: if you are stuck, Google it. YouTube is not just for cat videos. There are highly talented teachers out there who can help you understand the specific method you need to get into. However, don't let your methodology insight rely entirely on online sources—rather, consider this a kind of automotive breakdown service to get you rolling again and to understand the literature in your specific field better. Welcome all readily available help to grow into understanding that baffling paper or confusing results table.

The most important thing about methodology, however, might be to consider it a help and not a hurdle. The idea that methodology can be a hurdle stems from trying to apply methodology that too far beyond your grasp. In all likeliness, your topic will not benefit from an overcomplicated methodology, since complication comes with risk, and obfuscates what is truly at the centre of your work. Many strands of methodology either become slightly ideological and sometimes even esoteric by becoming so finely delineated that there is little practical application, or leading into staunch debates about what's most appropriate to use where. In many cases, the selection of particularly high-end methodology comes down to which school you follow. Especially as a Bachelor and Master student, it is much more rewarding to develop a basic or intermediate level (key to this is that it should be well understood by yourself) and implement this methodology very well, rather than trying to implement a methodology you don't feel comfortable with and don't want to grow into.

Experienced peers' two cents

'Science rests on the three pillars of rigour, reproducibility, and responsibility. Ethics is firmly built into all three pillars. Responsibility, as a fundamental ethical concept, forms the basis for everything.

'What is rigour? Rigorous work involves everything that rests on the basis of intellectual honesty. Also, think about science as a constant process of self-improvement. This corresponds with the error-analysis concept that engineers are familiar with. Be well aware of how well you are setting up your research in terms of experimental design and redundancy—something that is important in the biomedical sciences. Be aware of people's own biases and fallacies. Another major issue when it comes to how to do science well or not well across disciplines is when people make numerous mistakes in terms of probability and statistics. All these points stand for the rigour component of science.

'Reproducibility is something that we feel no longer needs much emphasis; it was a sign of the times in the open science movement where everybody started realizing how little reproducibility there is. We enjoyed seeing how students themselves were asking for ways to do science more reproducible. We partner a lot with the open science community and seek direct practitioner inputs to learn how to make this possible. These are some of the concrete ways that we ask students to adhere to good standards for doing good science.

'Responsibility symbolizes our strong emphasis on ethics overall. We do teach Responsible Conduct of Research (RCR), but then people may put it in a corner and check it off. The fundamental attitude—the mindset of ethics—underlies everything that we do. Here, the idea of social responsibility has many connotations. On one hand is the (social) community you feel a responsible part of. On the other is the wider scientific community in your institution and in your field. The widest view is to see science as an enterprise in itself. Then there are societal aspects. We as scientists need to be good stewards of the money people give us for our research, but also of the trust people put in us as scientists. So, people need to be fundamentally committed to those values of doing good science. We function as a role model. People look up to us. We need to be responsible for the trust people put in us. This is a major fundamental thought underlying our programme. All programmes should do that.' (Gundula Bosch)

'Why do we need research skills at all? To help us in making informed decisions. Identifying what is "right"—even though "right" and "wrong" are relative terms. Scientific approaches help us to make informed decisions based on sufficient evidence. Not to take things for granted. That is why research skills do not only apply to the writing of a thesis and graduating, but to each and every sector of life. Even when our students start their careers, wherever they go. Scientific methods for generating knowledge and questioning taken-for-granted ideas is important.

'All student courses are for acquisition of knowledge—we learn a fact, we get information—but the idea is to help students to transition from being an acquirer of knowledge to being (to some extent) a creator of knowledge. This is a difficult journey for students, but that is the hope. When talking about the contribution of knowledge, we usually talk of PhD students, but a Master's thesis done well can also contribute to knowledge. On the contrary: if a PhD project does not go well, it might not contribute to generating knowledge even if it is expected. A Master's thesis project can therefore be indistinguishable from a component project of a PhD in terms of the contribution to knowledge.' (Madhu Neupane Bastola)

'Going beyond the research question: that may have something to do with the nature of the field. Economic phenomena and challenges in this part of the world are related with each other, obviously to inequality and poverty. We believe that students should be aware of the societal impact of whatever problem they study beyond the numbers, beyond the models, and beyond other published research. This is something important to us. This may be more discipline- and region-specific.

'So you need to be scientifically diligent enough to produce rigorous research, and intellectually flexible enough to integrate your research into the greater context. At the same time, you need to be able to avoid overwhelming yourself with the complex holistic view . There is a delicate balance here.

'Most publications (70%) in finance are geared towards practicability. Especially in FinTec. In corporate finance, too, publications are more on the practical side. For those who work in investment banking, most of their research involves studying practical problems. In some cases, economic theses are purely theoretical. Most economic theses will be applied analyses of practical problem, rather than scholarly works which contribute to the academic field of knowledge.

'Some people might take a recent paper on insights concerning Latin America, and then try to replicate the findings for the Middle East. That in itself is not a scholarly work, because the contribution has already being made. But such work adopts academic qualities, and its contribution is to verify whether this is applicable to another region.' (Samer Atallah)

'Hands-on experience is very valuable. But the ability to conceptualize a problem and pursue it in a disciplined fashion is also important. Critical thinking is vital in developing a reasonable practical set of skills. Part of what theses contribute is the sense that you as a student were able to achieve some sort of excellence of your way of thinking, and that you were actually able to produce something of great value. Students benefit from seeing how their work relates not only to the scientific community, but to the real world. That's what we're going for.

'Even senior researchers often make things overly complex. Too many hypotheses, too many variables, too many relationships. They don't define boundaries well. That's a problem with a lot of research. At all levels. And that's a way to think about it. Expectations at each level, a bite-size which increases over time. Start small, try to do something bigger. Bigger still as a PhD student. But even PhD students don't reinvent the world. Many PhD students believe they have to reinvent the wheel.

'I think it is a matter of balance. My list of paradoxes includes humility and confidence. I see students thinking on the one hand that they have to over-complicate things to make a contribution. On the other hand, they do not really understand what they're writing about. Transparency and clarity are very important.' (Steven Floyd)

Deduce the research design

What seems like a central, watershed decision is usually not yours to make, but is best derived from the state of your research field.

Metaphorically speaking

Research means making choices on how to reach your destination. In many cases, the destination itself will suggest or even demand a type of travelling. Island without an airstrip? You'll be taking a boat, it seems. Summit of a mountain—why not hike?

Consequently, while many aspects of your final academic project look like design decisions that are entirely up to you, many of these decisions are intricately linked. If you choose to scale a mountain top, this will impact what and how much you can pack. It will require good weather. This requires access to information on weather patterns and suitable scheduling. In case of any travelling, it is a good idea to have a plan B in case plan A turns out to be unsuccessful or even risky.

The two big methodological domains—qualitative or quantitative research designs—are the first of many design decisions in your thesis. In many cases, this decision will depend on your desired destination: the nature and character of your research question. This often hinges on the state of the research field you seek to contribute to.

Rough coordinates

Quality—'An attribute, property; a special feature or characteristic. A substance having a particular attribute or property; a substance of a certain nature; an essence. Originally: the nature, kind, or character (of something). Later: the standard or nature of something as measured against other things of a similar kind.'

The Student's Research Companion. Omid Aschari and Benjamin Berghaus, Oxford University Press.
© Omid Aschari and Benjamin Berghaus (2023). DOI: 10.1093/oso/9780192855312.003.0007

Quantity—'A specified or definite amount of an article or commodity; a (large, small, etc.) portion or measure; also without of-adjunct. Also (occasionally): an amount of something immaterial.'

Exploration—'The action of examining thoroughly; investigation, scrutiny, study; an instance of this. The action of travelling to or around an uncharted or unknown area for the purposes of discovery and gathering information; (later also) the action or activity of going to or around an unfamiliar place in order to learn about it.'

Confirmation—'The action of making firm or sure; strengthening, settling, establishing (of institutions, opinions, etc.). The action of confirming, corroborating, or verifying; verification, proof.'

Train of thought

Once they have found an audience, a field, a topic, and maybe even a research question, a proposal, or a hypothesis, many students ask themselves whether they prefer to tackle the topic qualitatively or quantitatively. Few realize that, by that time, the dice (for that particular research question) may have already been cast. Many suppose that the choice of methodological hemisphere is theirs, and decide to take a path that simply does not fit their topic. Let's fix this. It's easier than you think.

If you aim for purposeful research, you will try to add to the existing body of knowledge. As you will try to take the most efficient path to your goal, you will first try to identify what the current delineation of scientific insight is. If the field has already advanced considerably, you will find enough theoretic material to develop hypotheses and test these hypotheses to make a smaller contribution to your field. To test hypotheses, you will work quantitatively, ideally with experiments. If the field is still in its infancy, you will not find substantial theory on the subject, and cannot readily build hypotheses. You need to explore the foundations of the field before you can take further steps. To explore the foundations of a field, you will need to do qualitative work by exploring cases, conducting interviews, or other types of qualitative, exploratory research methodology.

In essence, the choice of a (predominantly) quantitative or qualitative research design is not one you make some time down the road, but a decision you derive from the development stage of the field you choose. The only wiggle room in this is the degree to which you can innovate within a field in order to continue expanding its theoretical framework. However, there will be powerful forces in that particular research community responding that your innovative approach is not needed since the gospel has been set for this field. The established researchers are on record with their findings. They have little incentive to see their findings challenged. It is up to you to decide to challenge them or instead play by the rules. What seems even less plausible is to try and do research through hypothesis testing in a field that simply has not advanced to that stage yet. Since you need theory to build hypotheses, you would be lacking the elemental building blocks to construct your research from. Of course, you might try to introduce theory from a neighbouring or conceptually related field, but you will need to make explicit why the transport of theory from its origin to your proposed destination will be appropriate.

The most important thing to keep in mind when thinking about whether you'd like to work quantitatively or qualitatively is that you should not take that decision after you have picked your topic, but instead deduce it from the state of your field. By choosing your topic, you will most likely work in a fashion that corresponds with the state of development of that field.

In any case, try to avoid the pitfall of believing that one or the other methodological realm is easier or harder. The central difference between both approaches is predominantly when and how the necessary effort becomes effective: in qualitative work, there is less preparation and more work after gathering data. Since you work with complex and unstructured data, coding of your work will take ample amounts of time and nerves. In essence, most qualitative research methodology is about trying to structure unstructured information. That's an art in itself. In quantitative research, there is considerably more preparation work involved in ensuring that your hypotheses are sound and that your data collection is not confounded. Appropriate sampling is a major challenge to most research projects that can only be solved by relaxing the expected explanatory power and thus softening the claim to being able to generalize insight to all cases. Both types of methodologies require focus, detail, and commitment to carrying out the project according to quality standards set and enforceable externally.

In essence

- The type of methodology you choose is defined by to the question you aim to answer and the advancement of the field you aim to contribute to.

- Be sure not to look at your research question, your field, and your research design as if they were disconnected. This is the backbone of your research project.
- You can, however, start designing your research project with the component you are most certain about. For example, if that is a certain methodology or research design, pick a field, a question, and an audience that would work well here.

To reflect

- Do I have a preference in audience, fields, research questions, or research design? Which one?
- Which of the preferences is the strongest and should take the lead?
- How can you align all of these elements in a way that they inform and yield to each other?

Two travellers' tales

Emma is set to explore a question in a thoroughly quantitative field of research because she wants to work in that area, and she has heard that the pay is great. Sadly, Emma has her problems with quantitative methods. She feels that numbers have never really been her thing. Consequently, she also does not really want to attempt to get into the quantitative methodology, but rather tries to solve a quantitative problem using qualitative measures. She does manage to pull together a rather unusual thesis, but finds it really hard to answer questions on why she picked this approach (and not give away the real reason for her methodology choice, which is not a logical deduction from the positioning of the problem and field).

Nian picks a field he's interested in and develops an overview of what's currently being published on this subject. He decides that the amount of published research is still scant and exploratory, with many areas left perfectly blank—a good place to start his qualitative exploration into a specific question. He knows that both quantitative and qualitative methods come with about the same amount of work, just differently balanced (quantitative tends to front-load much work, and qualitative tends to drag a big tail of work in the analysis). Nian does not mind either, since he knows that he'd need and want to work himself deeper into either type of methodology. He completes a good thesis and finds it easy to explain why he picked the path he followed (and what he learned along the way).

Devil's advocate

There are cases in which a traditional topic or field can benefit from an entirely atypical approach. However, this is risky. If you choose an atypical approach, don't attempt it on a hunch but base it on a well-calculated plan.

How to tackle

A thesis project comes together when there are no (unintended) 'sharp edges', no 'sudden turns' that suddenly emerge and pull all of your audience's attention to a break in the development of your report's narrative. This does not mean that your final academic project cannot contain surprising results or innovative turns. Rather, it should not contain twists that cannot be logically explained and deduced from the prior development. Above anything else, a scientific text needs to protect the integrity of its line of argumentation.

Since the choice of methodology employed in your final academic project is a very prominent decision, protecting the integrity of your final academic project line of argumentation is easiest when you can deduce the optimal choice and not simply follow with your preference.

To choose the appropriate methodology, you might first decide on the type of methodology. Do you want to work qualitatively or quantitatively— or maybe a combination of the two? Your best indicator for this choice will be the state of the field you want to contribute to. If the field appears still in its infancy, exploration needs to be done, so it will be easy to jus- tify a qualitative exploration into the domain. If the field appears already well-understood, your question will likely be more focused, and you have enough prior research to formulate questions. Consequently, arguing for a quantitative approach is much easier than the less efficient qualitative exploration.

There is also room for deviating from this norm. But if you choose to do so, this must be a situation in which your argument will need to be stronger than the traditional logic explained above. To a certain degree, this means going against the grain of what the researchers in the field are doing. Of course, this attracts more attention, but it is commonly also more difficult to convince readers that you are onto something that others have not yet seen.

The purposeful scientific entrepreneur

Think about your project like a social entrepreneur who happens to apply scientific methodology. This perspective prompts several helpful questions.

Metaphorically speaking

Research means that you get to organize, undertake, and lead an excursion to a place where no person has gone before. This is your enterprise. You determine the destination, the mode of exploration, you balance risk and return. This shows how indebted you are to yourself to pick a great destination worthy of exploration and not just aisle six in the supermarket. You may consider yourself tasked with nothing less than designing and leading your own research enterprise.

Consequently, try to see your project not as a requirement by your programme, but as an opportunity to build a platform for yourself. Since you are going to work on a self-defined project for many months, why not pick and set up a project that you would want to build a reputation from? Certainly, much of the project's potential will only become apparent during and after the project. But if you plan your excursion to a place you do not care for from the start, it's certain to generate limited potential.

While it is common to look at the final academic project as an examination, that is just about the least inspiring, motivating, and exciting way of understanding it. Consider it an official instruction to illustrate what drives your curiosity and how you channel your curiosity to reach your goals.

Rough coordinates

Entrepreneur—'A person who owns and manages a business, bearing the financial risks of the enterprise; (now) spec. a person who sets up a business or businesses, taking on financial risks.'

The Student's Research Companion. Omid Aschari and Benjamin Berghaus, Oxford University Press.
© Omid Aschari and Benjamin Berghaus (2023). DOI: 10.1093/oso/9780192855312.003.0008

Investment—'The devotion of time, effort, etc., for a particular purpose, with the expectation of a worthwhile or beneficial result; an instance of this. Also: a purpose or activity to which time, effort, etc., may be usefully or advantageously devoted.'

Returns—'The yield of some productive thing considered in relation to the original amount or expenditure.'

Stakeholder—'A person, company, etc., with a concern or (esp. financial) interest in ensuring the success of an organization, business, system, etc.'

Train of thought

One of the key image problems of final academic projects is that they appear to be a load of work that's mandatory in order to complete an academic programme. There appears to be a great risk of messing up one or the other element and, by extension, damage an otherwise good or great evaluation of the previous achievements during the programme. Grades of final academic projects are commonly heavily weighted and influential on the overall assessment. In short, final projects appear to have many downsides and little upsides. They seem like that odd-looking, ill-maintained rope bridge right before your destination, ready to collapse under you. Who would ever like to engage in that?

Of course, you might see your next journey merely as an experience that will be over on the day that you complete it. However, wouldn't that be a considerable waste of your time? Given that you hopefully picked a particularly interesting area to explore—why not, at least for a while, act as a tour guide for others? Who knows—maybe there are professionals out there who would love to hire your experience to learn from you? Maybe you would like to share your insights by writing a book on the place you travelled to? Potentially you find something at your destination that could serve well as a basis for your future business, for consulting, for teaching? Of course, all of this supposes that you picked a place that is worth travelling to. But if you did: who is to stop you making the most out of your experience?

Try to take a few steps back and consider how the time and effort to be invested into your final project might be considered from the standpoint of a scientific entrepreneur. Since your investment is considerable, it is only prudent to ask about the types of return you might generate. For your own, personal gain, you should consider how your project will aid you in building a personal positioning on a certain subject, how you will mature during the project, which skills you wish to strengthen, who you might come in contact and collaborate with, etc.

True satisfaction, however, lies for many in how their project can contribute to the gain of others—how can you contribute to solving challenges experienced by others? Is there a way to design your project to strike not only one tone but a whole chord of benefits? That is what our suggestion of thinking about your final academic project like a scientific entrepreneur is all about.

The foundation of your final academic project becoming an entrepreneurial project is relevance. You cannot build an entrepreneurial project on something that you cannot imagine the use of and the target group for. Be sure that this relevance is not only something that you cunningly identify a market for, but also something that you feel happy about pursuing.

Once you've identified something that you enjoy creating and that you know is relevant to a certain target group, you ought to consider the system of offers that you can provide to those involved in your research. What can you do for those who participate in your interview series? What can you do for the peers who are, just like you, interested in the subject?

In essence

- If you allow it to be, the final academic project can be much more than the chore of an examination.
- Try to approach your final academic project like a scientific entrepreneur by investigating whom you would like to contribute to by conducting research. This will not only provide you with more purpose in your work, but also with opportunities to look beyond the thesis.
- Your final project can be a great opportunity to grow into the person and professional you want to become. Pick the direction in which you grow with the mindset of a strategist ('that will make sense long-term') rather than a brilliant tactician ('that sounds like a quick win').

To reflect

- Do you want to make your next months an examination or to a platform that you can build on?
- Which audience do you deem attractive and worthwhile enough for you to spend months contributing to solving one of their problems?
- What is this problem, and how can you try to help tackle it?

Two travellers' tales

Greta simply wants to complete her study programme. The thesis is a final to-do. But, more importantly, the thesis is something that no one (besides her supervisor) will likely ever read. Except for her parents, possibly. But they'll then only nag her as to why she didn't study that other programme. In short: there is little to be won here, life starts thereafter. Greta completes her thesis without giving the project hardly any opportunity to produce additional benefit, since she simply did not see such benefit.

Paul sees his thesis not as the final project of his studies but at least as a bridge into what he wants to do after studying—if not even the first project of his 'life after his current programme'. He sees it as his trajectory out of his current status and into a new one. Consequently, he tries to frame his project in a way that will serve as a springboard into a promising new direction. He figures: 'That's the only way I can justify the learning I shall have to do anyway to complete this successfully.' Paul manages to build a useful bridge to beginning his career, since his research not only included exchanges with practitioners and researchers in the field in which he wants to continue, but also presented his results at a local practitioner conference that happened to take place at the time.

Devil's advocate

All useful reinterpretation aside, the institutional role of the final academic project never stops being an examination. However, there is no harm in extending the goal when a successful project can and should be much more than an exercise. Indeed, it's a bureaucratic waste to spend so much effort on something that you would otherwise just view as another administrative requirement.

How to tackle

Whenever anyone tasks you with an examination and explains that this examination will take the better part of a year, of course you would immediately start looking for ways to make this challenge about more than jumping through someone's examination hoop. Even better: you get the support to conduct this examination—so why not leverage this opportunity to reach some of your goals as well?

However, the best practice recommendation is not to exclusively look for your personal gain, but to make sure you will make a contribution to a community you truly want to support. Making that contribution means, first, finding out how you can make a contribution and to whom, exactly. Those are the starting points for a well-integrated final academic project that can tick all of the university's boxes in terms of its examination format, but also can tick all of your boxes in terms of making this time worthwhile.

The advantage lies in the compatibility of thinking of yourself as a scientific entrepreneur and as a good researcher: you employ your resources to construct a project that delivers a benefit. You will need to manage the limitation of your resources, you will need to (learn to) lead yourself, you will need to find out exactly what it is that people want you to accomplish, and you will realize how much of a marathon it all is.

All of a sudden, this dire chore of writing 60 pages and handing them in on time has turned into something else—ideally into the first project of your life after your academic programme because you could build further on your experience. Maybe not in every case as the immediate foundation of your career, but certainly as the experience of having successfully produced a useful project that you take away from your final academic project.

Experienced peers' two cents

'If you define success as making a contribution, the question is always: a contribution to whom? There needs to be an audience for what you are writing to be a contribution. It reminds me a little bit of the first step in the entrepreneurial process: successful entrepreneurs start with asking, "What do people want?" They talk to people. They ask for responses to their prototype. They interview a hundred potential customers before they start to write their business plan. Get out in the world a little bit first.' (Steven Floyd)

'The strongest mindset that I try to maintain is curiosity about the world. To try and avoid taking too many things at face value. One of the things that companies benefit from is having a regular influx of new ideas and outside perspectives. If no one is asking questions, if no one is questioning the world around them, then we stagnate. We don't grow. Growth and evolution happen through questioning, wondering. I'm trying to imagine, "What if we tried it this way?" "What if we tried to change this process that we're undergoing to improve this?" "Why are we talking about customers in this way?"' (Matt Farmer)

'Going beyond curiosity is the researcher's ability to link things together. To go beyond the research question and to understand the subject beyond the research question. To understand that what they are studying has implications elsewhere.' (Samer Atallah)

'In an applied discipline like management, relevance is of critical importance. That does not imply that there is no place for theoretical, basic research. It merely means that if we fail to provide actual help to practitioners, our discipline loses the legitimation in the eyes of those who we should aim to serve.' (Günter Müller-Stewens)

'In their thesis, I expect students to produce insights that are stimulating for the field of practice to allow for a more profound thinking on a topic. In my field of qualitative research, I put them in a consulting context where they get lots of empirical experience with our partners, develop insights, and present them. The feedback of the partners is very important. My role as supervisor is to help them level up the quality of their work by phasing in my knowledge, too. The objective is to generate an experience that is unique for the students and added value for the partners.' (Urs Jäger)

Renewable research energy

Maintaining motivation to work on your project is crucial. Fuel your progress with curiosity first, and switch to discipline when you run out.

Metaphorically speaking

Research means a long walk. A very long walk. Sure, there are short excursions available here and there. But the longest walks seem to have the greatest chance of imprinting themselves on you. Thus, motivation and stamina will likely become an issue. It is one of the key capabilities of a researcher to lose neither your heading nor your propulsion.

Consequently, successfully conducting your research project in a fundamental sense means successfully defending your continuous advancement. In this context, maintaining, sustaining, and replenishing motivation are key activities. A good traveller knows his or her preferences for travelling, times of day more or less fitting for this or that task, and the necessity to account for and replenish energy lost in times of relaxation.

Part of becoming a good researcher is becoming a researcher who is not burned out after one project. One solution is making your project a part of your day which you do not continuously perceive as a burden you take up with disgust. If your project or your way of handling your project feels off, try to set aside worries about what you do and consider reflecting about how you try doing it.

Rough coordinates

Curiosity—'The desire or inclination to know or learn about anything, esp. what is novel or strange; a feeling of interest leading one to inquire about anything. Scientific or artistic interest; the quality of a curioso or virtuoso; connoisseurship.'

The Student's Research Companion. Omid Aschari and Benjamin Berghaus, Oxford University Press.
© Omid Aschari and Benjamin Berghaus (2023). DOI: 10.1093/oso/9780192855312.003.0009

Motivation—'The general desire or willingness of someone to do something; drive, enthusiasm.'

Stamina—'Vigour of bodily constitution; power of sustaining fatigue or privation, of recovery from illness, and of resistance to debilitating influences; staying power.'

Nuisance—'That constitutes a nuisance; possessing the ability to annoy, irritate, or harm.'

Train of thought

The final academic project is a requirement to finish your programme. No one undertakes a final project simply because they would like to do one—they need to do one. You can simply complete your duty—nothing wrong with that. But you can also find inspiration in your project. You can believe in tackling a problem that you find worthy of tackling. And you can try to help people. Even if you simply want to capture a topic and make it your own by willpower and curiosity—all of those motives point you to different sources of stamina. The core difference is whether you engage in your project as a task driven by discipline or as an opportunity driven by curiosity.

There are different kinds of trips you take when you travel. Some journeys you take out of necessity and others you take because you look forward to them, because you see a sense in them. Needless to say, that commuting takes discipline and a hike to explore a landscape merely needs some curiosity. While the former will require some energy and tend to make you more efficient to convert that energy, the latter might even set some energy free in terms of inspiration, new impressions, and enjoying the experience—even though you put in comparable amounts of work. Thus, the motivation why you travel imprints on how you will approach your journey and, in turn, the resources you can tap into.

When approaching your final academic project, try to get your mind into a perspective of exploration rather than diligence. Most of us only have so much energy to spend—even when diligent and disciplined—and once that energy has been spent, it only regenerates slowly. Thus, it's wise not to see the project as a large sink for your personal energy, but more like a system of energy storage, conversion, and sometimes even generation: you put some effort into your project, you work on it and think about it. You make it the best it can possibly be (and there are limits). As soon as your project has reached some critical mass, allow it to return some energy to you. This return might come from actual curiosity about how questions will be answered, from pride about advancing to become an expert in your field, from happiness about having figured out a particularly complex or otherwise tricky set-up of a methodology.

While we all agree that research projects take energy first, there are numerous ways to extract energy from it—and most of these ways offer themselves before the project is complete. While those who are investing diligent and disciplined work into efficiently solving the task need to be economical with their fuel, you might opt for the approach of seeing yourself in an exchange relationship with your thesis: invest energy, but also draw energy from it. Turning a research project into a source of renewable energy is one of the most useful ways to avoid becoming completely drained in the process of completing.

Granted: this perspective is not to be implemented religiously. A final academic project, after all, is a requirement that you need to complete in order to advance. However, there is no strict rule that you should not understand it as an experience that will both take and provide you with motivation. Certainly, there will be days during which you will experience your final academic project as a great opportunity and others that will leave you stranded thinking that your final academic project is the worst project you ever attempted (it's really not as though you had a choice).

However, steering your mind to experience more days in the first condition and fewer days in the latter condition is the whole point of this recommendation. Don't let your final academic project be a nuisance you can only get rid of through discipline. Let your project be just as much a destination of your efforts as a source for your motivation. Remember that the latter approach will refuel your motivation along the way, like a source of renewable energy; the former tends to ignore those opportunities in favour of experiencing return after 'the damned thing is done'. Don't let your final academic project become a 'damned thing' (there are enough days when it will, regardless).

In essence

- Especially when well-positioned, the final academic project can be such a fulfilling project that the only thing missing might be the energy to enjoy the process in and by itself.
- A critical but hardly ever discussed factor in success is to protect and replenish your energy and motivation reservoir through being aware of the drain and actively planning to regain some of the energy invested.
- Do not accept research as a positively exhaustive exercise—especially if you are thinking about turning research into a career.

To reflect

- Are you sensible and aware enough to consider your own energy levels?
- What is it about project work that draws most of your energy? How can you hedge this abstraction of energy?
- How can you replenish your energy most effectively? Do you have a plan in mind for regular replenishment?

Two travellers' tales

Vafi knows that the thesis will draw a lot of energy from him. Thus, he tries to boost himself at the beginning of his project and throw himself into work with full force. This works like a charm for a couple of weeks. After a month, it starts to wear on him. After month two, he is exhausted, and after the third, he is beyond exhausted and tends to hate his project—or his approach to it (he is no longer quite sure). He takes a long time out from the project and ends up extending his deadline. He completes his work, but feels as though this was even more exhausting than expected. Never again!

Hanna knows that the thesis will draw a lot of energy from her. Thus, she tries to be mindful of balancing the load of work with releases of stress and opportunities to replenish energy. She also makes a pact with a couple of friends who are also working on their theses to take care of each others' stress levels and—if need be—use a veto to initiate a weekend away to simply have some fun. Hanna is aware that the thesis is a longer dive than she can hold her breath for. Consequently, she becomes more aware about coming up to the surface reasonably frequently so that the journey can be a productive but also pleasant one—at least not a strenuous one. She sees the thesis also as an opportunity to learn to manage her energy levels during demanding long-term projects. This will likely be the norm when she's working: better try and adopt good self-awareness before then. Hanna manages her stress levels well during her thesis. Still, it's been a wild ride, and she's more than earned that holiday afterwards. But big projects can no longer scare her easily =—she's got the evidence that she will cope well.

Devil's advocate

Research means performing at the peak of your abilities. Find a good balance between performing at your best and being able to performing long-term. When in doubt, cut yourself some slack.

How to tackle

You will only complete your final academic project if you don't exhaust your energy while working on it—it is as simple as that. Your energy level is the most critical resource to manage, protect, and care for during your project.

Heighten your awareness of your energy level. If it helps you, put a recurring event in your calendar, maybe every other week, to take a moment to actively reflect on what currently weighs you down, what lifts you up, whether those are in a good balance for you, and if not, how you might change that. It might be a good idea to team up with another friendly thesis-writing student to cross-reference and buddy-system yourselves together.

When you feel that you are losing energy at a rate that is too great or that you are coming too close to being exhausted, take a break earlier rather than later. It is more difficult, takes more time, and will cause more delays to replenish your energy from a perceived 10% level (needing to regain many multiples) than from a 60% level (needing to regain 80% to feeling fully recharged).

All that said, during the thesis, you might feel that you never truly, fully recharge and relax, since in the back of your mind, your project and its deadlines are always looming. This creates a constant draw on energy which must be accounted for by being mindful, aware, and careful with your own and other's resources.

On the way, you will encounter many others who work themselves to exhaustion. This does not mean that you should. They may just be behaving recklessly. Also, different people have different capacities for energy. If another person has much more or much less energy: leave them be. This is an individual challenge.

Experienced peers' two cents

'I always advise students to do something that is genuinely interesting to them. It helps them to keep their motivation up for the duration of the thesis. A thesis project is a new experience for many students. Students have never actually worked on a piece that is so expensive in terms of time effort.' (Ansgar Richter)

'For too long time, people thought we would just bring a group of highly specialized experts into a room and they would connect and then create something great. This can work, if the individual has a certain attitude and mindset enabling them to think outside the box. However, not many people can do that.

'People, including students, think in a very entrenched manner in their respective disciplines ("rabbit-holes"). We found that for most individuals it is necessary to formally teach this broad thinking. It is almost as if a certain part of the brain is not trained. You have to animate it again. People often claim that they are thinking outside the box, but it is not what they are really doing. Maybe they are opening a tiny box within a bigger box.

'Outside-the-box-thinking starts—based on conversations with colleagues from multiple disciplines around the globe—with communication issues. The challenge is to find the same language, given the different educational backgrounds, e.g. social studies, the arts, or biochemical studies or health. We found that for adults it is more difficult to overcome this challenge (similar to the challenge to learn a new language).

'At the same time, we found that the younger individuals are seemingly more open to applying concepts to different areas, more curious, and, in a constructivist sense, less entrenched in established patterns. They do not submit to pre-made patterns as easily. Their boxes are not out of metal or wood, but out of rubber, or plasticine. It also seems that students enjoy this process more and have less fear of being judged. The curiosity is still there. It's key for programs not to kill that curiosity.' (Gundula Bosch)

'You have to enter into discussion with yourself. What are your life plans? What is the design of your life? OK, maybe at the moment you don't know exactly, and you can only do it like the start-up scene and go with prototyping and testing. Try if your heart beats in the direction of theoretical work, or are you more a type of consultant? You need a decision. Not from the beginning, but when you are saying to go to academia or at least you want to keep this path open to go to academia; later, in our times, you will have no choice but to learn the craft of publishing, of doing empirical research. There is no choice here. But even on this path, there is a choice of how you allocate your time. You have people who want to go to academia, they still have the time to study interesting practitioner cases to get better insights into their research questions. There are others who stay in their study lodge and don't see company any more. Even there, you have options. It's a way of self-discovery. You have to explore yourself and to feel where your heart beats.' (Günter Müller-Stewens)

Why even bother?

A final academic project can generate a great variety of returns. Required are your will to invest and your imagination to generate use out of the outcome.

Metaphorically speaking

Research is the type of journey that releases more of its reward by experiencing progress rather than by merely having reached a destination. This progress can come in many shapes and forms: the training, meeting the challenge, growing your experience, becoming able to tell a story, becoming able to guide others, and many, many more rewards—if you are willing to imagine and derive motivation from them.

Consequently, reconsider what makes your journey relevant to you. Certainly, there is this ubiquitous and sadly crowding-out sense of 'regulations make me jump through a hoop for me to receive my degree'. For a moment, try to imagine your desired return from a project that you undertook on your own. What would you want a project to return to you that you undertook of your own accord? Start with a long list, prioritize your items, and attempt a few on your high-priority short list.

Part of becoming a good researcher is becoming a researcher who likes doing what they do. Another part is the creativity to imagine and drive to implement a network of motivating outcomes which help motivate you on a day when you lack motivation. If you know the answer to 'Why even bother?' even on a bad day—and that answer encompasses more than 'Because I have to do it'—it will be a less bad day.

Rough coordinates

Goal—'The finishing point of a race or a marker by which this point is signified; the finish line, the finishing post.'

The Student's Research Companion. Omid Aschari and Benjamin Berghaus, Oxford University Press.
© Omid Aschari and Benjamin Berghaus (2023). DOI: 10.1093/oso/9780192855312.003.0010

Expectation—'A preconceived idea or opinion based on what a person has hoped for or imagined regarding a future event, situation, or encounter.'

Returns—'The yield of some productive thing considered in relation to the original amount or expenditure.'

Basis—'The bottom of anything, considered as the part on which it rests or is supported; the foundation, base, foot.'

Train of thought

We live in peculiar times: while an increasing number of people appear to be more and more focused on the purpose of what they are doing, we still find it difficult to let go of the more traditional, transactional idea of return: if I do that, what do I get in return? Most sceptical people follow that idea to the conclusion that 'surely, nothing will come of it' and 'I'd better not invest too much'. For final academic projects, however, you can expect a more or less direct relationship between your investment and return, if you consider a few guiding thoughts.

In the world of our metaphors, this chapter deals with the motivation behind your journey: do you simply want to get there and be done with travelling or do you see the travelling itself as equally or even more important compared with being at your destination? In the former condition, travelling is a mere nuisance, a means to the more important end—in the latter, travelling is the whole point, and 'getting there' is just the final stage of your journey. It's the final step of this project and adjacent to your next journey. Let us suppose that the journey is your final academic project. Then, the act of travelling represents the sensation of taking in the experience of your project, the sensation of learning, and building a result that you may be able to construct the first steps of a career on.

Since the return from your final academic project is rooted in what you worked on and how much you took away from your thesis, adopting a more immersive and invested approach to your project is a critical prerequisite to any sort of result. The good news is that there is a certain automatism about return from research: the more you involve yourself with it and the more you allow it to teach you, the more you will generate in terms of return. Research—just like learning—is respectable inasmuch it will not cheat you out of your returns if you define the returns appropriately. No, a great final academic project does not ensure a quick rise to power, riches, or fame. Yes, a great final project will be certain to provide you with a solid experience in a subject, some methodological experience, some actionable insight into a topic of importance with an audience you'd like to work with, and the potential to build a platform based on all of the above. Thus, generating return from a final academic project means, as well as making that considerable and sound investment of mind, time, and immersion, making sure that you expect returns that a final academic project can actually provide.

When considering your final project in an investment–return equation, be aware that if your goals are compatible with what an academic project can provide, there are some challenging requisites. You will need to commit to the project, immerse yourself, try to be aware of things you can do to improve the outcome, and be careful and entrepreneurial about how you spend the effort you invest. All of this involvement will facilitate your learning experience and the potential for future return. Trying to avoid the work and immersion involved and instead cutting corners to more directly reach the accreditation of your degree will make your journey quicker, but also less of a basis from which to generate return.

In essence

- The final academic project represents a considerable investment of time and effort, whether you consider and build it to bring returns or simply conduct it to graduate.
- Think through your final academic project in terms of what you want from it. Think broadly, prioritize, and attempt to realize a few of these returns.
- On a good day, you'll enjoy working on your thesis. On a bad day, you'll at least have a couple of supports, since you have extended your answers to 'Why even bother?'

To reflect

- If this project were not mandated by your programme: what set of returns would it take for you to conduct it? Try to think diversely here—neither all intrinsic nor all extrinsic motives.
- Which of these returns appear to have the greatest long-term use and impact for you?
- How can you try and implement a system that delivers these returns to you?

Two travellers' tales

Ingrid does not expect much from her thesis project: 'That's what needs to be done—so I'll do it. At the very least, the project should be something I am interested in.' But that's about it. Ingrid made sure that the scope of her project was as limited as possible, and invested a frugal amount of time into it. This worked out: Ingrid did not expect much, and she did not get much: a grade that she can comfortably complete her programme with. But that's it.

William expects his thesis project to require a considerable amount of investment from him. Consequently, he feels that he can expect more than a grade from his project. He thinks about how what he wants to research can help others (who might, later, become employers), he thinks about what he needs and wants to learn about the field and the methodology involved. He tries to align his project with actual questions raised by people in the field. In the end, he invests more than Ingrid, but he also receives more: a plausibly and convincingly positioned project that generates some attention among several of the practitioners and even some researchers he involves. He generates resonance. Since he felt this resonance develop during his project, this also served as a source of motivation for him. In the end, he had many strong points on his side so that his supervisor found it very difficult not to give him a very positive evaluation. William involved himself with his topic.

Devil's advocate

Certifications, grades, and published articles matter—both in their own terms and also in terms of what they can enable or disable. But see them in context. Ideally, you have a broader set of returns and motives stimulating your progress. Diversify your propulsion.

How to tackle

Your final academic project can generate two handfuls of different types of return for you—not just one, graduating. When you approach your project, consider the different types of return and score them by priority. Keep this in mind or maybe even on your desk: this tells you why you are investing a lot of energy into a project that, at times, can feel overly complex, uninteresting, and even pointless.

Try to think broadly and diversely—consider objective and subjective types of return, intrinsic and extrinsic types, ways in which the experience could shape, transform, and develop your own capabilities, horizon, and perspectives. But, certainly, don't forget pragmatic views in terms of your future career, professional visibility and association, ways to earn your livelihood; maybe even pursue a business idea.

Keep in mind that your priorities might change while you are conducting your research. Just be sure to consider these original high-priority return plans not just as lifelines for you to shed and write off through your project, but also plans to protect and fight for, energy permitting. If you want to build a reputation on a subject, let that information inform your actions. Don't just cross it off because you felt it was unattainable on one bad day.

Experienced peers' two cents

'There should be a purpose to a thesis, but it does not have to be a purpose in the sense that is directly related to your work or conducive to your next job. I tell students that to some extent their studies may be the last opportunity to do something that is different. I would not set the parameters too narrowly. The thesis should satisfy their curiosity, e.g. the thesis work may have an aspect concerning the topic of sustainability to it, even if it is not directly related to later professional work.' (Urs Jäger)

'I think there is such a thing as being "stuck in the middle" if you are trying to perfectly balance between academic and practitioner worlds. To my mind, any kind of work is also something spiritual. This does not have to be a religious term—"spiritual" means that there is a spirit and the spirit delivers you power for your work. You have to discover where the power for your work comes from. Sometimes, you are very deep into the theoretical papers, sometimes you are working on the practitioner case. It's only at the end of the day that it becomes a mixture. When you try to get deep enough to really discover something, then probably you need focus—focus on theory or focus on the practical work. Then, at the end of the day, you have to try and find again the right balance between the two poles, the two horns of the dilemma. It truly is a dilemma. If you are working really hard on one of the horns, you miss something on the other side. It would be much nicer not to sit every day for twelve hours reading papers—it would be wonderful to do an interview. But then I'd say: do it! Follow your spirit!' (Günter Müller-Stewens)

'I have learned for myself not to challenge students concerning their particular perspectives on how to approach knowledge. Rather, I test them where they come from—without trying to change them. After all, it is the last component in a longer educational process that the students have gone through. They have already had substantial amounts of education and are now giving a last effort that is pre-defined by their previous educational experiences.

'When students come with the perspective that knowledge is objective, then I refer them to faculty colleagues who happen to share that perspective and who have a certain way of handling it, typically using a relatively hierarchical, authoritarian, and method-driven ('learn the literature') approach—highly structured and context-free. Often, the focus is on quantitative methods. A supervisor, one who communicates this perspective well and invests care in accompanying the student during this process, can help that student to obtain a relatively high standard of methodological knowledge, recognize where science stands today, understand what knowledge means to today's mainstream academics, grasp how science is organized today (journals), and acquire an idea what academic careers entail.

'When students have a career perspective, their predominant interest is to find a job as quickly as possible. Interest in writing a thesis for the purpose of researching a topic is low. In my experience, most students fall into this category. Hence, it is important to find a supervisor who is on the same wave length, and is willing to invest time and energy despite the limited interest of the student. A university can handle this situation efficiently.

'This has much to do with the expectations of the supervisor as far as the student is concerned. I do not expect students to develop insight on the basis of a state-of-the-art methodology of science. An MA thesis is way too short, simple, and unconditional to allow us to expect an extraordinary insight. Quite the contrary: the value of a thesis has much to do with the context. Generating knowledge in a field already filled with high-level knowledge reduces the probability of someone taking note of it. But if you generate knowledge in an environment which is new to most, the probability is high that someone notices and inquires.' (Urs Jäger)

'I tell PhD but also MA students that they have a journey ahead of them, that I as supervisor can't tell them exactly where it will go and where it will lead. In an MA programme, the parameters are more set, but the time duration can be somewhat extended. However, I can't tell the student in advance whether he will complete the project in the set time. In a PhD thesis, this is even more important. I have known plenty of students, in particular from consulting firms, who have expressed an interest in doing a PhD that can be completed within two years. But I don't give them a guarantee. They cannot burden me with that perceived risk. That is not the right mindset. Over time, some people came to accept this.' (Ansgar Richter)

Preparation determines motivation

First impressions are key to initial motivation of those you engage. Sustained positive impressions are key to the stamina of a collaboration.

Metaphorically speaking

Approaching research means drafting and fine-tuning a travel plan. Since research is much more akin to a journey than arriving at a destination, the whole project revolves around designing an itinerary. The more complete, clearer, and plausible your plan as a pilot, the more motivated your air traffic control (supervisor), and the more confident your passengers (external contacts like interviewees).

Consequently, showing that you have already developed a good understanding of where, why, and how you want to travel is recommended before reaching out to your supervisor. This does not mean you have to have every detail nailed down before you seek your supervisor's initial evaluation. Simply prepare an extended abstract of your current idea of the journey.

Research also means stating what you would like to achieve. Do not look too intensely towards your supervisor to tell you what you should do, should want as a return, or ought to consider a good experience. Develop an idea and capture it on paper, then discuss with your supervisor.

Rough coordinates

Leadership—'The dignity, office, or position of a leader, esp. of a political party; ability to lead; the position of a group of people leading or influencing others within a given context; the group itself; the action or influence necessary for the direction or organization of effort in a group undertaking.'

Ownership—'The fact or state of being an owner; proprietorship, dominion; legal right of possession. The fact or state of being or feeling responsible for solving a problem, addressing an issue, etc.'

The Student's Research Companion. Omid Aschari and Benjamin Berghaus, Oxford University Press.
© Omid Aschari and Benjamin Berghaus (2023). DOI: 10.1093/oso/9780192855312.003.0011

Involvement—'The action or process of involving; the fact of being involved; the condition of being implicated, entangled, or engaged; engagement, embarrassment; financial or pecuniary embarrassment.'

Commitment—'The action or an act of obligating or binding oneself or another to a particular course of action, policy, etc.; the action of giving an undertaking, either explicitly or by implication. Also: an undertaking or pledge of this kind.'

Train of thought

When engaging supervisors, students commonly make a comfortable but unfortunate mistake: they come largely or entirely unprepared. The general state of mind seems to be that you could not possibly foresee the expectations of your future supervisor without having being told, so you do not need to try too much. She will tell you what to do. He will explain to you what I need to do to get this thing done and over with. Even though this state of mind is readily disguised as a way of accepting the supervisor's preferences, that is still only a disguise for trying not to involve or invest oneself too deeply in this project.

On your final academic project, you ought to take on and demonstrate ownership. You hold the responsibility, you must motivate the project team, you must know where you want to go, and everyone gets to look to you for orientation. Fortunately, final academic projects don't comprise many people to lead—it is mostly yourself—but your supervisor is generally not the person to look to for motivation, direction, sense, or purpose. That needs to come from you. Of course, you can build on her or his perspective to make sound decisions. But your supervisor is generally not the person who tasks you with a project and who will be your boss. They will be your peer, there to check on you.

While there are many consequences of this general rule of thumb, one speaks to how you approach potential supervisors. Come prepared. You need to have a first draft of a plan of what you would like to research. You should generate a first impression of what the literature on your subject looks like, and where you expect to find the gap to fill. How do you plan to contribute to filling this gap? Above all else: why is it important or interesting to engage this particular research project? Try to have these points squared away on one or two pages of text, one paragraph per topic.

When students are looking for supervisors, they are looking for 'the best supervisor for my project'. They suppose that there are a few superb supervisors, many mediocre ones, and many less-than ideal selections. By following these expectations, students commonly ignore the fact that the quality of their supervision has less to do with people's constant traits and more to do with their variable motivation.

You can push any supervisor's motivation—and by extension, their eagerness to supervise you excellently in their own way—by demonstrating that you know what you want, that you have a plan, that you are capable enough to capture and draft a rudimentary project draft. Supervisors are investors of time—a particularly scarce resource. They will invest in you if you quickly convince them that their time is not lost motivating you to undertake your own project. The easiest way to achieve this is to come prepared.

In this part of the book, the approach, we are mostly discussing the relevance of being prepared towards possible supervisors; but there is another important group that values preparation: external actors who may or may not support your project by providing expert insight, data, guidance, or mentoring. If you come prepared and manage to fuel their motivation to support you, your project will fly through much less turbulence than if you do not give them the impression that they are dealing with someone who values their time enough to make the interaction an enjoyable and productive experience. Much of this can be conveyed by a productive communication of respect towards your supervisor. If that communication fails, a lack of motivation is inevitable, and can damage your reputation with whomever you are trying to work with.

In essence

- Engage potential supervisors and external actors in a well-prepared way to maximize your chances of getting accepted as a supervisee and to win support as a researcher.
- To many supervisors and external actors, the degree of preparation by the potential supervisee directly correlates to how high the return of investment into your project will be.
- You can motivate almost every potential supervisor to be generous with time and insight if you are sending the signal that you will not be a drag on them, but will work self-sufficiently, in a well-organized way, and successfully.

To reflect

- What am I prepared to invest in the final academic project, and how can I demonstrate this willingness to invest through my preparation?
- What would a supervisor look for in an enjoyable, productive, and worthy-of-support colleague?
- How can I provide that?

Two travellers' tales

Xavier considers his thesis as an exam set by the university which he needs to complete. Thus, he expects to be provided with a problem or question which he can then work out—it is as simple as that. Consequently, he seeks an appointment with a potential supervisor and expects the professor to explain what she wants from him. Somehow, the meeting runs less well than he thought. There was just no (positive) energy. The professor seemed uninterested and somewhat annoyed at Xavier's lack of energy. They worked things out, the project came to pass—but all it ever came to be, was a formality on the way to graduating.

Judy thinks of her thesis as a project that she can design and sink her teeth into. She considers it something that she might want to build a bridge out of to help her find a job or maybe continue in research. Thus, she carefully chooses her topic and identifies a few interesting options to frame a research question. She familiarizes herself with some of the key literature and drafts a first proposal for a topic. With this proposal, she engages supervisors who appear to do research in a comparable area. Her supervisor picks up her proposal, suggests a few changes, and is happy to encounter an apt student who shares her interests and demonstrates the drive and self-sufficiency that will likely help her to complete the project not only successfully but also without much help. Judy implements her work and finds her supervisor open and engaged to help, since she makes a habit of coming prepared to their calls or meetings. This signals to the supervisor that investing time in Judy will pay off in a great project.

Devil's advocate

Developing your own idea is a great start and helps your supervisor get an idea of what moves you. Do not underestimate the advantages of allowing his or her views and experiences to shape and inform your plans. A great and efficient final academic project can end up being an intellectual co-creation. Have an idea of where you want to go and then allow your peer to help you get there— even if, at first, she or he comes up with an idea that appears hard to reconcile with your plans.

How to tackle

There are many ways of approaching a final academic project, but let's focus on two kinds: either you approach your project by being person-focused and knowing whom you'd like to work with as a supervisor, or you approach it by being topic-focused and knowing what subject you'd like to work on. Depending on which come first—egg or hen, topic or supervisor—you'll need different preparations.

If you are person-focused and know whom you'd like to work with as a supervisor, it helps to have actively participated in their lectures or seminars so that your face is known to them and carries positive associations. Maybe speak to one or two students who are currently writing their final academic project with this supervisor to get a sense whether the supervisor has a supervision style that works for you, or so that you at least know what to expect. Next, you review which projects they are working and publishing on, and check whether these specific topics—at the level of their specificity—are interesting to you. Check if they have an open final academic project topic announced somewhere. If yes, develop a one- or two-page proposal on their topic announcement. If no, try to work yourself into their publications and the publications they reference, and develop a first (one or two pages) proposal for a project that would be compatible with their work. Try to speak to them in person after class, and send in your proposal after having spoken to them.

If you are topic-focused and know what you'd like to work on, try to identify which supervisors might be available in the related field. You may come up with three or four at different levels of seniority. Immerse yourself in the literature on your subject. Check which publications the supervisors publish in, and compare with the literature you find interesting and accessible. It's likely that your supervisor may ask you to collaborate on a paper for one of the journals they have previously written for. To win the support of a supervisor it helps to keep in mind six things. First, are they interested in the same questions as I am? Second, do I understand their context and motives for supervision? Third, how do I help satisfy these motives? Fourth, does their supervision style work for me? Fifth, do they publish in environments that I find interesting and accessible to read (and maybe also to contribute to)? Sixth, would a collaboration with this person yield an opportunity for a growth sprint for me if I invested enough energy? Based on the answers to these questions, you can decide if that individual is suitable to apply to, and if so, develop a plan on how to pitch your project to them.

Experienced peers' two cents

'Your supervisor is not your boss, not your examiner, but your peer. My approach to this: I am not going to write the thesis for you. My job is to tell you if you are building momentum in the right direction that will lead to a successful piece of research. To guide you where you can find the areas that can help you write your thesis. My role is not to have all the answers for you. The role is that of a more experienced peer who provides guidance to ensure that the piece of research is coherent, meaningful, and well-founded. It's a form of friendly peer review.

'Unfortunately, I have to say that people tend to understand the supervisor as someone who spoon-feeds the learner as to when to write and what to write, exactly. That has a lot to do with ownership over the substance of the project. A curious person will have, assume, and defend ownership, and a non-curious person will not have that type of ownership.' (Samer Atallah)

'We have different types of students, and they seek different types of experiences in their thesis processes. If you try to impose the structure too heavily on them, some may be delighted, others might be very unhappy.

'When I did brainstorming with my students, they would come to my office and we'd book an hour and do brainstorming. I want to study this and this and this is how I would like to do it—and I'd say: great, go for it—if it passes my criteria for a valuable idea. But some of them would come to the office and say: I'd like to study corporate finance. Can you be a bit more specific? Look at the literature, look for questions that interest you and need answering. Then, come back. This is what I want to do—could you do this and that on top of that?

'Writing a thesis—if this is their first project—can be a very, very painful experience if they don't like what they are doing. It is important that the student sees the value in what they are doing, and that they are determined to turn over every stone to seek the truth on whatever they are doing.' (Timo Korkeamäki)

A peer called supervisor

Consider your supervisor a more advanced peer. Many other perspectives are based on common but misleading assumptions about what to expect.

Metaphorically speaking

Research in your final academic project means planning and conducting a journey during which you have recourse to a peer whose advice and assistance you can seek if you are stuck and cannot solve a challenge on your own. This is not your tourist guide, this is not your travel insurance, and it's also not the designated first responder. But it's a peer who has been around that particular neck of the woods and who can provide you with insight.

Consequently, try to consider your supervisor as nothing more and nothing less than a person who may be able to provide you with useful insight. Peers are not all-knowing and all-powerful. Their schedules are busy, and they are, in numerous instances, on their own journey. There is a good chance that your supervisor can provide you with useful information, but the further you are away from their field of expertise, this probability dwindles. Sometimes, supervisors are wrong in their recommendations.

In the end, your responsibility to your project is to arrive at valid, reliable, objective, and relevant insight. It is not to blindly follow your peer's instruction. It is not even to make her or him particularly happy. Your responsibility is to generate what you feel comfortable arguing is worthwhile research. Sometimes, your supervisor can help. Most of the time, it's really and truly all up to you.

Rough coordinates

Supervisor—'A person who has charge of or responsibility for a business, institution, department, etc.; an overseer; a person who directs or oversees a task or activity. A person who oversees the work or conduct of another or

The Student's Research Companion. Omid Aschari and Benjamin Berghaus, Oxford University Press.
© Omid Aschari and Benjamin Berghaus (2023). DOI: 10.1093/oso/9780192855312.003.0012

others; (now) esp. a person directly in charge of an employee or workforce; (sometimes) a person's immediate manager.'

Peer—'A person of the same civil or ecclesiastical status or rank as the person in question; an equal before the law. A person who equals another in natural gifts, ability, or achievements; the equal in any respect of a person or thing. A person who is associated or matched with another; a companion, a fellow, a mate; a rival.'

Mentor—'A person who acts as guide and adviser to another person, esp. one who is younger and less experienced. Later, more generally: a person who offers support and guidance to another; an experienced and trusted counsellor or friend; a patron, a sponsor. An experienced person in a company, college, etc., who trains and counsels new employees or students.'

Experience—'The actual observation of facts or events, considered as a source of knowledge. The fact of being consciously the subject of a state or condition, or of being consciously affected by an event. Also an instance of this; a state or condition viewed subjectively; an event by which one is affected.'

Train of thought

When starting your research project, you will encounter a new instrumental role in your academic life: your supervisor. Supervisors are different from teachers, parents, bosses, friends, and any other roles you met on your path to get here. It is easy either to be unsure of what to make of her or him, or even to confuse their role with something else. Since many supervisors are often unsure, inconsistent, extremely strict, or very lax about their role, plenty of strange relationships emerge—many not to the greatest benefit of the learning experience. For supervisor–supervisee relationships to work well, it is helpful to adopt the most suitable mode of operation:

Consider your supervisor a more advanced peer. Nothing more, nothing less. If you grant your supervisor more command over your project, you will likely turn out to be a passenger on the ride that is intended to be your project. That is not ideal: the research project is most helpful to you if you hold its reins yourself, and if you choose your direction yourself. If most of the creative choices are taken from you, there is very little to be proud of after the fact other than having endured the experience. On the other hand, if you disregard each and every instruction issued by your peer in good faith, you will not benefit from the experience that she can provide you with. As most scientific projects worth undertaking are building on decades of insight, you will not be able to perform half as well if you do not heed your more advanced peer's advice.

Working with your supervisor should resemble more of a scientific mentor–mentee relationship than anything else. Yet, there is an additional element: your supervisor may be either solely or partially involved in the evaluation of your work. Many apparently savvy students try to optimize for their supervisor's role in evaluation, and in the process turn them into the boss whose instructions are to be carried out. For your learning experience, we'd advise against this strategy: you will simply not learn as much. Rather, you will learn how to 'play the game' that is only played in this particular instance. You will learn how to implement means so that they generate ends.

Of course, some see the final project as a piece of work and the grade as the reward. We'd like to encourage you, instead, to see the final project as a challenge, the learning during the process as your reward, and the evaluation as one external voice mandated and paid for by the university to have some figure or letter to write on a piece of paper that institutionalizes learning. The evaluation, the figure or letter, and the piece of paper are not the point of your attending university. The point is your growth. That's why you and/or the society around you pays a considerable amount of money for your education—don't let that be spent on you optimizing for some letter or number on a piece of paper.

Even though some supervisors might suit you better than others, the single right supervisor for you does not really exist. Consequently, it makes sense to focus on the working relationship you build with the supervisor you end up having. You will fare best if you tend towards expecting little, but propose and follow through with a clear scheme of interaction that also works for them.

In essence

- Your supervisor is different from any other type of role you may have encountered so far. A suitable way of thinking of your supervisor is as a more advanced peer.
- Do not expect too much from your supervisor. Your best bet is to be well-prepared, efficient, and reliable in your interactions with her or him.
- Supervisors can become excited about and invested in one or more projects, but that depends on what they are allowed to witness.

To reflect

- Which kind of supervision relationship do you seek?
- What can you do to professionalize and streamline your interaction with your supervisor?
- How can you express your excitement about your project?

Two travellers' tales

Otto thinks of the thesis as the final chore that he has to complete before finally escaping university to go to work. Consequently, the thesis really is more of a task that he has to fulfil to his supervisor's specifications. He has very little ownership of this project—no more than with any other exam before, really. He sees his supervisor as someone akin to a superior at his last internship. 'The boss just needs to tell me what I need to do, then I do it.' Otto managed to complete his thesis, but never understood the thesis as something different from busywork. He did not learn much, and was surprised that on several occasions his supervisor got cross with him and did not want to tell him exactly what to do.

Faika sees the thesis as one of those projects at university which require you to take ownership and develop something on your own. She's excited to take on the opportunity, but also slightly uncertain about whether she brings all necessary capabilities to the project. Knowing that she has an older research peer who can be called upon when she really does not know the next step, or which option to choose, helps her to relax a bit. Faika certainly does not want to see her supervisor as her boss—she's much too independent for that. If this is her thesis, it will be *her* thesis. Faika completes a thesis that made her proud because it was thoroughly her own production, and a by-product of her learning more about the methodology she applied and a field she finds interesting.

Devil's advocate

Research means performing at the peak of your abilities. Find a good balance between performing at your best and being able to perform long-term. When in doubt, be merciful to yourself.

How to tackle

Try to build a working relationship with the supervisor you end up working with. Agreeing on a schedule might help both of you to structure the collaboration, if the supervisor agrees and does not have any other established systems of supervising their students.

For a six-month project, consider proposing meetings every six weeks. For the first meeting, about a month into your project, you might prepare a more detailed overview of your project and input on your overall trajectory. As subject of the second meeting, you might have a plan for gathering data, and also make sure that the plan makes sense to her. At the third meeting, you might debrief her on the data collection and give an update on the data analysis. Finally, you conclude your project by doing a debriefing about a month after having completed your project. This keeps the interaction in a constant and usefully spaced, not overburdened rhythm. You have ample time in between two touch-points, but also not too much time to get lost.

If your reality deviates from what we propose above (and most do), simply try to steer your project towards what you consider ideal. Nothing should keep you from getting in touch with your supervisor, even after a long gap—certainly not the feeling of your not being up to speed.

Experienced peers' two cents

'A lot that goes on in that external environment of the self as the candidate that impacts upon someone's ability to have a positive experience. A candidate may not feel valued by their supervisors, or that they're a part of a research culture. If you're not a part of some kind of community, then it's very difficult to see the worth in your own work when nobody else does. There's this to-ing and fro-ing between having that positive affirmation. Yes, this work is valued and affirmed by others. At the same time, by getting that feedback, you can then see the value yourself. So, we need, as institutions and lecturers and staff, to take responsibility for the way that we treat those who are conducting research. We need to value their contributions and to recognize that they are on a journey. And these can be very demanding journeys to try and support somebody on for supervisors as well. But researchers need to feel that they are personally valued and professionally making a contribution of value. And

I don't think we always do both or even only one of those things actually terribly well.' (Kim Beasy)

'Students must know what they want to achieve. They have to ask the right questions, and answer them. The appropriate supervisor can help them accomplish this. It's an illusion to think that a Master's thesis is a scientific paper and context-independent (developing knowledge that draws you closer to "truth"). Everything has to do with context, relations among people, relations to data, relations to science itself. Students must be clear what they are buying into, before starting research. The challenge is that students often do not know which questions are relevant, as these emerge during the process. Besides the supervisor, the institution of the university (and how it organizes this process of match-making and helps the student to ask the right questions etc.) is important in helping them solve this issue.' (Urs Jäger)

'I think what happens too often is that all the mentoring is around the substantive issues, the content. Mentoring might have somewhat of a blind spot on the process of research, like managing your personal workload, understanding the unwritten rules of the field, working through a reasonable process, that has boundaries, that is focused. I think part of making that more transparent to new supervisees in particular is to formalize it. To make explicit ideas such as "What constitutes a theory?", "What is an audience?", "How do you structure papers?" These kinds of things—formal work taken in as part of the curriculum, not just role-modelling, but actual formalization—helps supervisors (and in turn students) to internalize these ideas.' (Steven Floyd)

Countless shades of supervision

Supervisors are free to interpret their role as they see fit. Work with one who interprets their role in a way that you would like to be subject to and learn from.

Metaphorically speaking

While research can be a lonely journey, there is always a base camp somewhere. That's where you will find your peer. Peers are people and have different types of personality, goals, ways of thinking and operating. The more open and attentive you manage to be when selecting and collaborating with your peer, the more productive this relationship can be.

Consequently, try to distance yourself from the perspective that potential research peers are mainly to be differentiated by their fields of interest. Instead, consider that every peer has their individual set of goals, methodologies, convictions, and processes. A peer experienced in a field that seems interesting to you might be less fitting in supervision style to your personality than another in a field that seems less interesting. But who is to say if a great collaboration in a less interesting field is better than a miserable collaboration in a positively exciting field? That is for you to decide.

Research, to a degree, also means interaction among people. This interaction can be inspiring and fruitful, and it can be demotivating and painful. The quality, however, does not depend only on the researcher or their peer, but also on the collaboration they manage to create. A fit in styles can go a long way.

Rough coordinates

Flourishing—'To thrive, display vigour in, of, with (something specified); also, to abound in, overflow with. Of things (e.g. art, science, an institution): To attain full development; to be prosperous or successful, be in vogue; to have many followers or patrons.'

The Student's Research Companion. Omid Aschari and Benjamin Berghaus, Oxford University Press.
© Omid Aschari and Benjamin Berghaus (2023). DOI: 10.1093/oso/9780192855312.003.0013

Environment—'The social, political, or cultural circumstances in which a person lives, esp. with respect to their effect on behaviour, attitudes, etc.'

Supervisor—'A person who has charge of or responsibility for a business, institution, department, etc.; an overseer; a person who directs or oversees a task or activity. A person who oversees the work or conduct of another or others; (now) esp. a person directly in charge of an employee or workforce; (sometimes) a person's immediate manager.'

Style—'A mode of deportment or behaviour; a mode or fashion of life, esp. in regard to expense, display, etc.'

Train of thought

Different people need different environments to flourish. There is little use putting a mind of great creative capabilities in a context of restrictions. Likewise, there is little sense in putting an efficient mind in a place where there are no systems established to work with. Even though those two considerations appear plausible, many students find themselves at odds with the work context they find themselves in when writing a thesis. Even though final academic projects are intended to be largely equivalent in challenge and dimensions, they commonly have many different shapes and sizes in terms of how much creative space there is, how much focus on exotic methodology, and what the functional outcome will be. Much of this has to do with the academic supervisor.

Selecting a fitting supervisor will make a considerable difference in your personal experience of fit between you and your thesis. This is commonly hidden from the student perspective, as you are only experiencing one, two, or maybe three theses and might end up feeling that your experience is simply what a thesis feels like.

Supervisors come with different sets of motivation: one might be thoroughly altruistic, the other sagely restrained, the next entirely disinterested, and the last very demanding—and a fifth combining all of these traits. From the perspective of a student, these differences might not mean much and could be simply ascribed to personal characteristics and maybe even mood. If you look behind the curtain, however, you find the systems that drive these behavioural patterns: the professional realities and motivational systems that supervisors are subject to.

Let's start with the altruistic or the sage: commonly, you have senior, tenured professors who are nearing their retirement. These supervisors have ample experience, and they know that refraining from making decisions for you will yield the most substantial learning on your part. Professors nearing their retirement commonly do not relentlessly pursue their research profile, since they've reached what they wanted to reach: they have already built their scientific legacy. Common among the silverbacks, you might run into the free-ranging, the openly curious, the rather demanding, the self-focused, and any mixture of the above.

Then you have the professors in the midst of their career. These are the backbone of academia. Some might have tenure, many will not. Especially for those who do not have tenure, work will mean not only research and teaching, but also winning third-party funding for their position and the financing of their department. That means that your final academic project may likely play a lesser role in their priorities—the top of the list is already pretty crowded. As incentive structures at most universities are set up, most associate and younger tenured professors will reasonably place research and third-party funding as a first priority and teaching as a second. As most associate professors will have one or a few PhD candidates as research assistants, they might not consider your final academic project as a contribution to their research, but rather as part of their teaching commitments. All of this suggests that the context of associate professors is commonly suited to final academic projects that are less guided and more of a place to use creative space.

Finally, you will encounter younger associate and assistant professors. These academics are still establishing themselves and their research in the field. Due to the particularly competitive nature of this phase of their career, you may expect these researchers to be those under the highest pressure and equipped with the least comprehensive experience. Here, you will find those who are most interested in, focused on, and versed in cutting-edge research niches: these highly competitive people are building their career hopes on competitiveness in publishing articles that will propel their advancement. You will find young researchers on a mission to build a reputation in a field.

Your final academic project might play a considerable role in this, as younger academics commonly do not command a team of PhD students, and Bachelor's and Master's theses can make a contribution to exploring a field to evaluate whether their own time would be wisely spent in that direction. The characteristics are that you will be more closely guided, and your trajectory will be predetermined. With closer guidance comes less freedom but, if you perform well, a greater chance to co-author a published paper. Supervising you pays off for the young academic insofar as you might contribute to a publishable project.

In essence

- Different people benefit from different environments to flourish.
- There are several types of supervisors as well as countless gradations in between those types. Having a supervisor who fits your preferred style of work and your goal of a successful project helps build a good and productive relationship.
- When considering different potential supervisors, try to empathize with their roles, styles, and likely motivations. Reflect on what that might imply for you as a supervisee.

To reflect

- What kind of work environment do I prefer when conducting potentially challenging and complex projects?
- Based on their topical positioning, which potential supervisors might take on my project? ('Long' list)
- Out of these potential supervisors, who seems to have a style that is complimentary to what I benefit from in terms of a collaborative environment? ('Short' list, considering their career stages and potential motives)

Two travellers' tales

Zach focused his entire attention on the research subject when considering supervisors. He picked a professor who had published on this subject before and who had good connections with practitioners in this particular research area. Zach is a highly engaged and very creative student who loves ownership. He signs on with his preferred supervisor. Sadly, the preferred supervisor is so highly engaged in research and practice that under him, Zach feels as though he has become an intern who is being assigned project work in an existing project, but not his own. Yes, Zach learns 'how it's done'—but, truly, he would have preferred a little bit more freedom in designing his own project instead of signing up for an unpaid job as a researcher. Zach pulls through and completes a good project—albeit different from what he would have liked.

Lara paid equal amounts of attention to the subject and careful choice of supervisors. She is an efficient worker, and knows that she will flourish under closer guidance and greater project integration. She is willing to accept that this means less freedom in exchange for greater efficiency. Lara excels at her project—both substantially and experientially. She found an environment that worked well for her, and she will build on this experience to choose her first employer and superior.

Devil's advocate

Especially if you (or your supervisor) decide to (decides for you to) mostly work on your own, the collaboration style fit is less important. In other words, that is one type of collaboration style: none. Check for this, too. If you want to be a lone wolf, seek a laissez-faire supervisor.

How to tackle

Your final academic project experience will greatly depend on the degree to which there is a good and productive chemistry between you and your supervisor. As a rule of thumb, almost every supervisor can be motivated to become a good supervisor and act as a scientific mentor, if the chemistry works well and each understands what the other person seeks (the exception being academics who might be harmfully overworked themselves). Conversely, almost every supervisor can be a horrible supervisor if the chemistry does not work.

For your final academic project to turn into a desirable supervisee experience, reflect on what you want from your supervisor as a minimum, as an ideal level of supervision, and as a maximum. First, you need to try and understand what your goal is. It is also helpful to speak to other, like-minded students who have already completed a final academic project, to learn more about what you might want and might not want. (Try not to fall into the 'all-inclusive trap' here—in most cases, the true ideal is not to wish for the least possible effort involved, but a great outcome from a plausible investment.)

If you are in the position to choose between professors to try and convince them to supervise you, it pays to explore her or his style of interaction with other students, and what motivates and de-motivates this particular professor. Be careful what you wish for, here: the big-name professor might be less compatible with you than a younger postdoc. Speak to other students who worked with the particular supervisor to find out what might motivate them to support you and your project. If you have a choice, only engage those supervisors who are a good match for your preference.

Once you get a sense of what you are looking for in terms of a supervision relationship, review the shortlist of possible supervisors to see if a compatibility becomes apparent. Your list of potential supervisors should at least become shorter. You can then shorten this list further by considering whom on your list you can convince that taking you on will help them reach their goals. This has a lot to do with understanding what people are working on, where they publish, what they are trying to accomplish (and your own project being compatible with that). If you can make that case, you will have the highest likelihood of getting accepted for supervision.

Finally, it is a good idea to carefully discuss the mode of operation with your supervisor while not turning this into too much of an issue. Much of the collaboration will unfold as it happens. There will likely not be a detailed agreement between you and your supervisor on your collaboration. Still, it is a good idea to signal that you are mindful, and open to discussing ways to make the supervision of your project a professional and fluent experience for you as well as your supervisor.

Experienced peers' two cents

'There are different types of supervisors. And not all types of supervisors are open to discuss possible research ideas with the students. So, there are supervisors who are treating their students as "slaves" to delegate some of the not-so-convenient research work they have to do. But that's also, I think, the duty of the student to get information about the type of supervisor they are looking for.' (Günter Müller-Stewens)

'The way that an individual teacher treats supervision is his or her own decision, within a general, very loose framework. We have a minimum requirement in Master's theses; we have a minimal requirement by courses to ensure that these offers to write a thesis meet the minimum learning outcomes. However, academic freedom remains a cornerstone when discussing common guidelines or individual autonomy.' (Samer Atallah)

'I have learned for myself not to challenge students concerning their particular perspectives on how to approach knowledge. Rather, I test them where they come from—without trying to change them. After all, this is the last component in a longer educational process that the students have gone through. They have already had substantial amounts of education, and are now giving a last effort that is pre-defined by their previous educational experiences.

'When students come with the perspective that knowledge is objective, then I refer them to faculty colleagues who happen to share that perspective and who have a certain way of handling it, typically using a relatively hierarchical, authoritarian and method-driven ('learn the literature') approach— highly structured and context-free. Often, the focus is on quantitative methods. A supervisor that who works well from this perspective, and invests care in accompanying the student during this process, can help that student to obtain a relatively high standard of methodological knowledge, recognize where science stands today, understand what knowledge means to today's mainstream academics, grasp how science is organized today (journals), and gain an idea of what academic careers entail.

'When a student has with a career perspective, the predominant interest is to find a job as quickly as possible. The interest in writing a thesis for the purpose of researching a topic is low. In my experience, most students fall into this category. Hence, it is important to find a supervisor who is on the same 'wave length' and is willing to invest time and energy despite the low interest of the student. As part of a university, one can organize this situation efficiently.

'When a student invests time and energy in understanding what knowledge really means, they see it as a scientific adventure and bring with them a high 'naivety tolerance level'. They are open to admitting that they are lacking in knowledge. However, they perceive this as an opportunity to go ahead and start asking questions. In such case, I am eager to accompany such students along the path of understanding what knowledge really means. The relationship with such students is strong, similar to a PhD student. I treat them as if they are PhD students but in a more condensed form (BA/MA students). I provide them with texts, sources, and input from me about knowledge. They learn that knowledge is organized by humans. That a university is not representing a church, where one is supposed to discover truth, and professors are not priests. The students begin to understand what knowledge means and how to organize it. These are students who want to think deeply, and who are interested in the context (i.e. they are interested in analysing context that allows them to generate knowledge that can be used in other contexts). When such students appear, I help them to apply empirical projects and to get contact with relevant contexts. They learn methods of qualitative research. I accompany them along their learning path.' (Urs Jäger)

'Students should think carefully about what their potential supervisor's interests are. In the end, you have to work within those interest boundaries. Since supervision also means a commitment on the part of the supervisor,

ensuring that the student can work successfully within these interest boundaries makes it much more likely that a thesis project gets accepted for
supervision.

'There are those who like to supervise only those theses or dissertations
that are relevant to their own work. They want somebody to plough in their
own field and to make a contribution to what they're interested in. Others
are much broader in their commitment, and merely want to cultivate good
thinking. The potential supervisor can ask himself or herself: "What is the
payoff for me if I supervise this particular student?"

'Mentoring depends very much on where the mentee is in terms of their
development. They are not all the same. Some come with a question they
really want to pursue, and have already done some work on—particularly in
the PhD programmes, when a student has previously worked at the Master's
level on a topic. Some students are just naturally more disciplined. Some students have very fragile egos and have a greater need to be protected. Each
individual is unique, and the mentoring process has to be tailored to the
individual.' (Steven Floyd)

BEGIN

There comes the day when you take your first step out of the door. You'll be thoroughly excited and eager to progress quickly. To make your steps count, be sure to focus some attention on the following ideas. It pays to set things up in your favour to avoid pains and/or the need to redo something a few weeks down the road.

Conduct a project

Think of your thesis or dissertation as a project to be conducted. The resulting document merely reports your project and is a component of it.

Metaphorically speaking

Research is the sum and interplay of experiences you encounter when conducting a worthwhile excursion into a topic. It is not just the mechanical act of walking, but your plans, your modes of travel, your thoughts, your impressions, your insights. It is the decisions you made, how you carried them out, and what you unlocked through them.

Consequently, to appreciate and understand research most appropriately, consider it a complex and integrated experience, not just one facet of it (documentation). This recommendation is more critical than it might seem at first glance. Only if you appreciate research in all its facets will you be able to foresee, provide for, and mitigate challenges. Only if you appreciate research holistically will you be able to recognize the interactions between carrying out and documenting a project, between reading literature and phrasing your question, between writing, thinking, and revising—and so on.

Research, once understood as project work that includes many capabilities and 'trades', can be managed much more efficiently and effectively than if it is misunderstood as mainly revolving around one task—writing—with all other tasks merely tacked on.

Rough coordinates

Research—'Systematic investigation or inquiry aimed at contributing to knowledge of a theory, topic, etc., by careful consideration, observation, or study of a subject. In later use also: original critical or scientific investigation carried out under the auspices of an academic or other institution.'

The Student's Research Companion. Omid Aschari and Benjamin Berghaus, Oxford University Press.

Project—'A planned or proposed undertaking; a scheme, a proposal; a purpose, an objective.'

Document—'Something written, inscribed, etc., which furnishes evidence or information upon any subject.'

Decision—'The action, fact, or process of arriving at a conclusion regarding a matter under consideration; the action or fact of making up one's mind as to an opinion, course of action, etc.'

Train of thought

The colloquial term describing a final academic project at the end of your programme, if it is research-based, is that you 'write your thesis' or dissertation. As with many colloquialisms, this is oversimplifying, at least to the degree of being misleading: you will likely spend only a rather limited time during your final academic project actually writing the document if you follow a plausible procedure.

Instead, you will be spending ample amounts of time thinking about what you are going to write about. You are going to research what others have written. You will try and figure out which kind of approach makes sense, and how you get your data. Furthermore, you will implement your data-gathering and analysis—and you try to make sense of it all. Then—only then—will you truly start writing.

There is one simple reason for this order of priorities. To write, you must first have something that you can document. And that's your research project. Most students realize this when they talk to parents and friends who love to ask, 'How many pages have you written already?' and find it difficult to comprehend that research is mostly implementing the project and only a limited amount of time documenting your work by writing.

There are a few implications that come with the insight of 'project, not document'. All these thoughts are linked to the notion of research being like shooting with a bow and arrow: they are logical implications, not necessarily choices.

First, since doing research means conducting a project and not writing a document, many technical guides on writing that your examination office will be glad to equip you with are less instructive than they seem. It is certainly great that you should use 11pt New Times Roman and double-spaced lines—not because it's the last word in typography, but because it's one of the few things you can be certain of. The same goes for margin widths and line spacing. Do not, on any account, invest any kind of creative energy into making your document submission-ready by deviating from these standards. It's not the point, and it will draw away your time and energy. That's the domain of the examination office, and since it's one of the very few external instructions you will get for the project, hold it dear. The one instruction that we would like to direct particular attention to is the number of pages to be submitted. Any academic peer will tell you that your finish line cannot be defined by a number of pages. Sure, they might suggest (and follow through) that a longer submission will not be accepted. But that will merely be based on the powers that be. Not because your 70, 50, 20, or 100 pages were not documenting a great project. The number of pages says nothing about the quality of the project. But since it's an all-too-easy restriction to define and to uphold, not meeting it can easily lead to problems. Rather, consider the number of pages specified as information about the proper format—just like margins or font sizes—which provide you with an idea of how much space you can work with, how to break this space down, and how much space (and readers' attention) to assign to which types of content. While the number of pages or words cannot tell you when you are done, it is a great help in structuring your content. Also, no matter the page or word limit: once you get going, it is hardly ever enough.

Second, since doing research means conducting a project and not writing a document, adjusting your state of mind accordingly is helpful. The great news is that, initially, you can put aside your fears about writer's block, since you will not be writing for a while. Instead, plan out your traditional six-month final academic project like a project manager and consider instructive project stages, for example: 'Capture the problem', with much observation and little reading, for the first month (especially if you work independently and uninstructed, this will take time); during the next month, 'Confirm and confine the problem', with much reading and judging what it takes to solve the problem; in the third month, 'Prepare data gathering', with much consideration of data format and variables; for the fourth and fifth months, 'Gather and analyse data'; and for the last month, 'Document your project'. If you have everything lined up and ready to write down, you will likely not need more than four weeks to actually document a final academic project—to write what you did. These time frames may be useful proposals for Bachelor's and Master's, and can be multiplied three- to sixfold for PhD theses.

Third, taking an entrepreneurial perspective on your research project, you may feel like adopting an even broader perspective of how your next sixth months are going to play out and what implications are linked. It's no longer just about writing a text. It is about determining who your project should benefit, how to get in touch and learn from those people—and which type of relationship you would like to establish with them. Likewise, it will be about figuring out what provides value to them—what they would consider a true contribution. Once you know that: how are you going to make that contribution? What are you actually going to do? What are you going to need? And: who might be on your team to help you reach your goal? As a bottom line, what are you willing to invest, and what do you want from your project in return? All of these questions broaden your horizon to the degree that will be useful when getting a clearer and more complete sense of what it is that you are trying to do and how you might go about it. Certainly, your research project plays a part within this broader perspective. And part of your research project is your documentation, the text you are going to write and submit. But this is, for now, rather a minor facet.

Your final academic project is not a writing exercise. Or, rather, it can be so much more than that. Of course, it is always your decision whether to focus on either of the different levels. But if you choose to commit to a purposefully designed project that provides a contribution for an audience, just know that this is a valuable path to pursue, and that this might be one way of thinking about it. If you are considering it, rest assured that you are already far, far ahead of most supervisors' expectations. Be careful not to motivate them too much.

In essence

- Think of your thesis or dissertation as a project, not a document. The text you hand in is the documentation of your project.
- By thinking in this way, you immediately shift to a more suitable understanding of what will determine your success (e.g. not the number of pages written, but instead access to data).
- Consider your goal to be to design, conduct, and document a plausible and enlightening research project that helps an audience solve a problem by increasing insight into the challenge, and possibly by proposing solutions. It is not to write a short book.

To reflect

- At its core: what is your project about?
- Which components does your project consist of?
- How do these components contribute to your project's success?

Two travellers' tales

Maya does not mind writing. She's been writing essays and other assignments through most of her studies, so how hard can it be to write the thesis? Sure, it's longer, but it will not be that different. Maya finds an interesting topic and manages to work through the introduction and theory parts without much difficult. But now, writing gets more difficult. How is she going to set up her methodology? How is she going to analyse her data? What data? She seems to have underestimated the effect of having data access in facilitating her advancement. She bites the bullet and speaks to her supervisor. Her supervisor walks her through the project management part of her thesis that she has so far neglected. Maya gets back into her stride after getting stuck, finds a pragmatic data access, carries out her slightly rudimentary analysis, and finally returns to writing.

Adam sees the thesis as a project in which writing has two objectives: writing is a tool to help him refine his thinking about his subject, and it is a documentation effort at the end. In that sense, he actively uses writing to develop, test, and discuss his thoughts with peers. But he does not start finally compiling the documentation of his project until the final stage of his project, when most of the material he wants to write about—from research questions to methodology to findings—is known. He rarely gets stuck, since he always knows what he wants and needs to write about next.

Devil's advocate

Sadly, your writing will be the window through which your supervisor will look at your project. This is one of the reasons why writing has such a sizeable priority as part of the final academic project. Since it came to be as an examination, your writing is immutable evidence in this process. This cannot be argued away. However, your aim is not to produce evidence—it is to conduct a project and then document it to submit it as evidence on your performance.

How to tackle

As soon as you consider your final academic project a project to conduct and not a text to write, you open up to the opportunity to pick from many of the available tools that can help you manage and structure your project.

Plenty of these tools are predominantly procedural: how do you plan to go from A to B (i.e. visualizing your critical path in a Gantt chart)? Some of them actively steer your work through different types of activities (i.e. designing thinking approaches).

We keep coming back to the idea of a final academic project being usefully informed by a purposeful, scientific, social entrepreneurial view. Applied research on entrepreneurship has floated many different canvass-type structures that can help diversify your ideas about the challenge you are about to tackle. One concept we keep coming back to and thinking about is Osterwalder's Business Model Canvas.[1] We believe this captures many facets that can purposefully inform your design of a final academic project. The following diagram (see illustration 3) summarizes the discussion in the remainder of this section.

The Business Model Canvas is made up of nine spaces for you to consider and to bring to life. Of course, these spaces need reformulation for our purposes.

Working our way back from the result to the requirements, the BMC begins with customer segments as the first space which we might translate into the audience you aim to contribute to. Two spaces are immediately related to your audience. First, which type of relationship do you wish to build with them? Second, what are the channels through which you can reach your audience?

Centrally, BMC positions the value proposition. This is largely comparable to the contribution you aim to make. How does the contribution of your research unfold its value to the audience? Which problem can you help solve? Which insight do you plan to provide? These three questions are best derived from insight into your audience's challenges, gathered through the channels you can tap into and the relationships you aim to build.

Now that we have a first idea of what you want to contribute, let's work our way further back. What does the research design that can produce this contribution look like? Which resources do you need to carry out this research design? Finally, who do you depend on to provide you with access to these resources and enable this research design?

Finally, there are the two spaces that put your project into the context of a relationship between your personal investment of time, effort, stress, and possibly financial burden on one hand, and on the other the potential for return in terms of how your contribution can generate a benefit not only for your audience but also for yourself.

---

[1] See Osterwalder, A. and Pigneur, Y. (2010), *Business Model Generation: A Handbook for Visionaries, Game Changers, and Challengers.* Hoboken, NJ: Wiley & Sons

Support Structure (key Partners)

Who can help you? Who might benefit from collaborating with you? With whom do you share the same goals?

Who might help you set up and review your research design? Who might influence your research design?

Who might provide you with (access to) resources critical to your research project?

Research Design (Key Activities)

What do you plan to do? Which methodology are you going to implement? Why is this research design the best possible choice for this project?

Key Resources

What does your research design require as resources? Do you have access to these resources? If not: do you need to change your research design?

Contribution (Value Proposition)

Why does your project matter? To whom does it matter?

What is your project's contribution? How does your contribution become effective? What does it take to implement your contribution? How does your contribution compare to alternatives?

Relationships (Customer Relationships)

Which kind of interaction do you wish to establish with your audience? How do they and how do you benefit from the relationship?

Channels

How can members of your audience become aware of your project and stay connected with you? Which channels do you maintain?

Audience (Customer Segments)

Who is your audience? Why did you pick this audience? How do you relate to your audience?

What is the central challenge that you would like to help your audience with? What is the underlying problem? Any initial ideas for solutions?

How might your audience change in future? How are their challenge and solutions going to change?

Investment (Cost Structure)

What are you willing to bring to the project? Which different types of 'raw materials' – from time to skills, from effort to access – do you have at your disposal to contribute to this enterprise?

What will be an investment easily done? What comes at a higher cost to you? Can you shape your project to benefit from easy investments?

Return (Revenue Streams)

What do you want to generate as a return from your project? Which different types of 'products' – from learning to topical positioning, from insight to impact – do you want to realize through your efforts?

What is your timeframe for recuperating your investment of time and effort? What do you need to set up to generate this return?

Illustration 3: Thinking through your project as a scientific entrepreneur, adapted from the Business Model Canvas

Experienced peers' two cents

'Another skill comes into play here: independent study skills. Students need to select their topic, their area of focus, the resources that will be useful. Even if they will be getting support from their supervisor, there are so many things to do on their own which develop their independent study skills. That will be a lifelong asset for everyone who goes through this process—not only to complete their thesis but to pick up skills that will be useful in any field, wherever they go. Even if they do not pursue research degrees or further education' (Madhu Neupane Bastola)

Follow one trajectory

Align every component of your project with one common trajectory that leads to your project's goal. It pays to be critical with this.

Metaphorically speaking

At least the outline of a research project, much like a travel plan, ought to follow a consistent and logical development along a more or less intended path. Even if research reality often includes loops, surprises, and sudden changes of speed and direction, a journey rarely begins with a plan fraught with interruptions, accidental teleportation from one place to another, and disconnected segments would be as hard to follow as a research project whose individual segments do not link up convincingly. It is precisely because 'life will happen' while implementing your research project—that there will be plenty of twists and turns you will need to make sense of down the road, when writing your documentation—that you want to keep at least your initial plan quite straightforward.

Consequently, try to see your project, therefore, as a trajectory that your readers will be able to agree with. There should not be bends and breaks in your development that others find hard to follow. From another perspective, both the process and the result of research need to convince readers. Your chance to convince is threatened by each individual instance of disconnect. Maximize your chances by planning, conducting, and reporting your journey convincingly.

Research means producing and presenting a single piece of thought development. Thoughts are easily questioned and challenged by a critical audience. Researchers are by their nature among the most critical audiences you might imagine. This is why planning, implementing, and producing a seamless project is a central goal.

The Student's Research Companion. Omid Aschari and Benjamin Berghaus, Oxford University Press.
© Omid Aschari and Benjamin Berghaus (2023). DOI: 10.1093/oso/9780192855312.003.0015

Rough coordinates

Component—'A constituent element or part.'

Alignment—'The result of arranging in or along a line, or into appropriate relative positions; the layout or orientation of a thing or things disposed in this way. Also: a group of things forming a line.'

Logic/logical—'The branch of philosophy that treats of the forms of thinking in general, and more especially of inference and of scientific method.' 'Of or pertaining to logic; also, of the nature of formal argument.'

Progression—'Continuous action conceived or presented as onward movement through time; progress or advancement through a period, process, sequence of events, etc.; movement towards an outcome or goal; (also) such a process; a course (of action, time, life, etc.); a proceeding or process.'

Train of thought

When you embark on your scientific journey, the chances are that you will have not the same clear understanding of how the seemingly independent decisions build upon each other that you would have when you are actually planning a trip. You instinctively know that, to go to Australia, you need to pack your bags, get to the airport, take the plane, and organize local transportation to get to your final destination. When starting research, you have a certain idea of the components—theory, data, writing, your research question, and the conclusions you will come up with—but you should not be discouraged if you do not have the faintest idea of the order in which you can most usefully align them. And at the moment when you feel an anxiety attack creeping up, you realize that the most important consideration lies in the challenge you face: alignment.

When you start your research project, the initial conviction that you ought to adopt is that the individual components of your project need to be in alignment. A different way of putting this is that your goal is to generate a logical progression of thought and action. What does 'logical' mean, though? This is why our recommendation is that you should instead think of alignment and (to use an analogy) of hitting a target by shooting an arrow from a bow. If you hit the target—produce a good scientific project—all elements of the process—all stages of the arrow's journey—need to be in one continuous, flowing alignment. There will certainly be cross-winds, and you must account for gravity, so you might aim up a bit, but still: the arrow never jumps to the side and then flips backwards all of a sudden, it always tracks true from the moment you relax your index finger and thumb to let go to the moment when the tip of the arrow first touches your target.

The most powerful and efficient implication of this notion is that it shifts your perception of where your degrees of freedom are and which parts of the journey will be merely results of your initial decisions. In developing a guiding research strategy and setting off on a project, the instances of your actually having a say in how you want to do things are extremely, almost painfully limited. Most of 'how' you are going to approach the project will be governed by 'what' you are planning to do. There is more leeway in deciding what you want to do—but then again, less than you might think. In every field, there is a narrow band of borderland that is suitable for research—come too far inland and the topic has been researched and will feel dull; go too far outside the perimeter and you will risk rejection by your audience—you might become a free thinker ahead of your time.

If 'how' is mostly governed and 'what' is also quite limited, consider thinking yourself back to 'why' you wanted to invest your time into research (beyond the necessity to get your degree). Do you want to help people? Are you simply, genuinely curious about something? Do you really love working with data? Are you fascinated by people telling you about their perceptions of critical incidents? What is it that can be a source of joy in your research? The 'why' is entirely unregulated by any kind of scientific impetus. You may decide why you want to research. It is your choice of target, speaking of bow and arrow. Depending on your choice of target, you will make logical deductions on how far you need to pull back your arrow, how to account for gravity and wind. By pulling the string further back, you will automatically tighten the grip of your fingers and flex your muscles to charge your bow with the energy needed to propel your arrow. None of this is your individual choice—everything depends on your choice of target. That target is not the insight you want to generate, but the reason why you attempt it.

Adjust your expectations of what will be challenging about your final academic project. It is not a myriad of independent decisions one after another, but the necessity of understanding the red thread that weaves all of these decisions together to form one powerful vector in relation to your target. There is a reason why most people with little experience do not hit the target, and why those with great experience are more likely to score higher: this is part of the challenge that stands between you and a good research project. This capability is, however, also something mastered by many, and there are distinct, learnable competencies that can help you hit the target.

In essence

- Even though they sometimes appear independent of each other, most design decisions in your research project are logically linked, and depend on each other.
- Understanding and becoming able to appreciate the interrelatedness of design decisions is one of the central insights you can learn while conducting your final academic project.
- It is useful to understand the interrelated nature of research design decisions as helpful and not a hindrance: there will be plenty of white space left for you to create in—but where there is a logical connection between the state of a field, your choice of methodology, the type of data you generate and the type of analysis you will be running, you can relax and allow the logic take over some of the hard decision-making for you.

To reflect

- What are the design characteristics of your project that are (more or less) set in stone? What are the design decisions of your project that are still to be determined?
- Is there a combination of characteristics and decisions that fit together most seamlessly? Which decisions go well together (i.e. need the least amount of explanation, since they implicitly feel well related)?
- Which characteristics previously thought of as 'set in stone' might need revising? Do you need to adjust?

Two travellers' tales

Burt loves research. To him, drafting a research project is predominantly a form of creative work. He enjoys exploring the options open to him from stage to stage in a project. In his thesis, he gets to choose not only a topic, but also the way he wants to tackle it, the way he would like to analyse the data he generates, and his way of bringing it all together in a document. All goes well until he finds himself in a surprisingly stern defence of his project with his supervisor. She simply does not understand or follow most of the decisions he arrived at in his project. Burt is not sure if his supervisor is simply being complicated or whether he could have done something differently.

Nina loves research. To her, drafting a research project is predominantly a way of logically linking design decisions together in a robust chain. She knows that sensibly chaining together design decisions in her project will enable others to better follow what it is she has attempted. Whenever someone does not follow her plans, she knows to review the links of the chain where people were thrown off her train of thought. Nina has a certain sense of security that, even though there are countless ways of generating new insight, she can draw from her most fundamental choices—the subject of her analysis and the state of existing literature—to arrive at the most appropriate path to take. Usually, there are fewer than a handful of options from which she can choose in light of her individual situation as a researcher (e.g. resources available to her, access, her skills).

Devil's advocate

Life happens. You may have planned the most integrated and the smoothest implementation yet on a given subject, but still, reality struck your project and turned it into a wicked, crooked journey. That happens and—given an interesting subject—this is far from a drama. It is interesting! But finding something interesting based on an approach that was planned to run smoothly is more exciting than generating chaotic performance art from a project plan that always seemed disjointed and overly expressionist.

How to tackle

To align the design decisions in your research project—all little and big characteristics you can and need to determine in your undertaking—it is commonly a good idea to think back from the audience to which you would like to make a contribution. Here, you find not only most of the insight you need about the nature of the problem you aim to tackle, and the detailed state of research and previously tried solutions, but also a sense of the possible types, shapes, and forms of solutions that may serve to help your audience. Now you know what your audience might consider useful.

Based on the state of research, you will be able to determine if you should follow an exploratory (not much insight gathered yet) or a confirmatory research strategy (ample insight on which to build hypotheses). Also, the state of research will show you which methods have been employed before and what the conventions involved with these methods are. If you can generate a sense of what type of solution might be useful—merely insight, or instead an artefact like a procedure, test, or any other structure that people would be able to work with—you can compare if the sensible research strategy in light of the state of the field lends itself to generating (part of) the type of solution that is sought. Now you know more about what your contribution may look like.

Based on your deduction of which methodology might be most purposeful to apply, you can work your way back to test whether you already have or need to build up the appropriate skills to implement the project. Do you have access to the type of data that your research demands? How can you access this data, or do you gather it? If you need outside help: who can help you? Why should they? Do you know how to analyse this data? All of those questions need to be on the line that traces one trajectory. The conventions of the methodology used determine not only its implementation, but also its reporting. It pays to follow a rather orthodox path here. If you struggle with more advanced implementations, scale down the ambitiousness of your project and claim to contribute, rather than implement a methodology in a way that you do not feel comfortable defending it.

All of this leads you to the consideration of which research questions you can purposefully ask yourself to try and generate a contribution to your audience without over-promising on what your research design can validly, reliably, and objectively deliver.

In essence, learn about your destination and trace your steps in a logical progression back to your position today. It is not uncommon to find yourself in a position to be able to walk in the general direction of a contribution, but fully reaching it might seem impossible. Then you adjust what you can achieve to a reasonable and responsible degree. Compare illustration 4 to get a sense of the relationship among components of a well-aligned and a less well-aligned project.

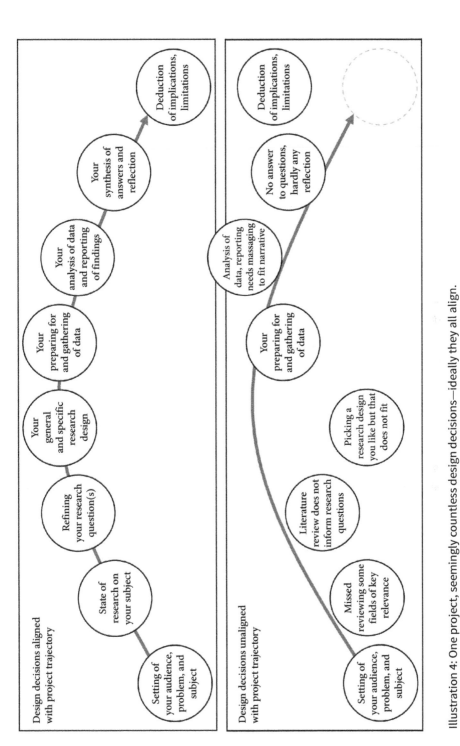

Design decisions aligned with project trajectory

- Setting of your audience, problem, and subject
- State of research on your subject
- Refining your research question(s)
- Your general and specific research design
- Your preparing for and gathering of data
- Your analysis of data and reporting of findings
- Your synthesis of answers and reflection
- Deduction of implications, limitations

Design decisions unaligned with project trajectory

- Setting of your audience, problem, and subject
- Missed reviewing some fields of key relevance
- Literature review does not inform research questions
- Picking a research design you like but that does not fit
- Your preparing for and gathering of data
- Analysis of data, reporting needs massaging to fit narrative
- No answer to questions, hardly any reflection
- Deduction of implications, limitations

Illustration 4: One project, seemingly countless design decisions—ideally they all align.

Try not to build roof-down

Identify and follow the logical progression of your project's compo-
nents. If stuck: are you still following that logical progression?

Metaphorically speaking

Research, like a journey, starts at home and ends at your destination. It is
impractical to start in the middle, continue with the beginning, and finish
off with the conclusion. Not only that—you need to have advanced from
stage to stage in your project, but you will also be picking up material in
earlier stages (e.g. data) that you will need to complete later stages (e.g.
analysis).

Consequently, try to avoid working your way through your project too
chaotically. Even though it might be that you sometimes feel more like
continuing on this or that part of your final academic project, do not discount the relatedness of research's stages. The big exceptions are circular
processes that are not uncommon in some research settings—e.g. conducting research, revisiting premises, adjusting your setup, and rerunning your
research. However, that commonly requires going through several steps of
your final academic project for every skip in process you undertake.

Research, just like a journey, does to a large degree imply procedural
advancement, not a spontaneous and random emergence of structures and
experiences. Plan your journey out and then follow through, one leg of the
itinerary at a time. Imagine how exhausting it would be to skip from segment
to segment.

Rough coordinates

Order—'The condition in which everything has its correct or appropriate
place, and performs its proper functions; the force for harmony and regularity
in the universe.'

The Student's Research Companion. Omid Aschari and Benjamin Berghaus, Oxford University Press.
© Omid Aschari and Benjamin Berghaus (2023). DOI: 10.1093/oso/9780192855312.003.0016

Chaos—'A state resembling that of primordial chaos; utter confusion or disorder.'

Progress—'Progression or advancement through a process, a sequence of events, a period of time, etc.; movement towards an outcome or conclusion. *in progress*: in the process of happening or being carried out.'

Stuck—'Held fast or trapped in some place or position; unable to move or be moved. Of a person, relationship, or situation: unable to progress or develop; blocked, stalled.'

Train of thought

Beyond coming to grips with all the elements needing to be in alignment for you to succeed, you also need to understand that having all of the project steps in logical sequence will make a substantial difference. While lack of alignment threatens your project's coherence, failing to follow a logical sequence threatens your own experience with carrying out the project. There are plenty of analogies to illustrate the value of great sequence: from putting the cart before the horse to trying to push a rope, you immediately get the sense that by confusing orders of logical sequences, you will quite likely ensure not having such a terribly good time.

Case in point: writer's block. Indeed, many blockages and frictions are there not only to bug you, but to possibly instruct you that you are doing something wrong or at least in the wrong order. If you try to write and nothing comes to mind, chances are you either don't know what your project is about (sharpen your project's positioning first) or you simply don't yet have anything interesting to tell the world (generate some new insights first by conducting your research project before you try to write). If you have a pressing feeling that you really should have a meeting with your supervisor, but you feel a bit ashamed that you have not advanced further on your own, that might actually be an appropriate assessment. And you know what? It happens to everyone, and the only way to avoid it is to pull together and get some stuff done and talk to her or him in a week. It is more problematic if you find out that setting up your survey generated systematic errors—during data analysis. Of course, you wish that you could turn back time to do some proper testing and pre-live analysis, but there you are, stuck with bad data. That happens, more often than many of us care to admit. The reason for such errors happening is commonly not only simply 'human error' and negligence. Rather, errors appear because conducting any research project means not only testing but indeed building your own capabilities. You are learning, and the chances are that during this process, you will not fly flawlessly. Thus, first part of the learning process is to learn how to recover.

Second, ambitious research projects often mistake complexity with quality. The more you observe and learn from senior professors, the more you will find that their research methodology can be greatly simplified in terms of technical methodology, and that freed resources can instead be invested in pitch-perfectly identifying the most apt formulation of the question and approach. While there may be some more occult research streams that require thoroughly elaborate, niche, and complex methodology, you should only attempt this if instructed closely. If this is not the case, err instead on the side of caution, simplicity, and ability to implement more or less flawlessly.

Many of the hardships of doing research are really not catastrophically problematic; it's just the lingering self-doubt and pity that can get to you. Even if your data is lost, you have an estranged relationship with your supervisor, you have writer's block from another planet, and no one likes your topic, there is really no way around getting through this rough patch. The sooner you sit up straight, take a deep breath, and plan to work your way out of the conundrum, the more quickly and easily you will leave the pit of sorrow. To some, a slight inconsistency in data with theory might feel like a substantial let-down, while it takes considerably more hardship to bring down others. In any case, do not be surprised if the final academic project provides those instances in which you really don't see much light. You will be able to work yourself out of this.

In essence

- Your final academic project will be a large undertaking. You might be tempted to try and work on multiple fronts at the same time, and productively procrastinate by avoiding what you really should be working on next.
- Try to avoid this. There is generally a sensible (or at least a most sensible) order in which you should work through your tasks.
- The central reason for avoiding this is not only efficiency and avoiding procrastination, but also avoiding the risk of getting stuck and not knowing why. The reason for getting stuck might simply be that you are trying to attempt things that are not possible before another step has concluded.

To reflect

- What are the tasks that I have to accomplish for my project to come together? What is the most sensible order in which I should work through these tasks?
- Are there dependencies among those tasks? What are those? Which tasks should I really not attempt to tackle before which other task has been completed?
- In case I truly need a little bit of variation to keep up morale: which parts can I always work on and progress with since they do not depend on other tasks?

Two travellers' tales

Olivia can't wait to finally get her thesis done. Technically, she already has a rather clear sense of what will be the result. The whole process of the thesis is more of a scaffolding to structure her thoughts. Since she wants to sketch out the general line of the whole document, she sets aside any thoughts about the tasks of her project to attack the challenge head-on and on all fronts in parallel. Her thinking is: let's have an overview first and fill in the blanks later. Not too far into the project, Olivia finds herself exhausted. Somehow, she's overstretched her mind to think of every challenge at once. She also finds it harder to generate the motivation to conduct her data acquisition and analysis—she already knows what will be the result. Her presuppositions and actual findings run into each other, with little delineation between one or the other.

Chris generally loves his freedom to pick and choose what he works on next, but realizes that his thesis will only offer limited opportunities to do so. If this project is to generate new insights, he needs to commit to openly and objectively conducting his data-gathering procedure, then look at the generated data, then write his findings; only then can he think about discussing the findings. To keep on track, Chris still drafts a complete introduction and even a rudimentary and uninformed first sketch of the conclusion, to consciously document his expectations and later see how his findings and discussion may or may not differ from his original expectations. Taking more or less one step at a time provides Chris with a good sense of how he is advancing and if he is still on track to finish on time.

Devil's advocate

Especially at the end of your project, there is great value in harmonizing the documentation of your project 'horizontally', across all phases and chapters. Then, editing your work will also entail synchronizing your introduction with your conclusion, linking to your discussion, findings, and maybe adding some missing literature references. This non-sequential work is, however, rather a part of editing than of conducting your project.

How to tackle

Identify the key tasks and the relationships among them. Don't invest too much time on parts of the project still inaccessible. To get some variation and keep up motivation, identify those parts of the project you can always switch to and work on. For the general progression of the major parts, consider illustration 5.

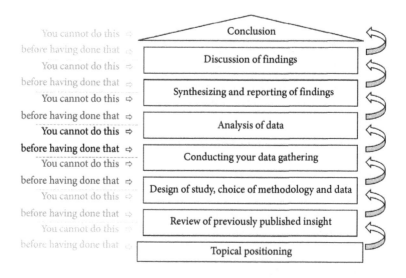

Illustration 5: Only tackle the parts of your project you have already unlocked through preparation.

Build well-dimensioned bridges

Your research ought to link what is known with what is not yet known.
Try to develop a sense of how far your project can reliably reach.

Metaphorically speaking

Research creates a product that will help connect the current status quo of insight (this side of the river) with a future state of even deeper, more discerning understanding of a matter (the far bank of the river), with you being the bridge builder and your project being the bridge.

Consequently, to select the most appropriate place to put up your bridge, you need to select a place where it is not possible to merely jump across (contribution unnecessary) but also where it is not entirely impossible for you to build a bridge (contribution impossible). You need a suitable space—not too far, not too close. Ideally with easily fortifiable bridgeheads on dry grounds—maybe a little island in the middle of the stream.

Research means balancing risk between the superfluously trivial and the devilishly risky. Plan that bridge too far, and people will find it difficult to trust it—even if you managed to pull off the feat (or did you?). Plan that bridge too simplistic or even entirely unnecessary, and people will discover it as such.

Rough coordinates

Bridge—'Figurative and in figurative contexts. Something resembling a bridge in form or function; that which spans a (physical or notional) gap between two things; esp. a person or thing which connects, reconciles, or unites different groups, events, periods, etc.'

Link—'A connecting part, whether in material or immaterial sense; a thing (occasionally a person) serving to establish or maintain a connection; a member of a series or succession; a means of connexion or communication.'

The Student's Research Companion. Omid Aschari and Benjamin Berghaus, Oxford University Press.
© Omid Aschari and Benjamin Berghaus (2023). DOI: 10.1093/oso/9780192855312.003.0017

Known—'That has become an object of knowledge; that is or has been apprehended mentally; learned; familiar; esp. generally or widely known or recognized, familiar to all, renowned. Also: that has been (esp. publicly) identified as such.'

Unknown—'That which is unknown; anything or everything which is outside the scope of existing knowledge or experience; that which is beyond the limits of human comprehension or understanding. Also: a condition, circumstance, or context characterized as unknown or outside the scope of existing knowledge or experience.'

Train of thought

The central challenge at the start of your final academic project is that you will likely not know which project to engage in. While you might know the subject, you find it difficult to judge how far you can and should reach with your research. In one instance, you consider playing it safe, and plan to investigate something that appears easily implemented. In another instance, you feel more confident, and play with the thought of truly aiming for some scientific advancement in your final academic project. You have this outlandish idea that might ring true, and believe that you could possibly pull that off. But how do you decide—should you go for hedging your bets, playing it safe, even risking investing considerable amounts of work into a topic that comes close to being superfluous? Or should you instead attempt a risky project, engage a worthwhile subject, and that might even get recognized by your research peers?

Consider your research project to be like building a bridge between two riverbanks. Building a bridge only makes sense if you want to connect a place where you are with a place where you'd like to be. Your research project needs to connect the current state of insight (the place where you are) with the desired new insight (the place that you and your research peers would like to be). This means that you should not build bridges from existing insight to other places of existing insight. That's wasting energy. Equivalently, bridges are not needed to connect two places that can be connected with a mere step: the new place you'd like to connect must be appropriately distanced to warrant the effort of setting up a six-month research project. Anything else is, once again, a waste of your effort. Finally, there's little value in trying to build your bridge between two riverbanks that are thoroughly uncertain in terms of distance and the types of waters traversed. This will change with experience (a PhD student can be asked to explore more uncertain and risky settings than a Bachelor's student). Still—at all levels of research, a final academic project that aims at making some form of contribution will need to demonstrate that the distance between prior and posterior insight is worth mentioning. Indeed, the distance you successfully cover is your contribution.

If your programme does not require you to make one (e.g. places low emphasis on evaluating the innovative performance of your work), make it your personal goal to contribute. If your programme requires you to make a scientific contribution (i.e. places a premium on innovation), be sure to balance the risk portfolio of your research. There is no particular fame or fortune in picking a particularly unwinnable battle and then failing. That's simply waste, spelled differently. Consequently, the most important recommendation for balancing your research project is to balance the risk and return structure of your project.

If your research project resembles a bridge that you'd like to build between the known and the previously unknown, you will be a substantial step closer to understanding what a research project ought to be: not a nuisance at the end of your programme, but a meaningful effort to put your new capabilities to work.

In essence

- When positioning your research project, consider that you are trying to bridge what's already known and what's not yet known.
- Try not to reach too far with your bridge—this will become risk your support not being strong enough.
- Try not to reach too close, either—this will seem safe but is also redundant. Don't set your project up to be redundant.

To reflect

- In your field of your research: what is already known and accepted as supported and published insight?
- What are other researchers currently considering as interesting to explore into further?
- What would be your options to position your research—from reaching too close to reaching too far and a couple of options in between—and which appears to be the most balanced and appropriate reach for your project?

Two travellers' tales

Dennis is uncertain about how risky his thesis project should be. He starts a project proposal on the very safe side of things, and proposes to explore the relationship between two concepts that are so close to each other that it is hard to tell them apart. 'Where there's no risk, there will be no innovation'—at least, that's what his supervisor tells him in their discussion of his proposal. Dennis takes this as carte blanche to make a decisive course correction. He now works on exploring the relationship among concepts previously thought of as unrelated—but he has an idea that he wants to test. Sadly, his experiments come up showing no relationship. Even though he knows that this finding can be as valuable as finding evidence of his idea working, he feels slightly let down by the result. No one enjoys developing seemingly smart hypotheses only to see them not confirmed in experiments.

Pauline is consciously balancing innovation and predictability in her research proposal. She feels that her design yields interesting insights, no matter how her research turns out. Part of this confidence is rooted in the way she combined her project's central hypothesis, which it seems she has a reasonable chance of confirming, and the sub-hypotheses which qualify the relationship under different circumstances. These secondary investigations in particular are new, and will be interesting no matter which way the effect works and even if the effect does not materialize at all. Pauline made sure to differentiate the risks she buys into when framing her project.

Devil's advocate

You are not always entirely free to define the characteristics of your proverbial research bridge. Sometimes, there are tactical considerations to be considered—possibly, your supervisor asks you to carry out a project that is merely intended to replicate a known relationship, or there's the chance of winning a grant for a particularly daring research proposition. However, be aware that specific contexts are exceptions to the general rule of trying to make a reasonable contribution successfully.

How to tackle

To determine whether you are projecting your bridge to reach too far or too close, testing your ideas with your audience is a good starting point. Try to get in touch with members of your audience and discuss with them a range of possible positionings and dimensions of your intended contribution. Given that your audience has ample experience of dealing with the challenge you are trying to contribute to, they will be in a position to provide you with a sense of what might be too small or too large in terms of scope, and which kind of positioning might yield the result that would be most readily understood, accepted, and put to use (see illustration 6).

Experienced peers' two cents

'In a particular case, you might lean more one way or the other. You might be more incremental or leapfrogging, more aggressive or less aggressive in terms of how far you stretch the wisdom.' (Steven Floyd)

'As we are looking for the research question, one key recommendation is that the more specific you can make your research question, the easier you will make your life for your thesis process. If your question is "What is the meaning of life?", your research will take a while. If you can frame the question very specifically, it will be much more motivating and easier to complete.' (Timo Korkeamäki)

'A thesis is an opportunity to do an original piece of research, more so than any other course during one's studies. Under the guidance and supervision this involves asking the right set of questions and figuring out what a good research question actually is. This is half of the work of decent supervisory work. For the student, it is to define a good research question and then go on to address and answer the question in the best way possible.' (Ansgar Richter)

'I always advise students to work with data of original nature, e.g. original empirical data (surveys, interviews, secondary data sets, meta-analysis technique). One can learn a lot from the studies, but it is important for them to involve themselves with an original data set. I do not encourage students to just do a literature review in the conventional sense. But I tell my students that the purpose of a thesis is to produce something that is genuinely new. It is about insights of a kind that has not been produced before. This may be more challenging with a BA thesis, but this would be the realistic expectation for a MA thesis.' (Ansgar Richter)

'We also sometimes gave research questions to our master students to help them write the thesis. But it's often because they did not make the effort to come up with their own research questions. Usually, we are open to discussing their ideas for a research question. Usually, they don't have the same access to organizations as we do—maybe a little, but not enough to discover

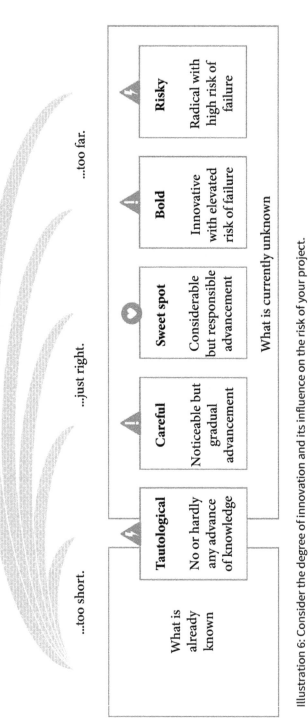

A bridge...

...too short.   ...just right.   ...too far.

Tautological	Careful	Sweet spot	Bold	Risky
No or hardly any advance of knowledge	Noticeable but gradual advancement	Considerable but responsible advancement	Innovative with elevated risk of failure	Radical with high risk of failure

What is already known

What is currently unknown

Illustration 6: Consider the degree of innovation and its influence on the risk of your project.

something interesting. But there are so many public talks by executives, end-less case studies, and if you are interested in a specific industry or company, there are so many interesting issues. Currently, for examples, there are many changes in society and the business world which I can also discover from an external perspective.' (Günter Müller-Stewens)

Impression management

Research is an exercise in humility. The academy, however, can be a place of ostentation. Avoid boasting. It distracts everyone's focus.

Metaphorically speaking

When travelling, you will encounter many other people. Many of them will be keenly aware of the pressure that seems to be exerted on them. Pressure makes people tend to inflate signals that demonstrate performance. In short, on your journey you will encounter others who will tell the tale of having climbed the highest peaks, wrestled the wildest animals, and found the most beautiful spot. If this inspires you, listen on. If it does not, disregard them.

Since motivation and drive are at a premium in challenging projects, try to protect yours as well as possible. If you encounter other researchers who not only tend to tire you with their stories but regard your own project as much less impressive, significant, necessary, or valuable, stand up and choose another camp fire to sit down at. If at all possible, do not carelessly engage in bragging yourself—even if you have something to brag about.

Research means that you are in a community in which many people around you are faced with some of the most challenging intellectual problems they have ever confronted themselves with. They are under pressure, and most do not thrive on increasing this pressure. Impression management increases this pressure and leads us down the least attractive path.

Rough coordinates

Ostentatious—'Of actions, events, qualities, etc.: performed, exercised, or displayed in a manner calculated to attract attention or admiration; pretentious, boastful.'

Pride—'A high, esp. an excessively high, opinion of one's own worth or importance which gives rise to a feeling or attitude of superiority over others; inordinate self-esteem.'

The Student's Research Companion. Omid Aschari and Benjamin Berghaus, Oxford University Press.
© Omid Aschari and Benjamin Berghaus (2023). DOI: 10.1093/oso/9780192855312.003.0018

Humble—'Having a low estimate of one's importance, worthiness, or merits; marked by the absence of self-assertion or self-exaltation; lowly: the opposite of proud.'

Critical thinking—'The objective, systematic, and rational analysis and evaluation of factual evidence in order to form a judgement on a subject, issue, etc.'

Train of thought

Your final academic project has many functions: it's a learning opportunity, it's a complex exercise, it's an opportunity to position yourself, it's an examination, and maybe even a few more things. Some functions are productive, while others can easily lead you in the wrong direction. Especially considering your thesis as an examination or positioning opportunity may suggest to you that it's all about making a particularly high-performing impression. And you are not wrong: impressions play a great role—but be sure not to try and fabricate impressions that help you less than they hurt you.

We've all been in the situation where we're planning a trip and looking around for some guidance in making the right choices. Commonly, two quite distinct personalities might offer their wisdom: one boasting of their insight on travelling, their knowledge of culture, spoken languages, experiences, and overall understanding of the world, the other rather sagely and reflectively pondering their experiences and stating that their travels left them with more questions than answers. Certainly, the first guide will provide you with clear-cut and seemingly 'true' answers, supposedly founded in extensive first-hand knowledge. The other guide might even confuse you with their questions rather than providing solid answers. Whichever path you take will need to be yours to discover.

The final academic project is an examination that you might mistake for a test of knowledge. It is that, too—but not predominantly. At its core, the final academic project is a test of conduct. Building your decisions on knowledge is merely an important part of your demonstration—but it is also somewhat deceptive. The more you learn about a subject, a methodology, or a setting, the more you persuade yourself to accept your knowledge as truth, as reality, and ultimately as dogma. If you find yourself arguing that you 'are not making this up on your own', but that you read and cite books and articles— that's not even half-way towards thinking scientifically about building your knowledge. The mere fact that something is written, published, and printed does not make it sacrosanct. Yes, reviewed and published knowledge is part of the canon on a subject, but this is only the 'state of the art' today—and you yourself are working towards expanding this state of the art. This brief excursion into the role of keeping a critical distance regarding your own supposed knowledge of the subject leads us to why impression management—in our case, the intended behaviour of overselling your own insight into the subject to appear more impressive—is not helpful. At least, someone more experienced and well-read will burst your bubble; at worst, you risk short-circuiting your scientific circuits by sprinting along the path from dedication to reading a lot to pride in knowing a lot to arrogance about not needing to learn more to ignorance—which ultimately defeats your purpose as a researcher.

Undertaking your final academic project means that you carry out an examination of your own scientific conduct. The key result of this examination should be that you don't come out of a scientific project any less of a scientific researcher than you went into it. Scientific work should not blunt your critical edge, but sharpen it. Scientific work should not make you try and impress others with your knowledge, but (if at all) with the questions you will be able to ask. The ideal conduct during a final academic project is not that you were able to learn something once, but that you have the facilities to conduct ever more efficient and effective learning and insight-generating projects. You demonstrate that you have learned what scientific work is about.

In essence

- Impression management is common. There are micropolitical instances in which this might be unavoidable. But if you are not in such a situation, avoid it.
- Impression management behaviour we should avoid: making results more impressive than they truly are, underscoring effects, massaging data, leaving others in our dust. This is contrary to what research is about.
- Impression management does not just contradict what research is about, it can also lead to an arms race of stagecraft, smoke, and mirrors. None of this helps, and some of this hurts others. Let's be humble and focus on what's truly interesting.

To reflect

- Do you notice impression management by others? Does it affect you? How?
- Do you join others or maybe even introduce impression management?

- What are good ways to curb or entirely shut down instances of impression management?

Two travellers' tales

Quinn is keenly aware that a university is a place where smarts are valued. So, why not put a bit of nerd flourish on your work and presentations? Just to make some work look a little more impressive than it really is. Often, she manages to impress her audiences—except for those instances in which her bluffs get called out. She does notice, however, that her audiences tend to get less and less involved with her material. She gets fewer questions and suggestions, and finds it harder to get a discussion going around her topic. All in all, she ends up taking away less from colloquiums. She succeeds with her project and finds it fairly easy to take the next step in her career. Impressions matter.

Eric is rather shy when presenting and tends to be more critical of his own work than others might be. To him, being understood is just as important as being able to present. He'd rather enable everyone to understand what he did than put a shiny veneer over his project. He is not here to impress anyone. Instead, he is here to wrestle more insight from the subject of his interest. Eric finds it harder to compete on particularly showy events, and is worrying about the academic job market due to his shyness. But he also knows that he does not want to take the career step that gets him into a circus of showmen and -women. Rather, he's looking for a place to dive deep and produce beautifully comprehensible, insightful research results. He was always more interested in the question than the answers (and how to sell those).

Devil's advocate

Just like avoiding bragging, there is much to be said for avoiding undue self-deprecation and shyness. It is a fine balance—but a key marker of academic capabilities—to report your achievements appropriately. Not only for others to follow, but also to allow others a neutral perspective on your achievements.

How to tackle

To avoid getting dragged into a match of impression management, a productive type of self-awareness and self-evaluation is useful. Consider the relationship between clarity and confidence. Clarity in expressing ideas often seems linked with confidence. It commonly seems at its highest in a state of well-balanced, productive, and positive confidence (but not in pronounced over- or under-confidence).

When authors become overconfident and claims tend to reach further and further, communicating ideas often becomes less clear as the claims presented seem harder and harder to justify. Blanks appear more or less synthetically filled in to make the claim more or less believable. Obfuscation starts to show here and there. When authors go into full overconfidence, this situation becomes even more pronounced. Claims start to exceed evidence by far; episodes of self-aggrandisement often flirt with boasting about what has been achieved, essentially moving closer to being intentionally misleading; so much political noise is added to the signal that clarity is severely harmed.

However, there are also problems with the opposite: when authors lack confidence in their ability to speak to a topic or project, presentations and writing tend to become more vague, less decisive, and less active in tone. The less confident an author is, the less certain and well-founded their contributions become, until they become chaotic or even unintentionally misleading. It is not uncommon to find texts with these defects arise when an author has written passages that they were not yet equipped to write.

Given sufficient evidence for your advancement (you will have none at the beginning, some in the middle, and most at the end of your project), your best bet may be to let a focus on the clarity of your writing or presentations determine the degree of confidence you will exhibit. Work with what you have. Don't write fiction. If your goal is to produce the clearest material you can on the status quo as it presents itself, you will automatically steer away from being either underconfident (you will not write what you do not feel certain of, yet) or overconfident (you will not write what has nothing to do with your evidence or insights) presentations of your work. If your goal is to communicate clearly (rather than impressively or over-cautiously), your risk of falling into either of these trap is reduced. Then, any deviation from that goal—to write clearly—will feel strangely awkward. Finally, a good use for that sensation.

Maturing your mind

If you allow your project to take a hold of you, the challenge will lead to your mind maturing. It is this maturing that enables you to complete it.

Metaphorically speaking

Travelling means not only getting from A to B but growing your insight into the world and your role in it. Just like growing up, any meaningful growth experience has the potential to subject you to emotional stress that may leave you exhausted at times. It is very likely that you will experience a challenge that goes far beyond what you were routinely used to before. However, there is little growth to be expected if your path does not ask more from you than you thought possible to give.

Consequently, if you feel as if your path through your research project is taking a considerable toll on you, that's generally a good sign that you are challenging yourself. However, you will be safer from getting stuck or feeling overwhelmed if you are prepared for the realization that a worthwhile project will not feel surprisingly easy once you are inside it. Try to maintain your awareness about your central tasks, the obstacles in your way, and the amount of energy you have available to work with.

Do not try to manage away and avoid everything challenging within your research project. The challenging bits and your response to them are what will make you grow.

Rough coordinates

Maturing—'To cause to develop fully (the mind, a faculty, etc.); to perfect the development of (a person) mentally and physically. To make ready; to perfect (a plan, work, course of action, etc.); to bring to full development.'

The Student's Research Companion. Omid Aschari and Benjamin Berghaus, Oxford University Press.
© Omid Aschari and Benjamin Berghaus (2023). DOI: 10.1093/oso/9780192855312.003.0019

Meaningful—'Full of meaning or expression, significant; communicating something that is not explicitly or directly expressed. Having a serious, important, or recognizable quality or purpose.'

Energy—'The collective physical and mental powers or efforts of a person, group, or other entity. A (hypothetical) metaphysical or psychic force underlying or driving all mental activity, often regarded as analogous to physical energy.'

Transformation—'The action of changing in form, shape, or appearance; metamorphosis.'

Train of thought

If you subscribe to the notion that final academic projects are implicitly geared towards your own learning and advancement, you can follow this thought a bit further: along with any meaningful learning, you will generally expect a certain sense of maturing. Through the act of having learned a meaningful new perspective, a new insight relevant to you, your own perspective on things changes. Your advancement has allowed you to mature to being a slightly different person. Of course, everything hinges on the term 'meaningful'—irrelevant lessons learned and experiences will not make such a mark on you as those which were important to you. If you follow us so far, there are a few interesting and worthwhile perspectives here.

If you have been on a particularly long hike, one where you might not even know every decision at every crossing, you may have found that, at one point, you will have fully subscribed to walking on your path. You have become one with your task to a certain degree. You have entered the flow of your objective and subscribed to it. While there may be still a few miles to go, you have become certain that you will reach your destination. You have a clear sense of your ability to complete your task. The coin has dropped.

During any demanding final academic project, chances are that you can differentiate the complete experience into the time before the coin dropped and the time after. Before, everything appears much more open-ended and uncertain. Before, it feels like a realistic possibility that the project could fail—a possibility to be feared and avoided. After, there is a distinct sense that the completion of the project is merely a matter of time and some more effort. Commonly, this moment of advancing, maturing, of generating a sense of having reached a self-determined standard, is much closer to the sense of graduation than the ceremony at the end of your programme.

However, while this moment of maturing during a final academic project is a great sensation, it is also fought for and won by investing considerable energy, nerves, many revisions, much rewriting, and several frustrations. You can imagine many of these investments as dues you pay when attempting this particular growth effort. If you attempt a project that is worth doing—that holds enough growth potential along the way for you—you will find yourself investing this effort and energy to fuel the transformation that this particular journey will cause in your mind. Hopefully, you will exit your final academic project a bit different from how you entered it. The whole idea of pointing out this peculiar effect that many experience during their final academic project is to allow you to consciously experience it and not make this transformation more exhausting than it already is. It's positively acceptable to be exhausted through this process—learning takes energy.

In essence

- One key characteristic of a final academic project is that, if you allow it to, it enables a phase of intellectual maturing. This sets it apart from most other tasks, experiences, or examinations you will have met with during your academic education. This is one of the reasons why theses are most comprehensively understood if they are not simply considered as examinations.
- Don't be surprised if fully engaging your project triggers emotions and behaviours you thought you had overcome long ago: lack of confidence, fear of failure, exhaustion, uncertainty, comparison behaviour, and so on. Those are coping mechanisms of a growth sprint.
- Keeping in mind that you are actively growing as you are working through a final academic project will likely be tiring. But the tiring can also be a sign to you that you are fully committing to the challenge.

To reflect

- Do you notice how your behaviour and your perspective on yourself changes ever so slightly in facing and gradually overcoming the challenge?
- If not: do you subject yourself to the project to a meaningful degree?

- If yes: which changes do you welcome? Which changes appear strange to you? Can you accept both types of changes and learn to curb those which you'd rather avoid in future?

Two travellers' tales

Fred is set to finally get his academic programme done and over with. If what it takes is to submit a thesis project—so be it. Fred has learned that university is a game which can be played successfully—efficiently—or unsuccessfully—causing a lot of headache and heartache. Thus, Fred checks the options to write his thesis as efficiently as possible. Like a stone skipping over water, he takes the thesis in a stride. As if it never touched him. And so, it came and went.

Samantha is happy to complete her academic programme and achieve a milestone in her life. Here is where she met most of her current circle of friends. Here is where she has endured much and also has taken away many interesting insights. She's got a sense of how university has shaped her way of looking at things, and would not want to miss it one bit. Consequently, this is also her expectation and ambition for her thesis. The idea is to try and undertake a project that will help her grow her abilities further. In the end, and it would be a shame for these months of work to just be spent on an examination.

Devil's advocate

There is an important point to be made for efficient solutions, avoidance of impossibilities, and picking your battles. Realism dictates that you will only be able to tackle so many challenges in half a year. Once again, it's up to your sense of balance to find a path. But remember: too easy is just as bad as too challenging.

How to tackle

The idea discussed in this chapter is rather an intuitive, self-adjusting process that will occur if you engage with the challenge more or less wholeheartedly. It is nothing that you would proactively design or steer in detail. Be aware instead that you are undergoing an experience that comes not only with practical, but also with personal growth challenges. This project can drain your energy in more than one way. Try to be attentive to how the challenge wears on you and how to negotiate your path so that it seems in sustainable balance between investing energy into growth and replenishment of energy.

Experienced peers' two cents

'A thesis might accomplish many things. First among those, a thesis is intended to help graduate students develop their research skills. We call master's theses "capstone projects", others call them "highly critical components" which synthesize everything that the student has learned during that programme. The thesis offers the opportunity to the student to work on their own to materialize and translate what they learned from a course at university into the reality of their research project. It is a major opportunity not only for learning, but for making big decisions and sustaining focus for a long time on one project.' (Madhu Neupane Bastola)

'One aspect of a thesis is to inspire somebody to want to continue on a research journey, or to at the very least understand the significance of research and the time and energy that goes into it. Also, let's not forget the significance of those epiphanies that happen within research, allowing the student both to discover the experience for themselves but also to have some empathy and appreciation for those epiphanies of others.

'So inspiration is something that can be achieved by a thesis. Unfortunately, we know that that isn't always the case. Quite the opposite, in fact. Writing a thesis can feel as if you're a slave to the thesis and a slave to the ideas of others. So this ideal achievement that some theses manage to realize can be lost. At the very least, the thesis should serve as some kind of ticket to somewhere else. But it remains true that a thesis can be a beacon of inspiration around the beautiful world of research. Here, it is important not to forget that it is an amazing privilege to actually have the opportunity to engage in deep thinking and research, whatever the discipline.' (Kim Beasy)

Comparing with others

Final academic projects are too complex to meaningfully compare progress. Comparing often yields not much more than resentment.

Metaphorically speaking

Research means performing. Performing suggests measurement. And where multiple performers act side by side, comparison and competition are close to inevitable—no matter if working at your desk or when competing to discover the best route to your chosen target. But since research is a complex, mostly qualitative performance, and true insight to compare multiple experiences are difficult, comparisons invariably lead you astray.

Consequently, while you might be interested to look left and right to inform yourself about how you are doing in comparison to others, there is very little point in doing so—except for procrastination. You will not be able to entirely and appropriately compare yourself to others and their project advancement to the degree of accuracy that would inform you meaningfully. In the end, the most useful question is whether you are advancing at a pace that makes sense for you, within your project scheme and given context.

Research projects are, in numerous instances, as individual as their researchers. Do not try to standardize and generalize your performance to make it comparable to that of others—especially not on a whim. More likely than not, your comparison will not take into consideration all relevant factors, especially if it is only developed and considered briefly.

Rough coordinates

Compare—'To mark or point out the similarities and differences of (two or more things); to bring or place together (actually or mentally) for the purpose of noting the similarities and differences.'

Transparent—'Easily seen through, recognized, understood, or detected; manifest, evident, obvious, clear.'

The Student's Research Companion. Omid Aschari and Benjamin Berghaus, Oxford University Press.
© Omid Aschari and Benjamin Berghaus (2023). DOI: 10.1093/oso/9780192855312.003.0020

Advancement—'The action or an act of going forward; progress along a course; (also) the condition of having progressed; the degree to which something has progressed.'

Complex—'Consisting of parts or elements not simply coordinated, but some of them involved in various degrees of subordination; complicated, involved, intricate; not easily analysed or disentangled.'

Train of thought

You are not the only one undertaking a journey—many people are. Many of your peers have set off to engage on their thesis project, maybe even at the same time. You might even have agreed to complete the final academic project within the same time-frame. The details are not relevant—what matters is that you go through the project together. You think. But only a few months into your research, you find that others are much further ahead. They seem to have it easier. They must have a better supervisor than you—or is it the topic that simply comes together more readily? No matter what, they are ahead, and you feel behind. There is this creeping, nagging impression of them being smarter than you are. What if you don't make it? Oh my, that's not out of the question? What if I don't make it?

For people without the most robust confidence, the comparison of performance in complex tasks is detrimental. If you compare yourself to others, you are trying to generate an appropriate self-evaluation (how am I doing?) in relation to external yardsticks (your impression of the performance of others). Given the complexity of the task, however, your impression of the performance of others will be incomplete. You will not have full information on the conditions your colleague is acting under. Especially in a situation of decreased confidence, four detrimental outcomes arise. First, you misinterpret the advances made by your colleague, since you only perceive her visible successes and do not consider her possibly still insurmountable challenges. Consequently, your confidence drops further—she must be smarter than you!

Second, you misattribute the advancement of your colleague to better working conditions, since you assume that she must have more help and less hardship. Consequently, your confidence is protected, but there's a kernel of envy growing with you—sure she's ahead, who wouldn't be?

Third, you feel that you are ahead, and the others are left far behind. Maybe you feel more confident and continue, perhaps you start asking yourself if you overlooked something important? All of a sudden, you find that your colleagues have developed much more thoroughly rooted theories, more advanced surveys, seemingly better research. Consequentially, you scramble for substance and tag onto your project elements that were never intended to be there—and there you have it: Frankenstein's monster project.

Comparing your own advancement or quality during the final academic project to appease any lack of confidence is an intoxicating brew. It might make you feel better and quench your curiosity for a brief, fleeting moment—but it will also sow the seeds of a toxic exchange with colleagues, and detrimental decisions. Hardly any outside yardsticks beyond your own research field are truly informative and helpful if they are purely meant to reassure your stance in the project.

When doing your research project, resist the urge to look left and right to identify who's leading the race. There is no race. The only journey that matters is your personal maturing from a state before your final academic project to the person you will become thereafter. That sounds very new-age, yes. However, if you weigh the advantages of knowing where others are standing against the disadvantages of misinformation and misleading conclusions from that information, you will arrive at the conviction that the only status quo that counts is yours. The more you focus on your project, the better. The more you can invest energy into making your project the best it can be, the better you will feel. From this positive loop comes the confidence that you can build upon. Not on perceived advantages over supposed competitors. Finally, comparing leads to alignment. Your final academic project, however, ought to set you apart from others. A good sense of alignment, therefore, will only serve to give you a false sense of security.

Even though this sounds opposite to what we wrote above: when writing your final academic project, certainly keep close contact with your colleagues. Not to compare, but to share their experiences. There is great value in learning more about your fellow researchers' experiences so that you can build more informed decisions for your own project. There is a substantial value in sharing the experience of researching because most people are going through the same ups and downs—albeit in different phases. Keeping a close-knit community of four to six friends who are going through this process together is helpful. But try to avoid comparing your individual performances. Where there's comparing, there is a lack of information. Where there's a lack of information, a lack of confidence is not far. Where there's a lack of confidence, there be dragons.

In essence

- The final academic project commonly leads to increasing comparison behaviour: many people left and right are on the same trek, you feel uncertain about how things are going, so you look left and right to learn about your own status quo.
- The problem here is that whatever you will find left or right will not be a complete impression of your colleagues' experience, their challenge, and solutions. It is common to draw inappropriate conclusions which might at least confuse or demotivate you and at worst lead you astray in the decisions for your project. Even if it reads like an adage: no two projects are alike. Don't force them to be alike just to draw the wrong conclusions.
- When writing your final academic project, try not to compare your advancement and achievements so far with that of others, but try to carefully and critically learn from your colleagues' experiences. Remain careful not to draw too simple and immediate conclusions.

To reflect

- Do you generally tend to compare your performance with those of others?
- If yes: how can you put a buffer between what you see in other projects and immediately comparing it with your project? Is there a way in which you can appreciate and learn from others while accepting their experience and performances as not comparable with yours due to dozens of little differences?
- What can you do to get yourself out of a temporary lack of confidence?

Two travellers' tales

Tonya has always been a rather competitive person. With the thesis, it's just the same: she's up for the race with everyone who signed up for the thesis in the same period as she did. When working through the stages of her thesis, she often compares her progress with that of her thesis colleagues and celebrates even small leads. Not everyone around her appreciates that. Some of her colleagues struggle more than others. They tend to withdraw from their writing sessions. Tonya considers this 'one more left in the dust'. She manages to pull through and reach the finish line first, after three months and two weeks—this must be some kind of record. After handing in her thesis, she wonders if that was what the thesis project truly was all about.

Gill is a rather independent person. He does not make much connection between his performance and that of others. In his mind, how his project is going is entirely unrelated to how anyone else's project is going. He really enjoys the thesis, since it seems to be one of those projects at university in which he can independently develop his thoughts, in his time, work on his project, and push forward. It feels as if a morning run to him—you have got to run these on your own as well.

Devil's advocate

There are instances in which comparisons are unavoidable. That is the case when, for example, applying for positions, grants, or awards. But even then, it is not up to you to evaluate and compare yourself; instead, it is up to the jury that evaluates your fit with the benefit you apply for. This comparison hinges on one critical element that you commonly do not have when directly comparing with competitors: a third, independent yardstick quality that you are being compared to.

How to tackle

This chapter rather suggests a 'how to avoid'—and it is not easy to purposefully avoid often unintentional and subconscious behaviour. One approach that might help you is to remain attentive to your behaviour and spot whenever you try to draw much information about your own progress by looking left and right. Consider this the first stage of becoming aware and evaluating whether this information-gathering truly helps you or instead distracts you. If the latter is the case, try to refocus your energy on your project.

Beyond this more subtle first stage, make sure you notice a more detrimental second stage: set out to spot when rough passages of working on your project coincide with you comparing yourself with others and drawing conclusions that drag you down, drain your energy, and make your progress not easier but harder. If you identify this negative effect of comparison behaviour on your experience of the project, you might need some distance from your project to refocus. You will have gathered enough observations to make yourself clear that comparing does not help your advancement by now. Use this to steer your attention back towards your project, and possibly to a discussion with your supervisor to get some advice on how you can develop your project further, given your specific setting and the speed of development currently possible to you.

The more evidence of detrimental effects comparison behaviour provides you with (and that you can spot due to your attentiveness), the more reason you will see to abstain from that behaviour. Some—particularly confident—people do very well with extracting useful information from the progress of others. Others do less well.

A researcher's humility

Build upon existing knowledge and always remain critical. Rather implement a simpler project reliably than a complex project horribly.

Metaphorically speaking

Research can be a journey. But any journey can only provide you with one impression (albeit a very well-developed and attentively documented one) of many possible impressions of the destination. You will not generate the irrefutable and single truth about your goal and the path to get there, but will capture one impression that is applicable as long as the path is not overgrown, the hill has not seen a mudslide, or that a new highway has not yet been built.

Consequently, be aware that your aim for cannot be an infallible and authoritative insight. You might generate a very valuable perspective and contribution to the subject. You might even find great resonance for adopting a unique or innovative angle on your research subject. But you should always remain aware that no matter how much you invest into your research being independent of your person as a researcher, there will be a final bit of subjectivity in your findings—simply because you set the project up according to your preferences. Your journey to your destination was your journey; and while others might follow in your footsteps, they may find a different experience depending on their perspective.

While research projects attempt objectivity, reliability, and validity, they will always be limited to a degree. Thus, while you may attempt to generate a true insight, it is generally more appropriate to speak of and attempt to generate evidence for a certain understanding of how, for example, actions are related to consequences.

Rough coordinates

Critical thinking—'the objective, systematic, and rational analysis and evaluation of factual evidence in order to form a judgement on a subject, issue, etc.'

The Student's Research Companion. Omid Aschari and Benjamin Berghaus, Oxford University Press. © Omid Aschari and Benjamin Berghaus (2023). DOI: 10.1093/oso/9780192855312.003.0021

Research—'Systematic investigation or inquiry aimed at contributing to knowledge of a theory, topic, etc., by careful consideration, observation, or study of a subject. In later use also: original critical or scientific investigation carried out under the auspices of an academic or other institution.'

Truth—'The fact or facts; the actual state of the case; the matter, situation, or circumstance as it really is.'

Theory—'The conceptual basis of a subject or area of study. Contrasted with practice. Abstract knowledge or principles, as opposed to practical experience or activity. An explanation of a phenomenon arrived at through examination and contemplation of the relevant facts; a statement of one or more laws or principles which are generally held as describing an essential property of something.'

Train of thought

Knowledge comes in many forms—derived from anecdotes, or from more systematic observation of one or more cases—but most knowledge consists of highly complex, sometimes convoluted, interconnected, messy insights that have limited potential to be transported to and applied in other settings. Theory is a refined form of knowledge which extracts the fundamental abstractions from messy insights. Theories may be unsubstantiated—a first draft of an abstract of how things might be interacting. Theories may have become substantiated —a draft on how things may be interacting, which has found some empirical support. But since science can never ascertain that there will not be evidence contradicting a theory, theories never attain the status of full, final, conclusive proof. This also illustrates the divide between what can be reached through science and the concept of 'truth': science builds theory, and defines theory as never fully qualifying as truth because that would undermine the fundamental scientific tenets of remaining critical, abstaining from dogma, and the defined objective of science—to learn. Science is not a destination, it is a process. Consequently, truth can only be relative: it is approachable, but not definable.

Thus, our analogy focuses on the journey rather than the holiday on the beach (which might be more akin to proudly contemplating your findings): just as science is a process, making a journey is about the travelling and not about reaching your destination. This will undoubtedly clash with today's reality of your final academic project efforts being rewarded by a grade and a certificate at the end of your journey. The focus on a reward for your work puts the focus back on completing, and draws your attention away from a useful, productive, and insightful process. It might be that institutionalized education simply has not yet advanced to a state where it can ensure a culture, appreciation, and certification of continuously appropriate scientific conduct. Today, scientific conduct most prominently reaches our attention when a scandal breaks due to lack of such conditions—not necessarily because we are regularly particularly attentive to great examples of it. Even academic awards are rarely exclusively known for being entirely based on the assessment of inspiring academic conduct; they are instead commonly whispered about in terms of a mixture of academic performance but also political, motivational, communicative, and other factors. Not many academic communities are particularly trained and effective in making excellent academic conduct visible and inspiring to everyone. This transmission belt seems to be difficult to activate.

In many environments of writing your final academic project, the only guidance that you will get for adopting excellent scientific conduct is your own drive to carry out a project that will train you best. The most important and at the same time most generic recommendations when building your own guidance is this. The qualifier 'scientific' tells you more about the process than about the outcome of a project—science is not about knowledge close to truth, but about continuous, critical reflection of existing theory or adding theory.

In more pragmatic words: when reviewing theory for your project, test the support for others' research, and be careful which other research you follow and build upon. But never expect any insights to be complete or irrefutable. Develop a sense of balance between testing, trusting, and building upon other insights—always trying to gauge the degree to which each contribution will remain reliable. Suppose you need to cross a hundred bridges to get a chance to build your own: you will need to become rather apt at assessing how reliably the bridges you plan to cross will support your weight.

In essence

- What makes your project an academic project is adherence to academic standards.
- Another key tenet of scientific work is never to consider your product a truth, but rather as a contribution to describing what looked like truth in your project.
- Consequently, the most likely fundamental training during your final academic project is sharpening your critical thinking. You will apply it to

yourself, but also to all literature that you choose to include in your work to build your initial understanding of the subject you research. Critical thinking is the muscle that you'll depend on most when hiking through your project.

To reflect

- How do you judge your own critical thinking skills? Do you have evidence to support or contradict your initial hunch?
- What can you do to increase your capabilities in critical appreciation of topical literature? How can you try and sharpen your senses when reviewing your research design?
- Your resources are limited; to what degree can you afford to become more and more critical and demanding regarding your own research design?

Two travellers' tales

Henry always loved to write—that's why he never really looked too fearfully towards his thesis. He's been writing essays for a literary journal, has been working on his novel, and loves working for the university paper. When he began his thesis, he was convinced that he would write the finest piece of literature he'd ever conceived. Of course, he includes theory—also some personal theories—and adds a methodology chapter on what should have been done (although he knows no one actually has done it). Based on less than a handful (but more than ever before when working for his university paper) of interviews, he develops a lovely text on his subject. When he hands in his text, he is fulfilled by the sense of finally having come closer to the truth of the matter. In an appointment a few weeks later, he finds his supervisor unclear of how to consider his text. He does not appear to consider it academic research.

Uma loves to take a closer look at things. While everyone speaks about writing the thesis, she shudders at the thought of writing several dozens of pages. What she looks forward to is setting up a project in which she can systematically approach a better understanding of her subject—maybe even better than what has been published before. Uma is meticulous about conducting her project. Still, she keeps in her critical mind the many ways in which she as a researcher has an impact on her own work. At the end of her project, she transfers and expands all of her notes about her project into a concise text, just long enough to fully illustrate all the necessary observations she made. Uma was surprised about how many pages it takes to describe a full project thoroughly. Writing came more easily to her than she thought because she knew what she was going to write about before she started. Even though some of her central hypotheses did not hold true in her experiments, her supervisor commended her diligence and good documentation, noting that a well-done and well-documented project will always be useful, no matter the outcome, since the results can be relied upon.

Devil's advocate

Perfection is hardly ever a good yardstick. It is simply often not attainable if you do not have an abundance of resources necessary to reach your goal. Thus, there is another balance to strike: how do you optimize your research design (on a strategical level) and your implementation (on an operative level) in a way allowing you to create a valid, reliable, and objective platform for your project? How far can you reasonably get to this?

How to tackle

This mindset encourages you to get highly invested into the traditional and fundamental academic trades and qualities. However, it is also necessary to find a balance between trying to approach an optimal solution for your project in terms of academic quality while at the same time being realistic about the resources you have at your disposal. Perfectionism is only a lovely thing to pursue when you have an abundance of resources and can easily ensure you'll reach your goal—otherwise, it is a burden.

Even though this might surprise you, the most mundane guidelines from your academic administration can help you to find a balance between becoming perfectionist and working in too relaxed a manner: if you have six months and 60 pages to document your work, there are certain limitations on what you can do. Your final academic project is one project, after all. It is not intended to keep you busy for too long. Include this information at the perimeter of building your project. Take inventory of what you want to do to strengthen your project, prioritize these tasks, and split your resources accordingly.

Experienced peers' two cents

'When they come to invest time and energy to understand what knowledge really means, they see it as a scientific adventure and bring with them a high "naivety tolerance level". They are open to admit that they are missing the knowledge. However, they still go ahead and start asking questions. They perceive it as a chance. In this case, I am eager to accompany such students along the path of understanding what knowledge really means. The relationship with such students is strong, similar to a PhD student. Thus, I treat them as if they are PhD students but in a more condensed form (BA/MA students). They receive texts, sources, and inputs from me about knowledge. They learn that knowledge is organized by humans. That a university is not representing a church, where one is supposed to discover truth, and professors are not priests. The students start to understand what knowledge means and how to organize it. These are students who want to think deeply and who are interested in the context (meaning that they are interested in analysing context that allows them to generate knowledge that can be used in other contexts). When such students come, I help them to apply empirical projects and to make contact with relevant contexts. They learn methods of qualitative research. I accompany them along their learning path.' (Urs Jäger)

'This is what makes progressive research. Progressive research is built on previous thinking, on what we already know, and we want to make progress. Don't always reinvent the wheel. We intend to speak to a real problem. We don't want to deal with research questions which are not critical. And one of the big challenges in the academy has been to address big problems that we face as a society in the world. So if you do really good research, good defined as theoretical but also relevant, rigorous but also interesting, you have to recognize that research must combine the qualities that are embedded in these paradoxes.

'Read the best research—not all research meets this standard—the very best research, like the paper by Wendy Smith and Marianne Lewis on just that topic ('Toward a theory of paradox: a dynamic equilibrium model'), you will find highly rigorous work. This deductive theory-building paper integrates a lot of literature, but the outcome is a foundational theory of paradox, which informs all kinds of experiences that people have in organizations and elsewhere.' (Steven Floyd)

'Officially, a graduate, who is supposed to write a MA thesis, must prove that (s)he can apply scientific methods in a correct way and to develop an interesting result. What I generally experience is that the expectations concerning the outcome of such thesis work is relatively low. Yet another assumption is that supervision of thesis work may just be a waste of time insofar as it cannot produce any meaningful results. At least, this is what I experience as concerns the general understanding about thesis work.

'I myself, have currently the following perspective. The first encounter with thesis work is to ask oneself what knowledge actually is. What does the student think is meant by knowledge and knowledge generation? Usually, this is the first discussion that I have with students who show interest in writing a thesis and ask me to supervise it. In this context, I detect various perspectives.

'The dominant perspective is that knowledge is objective and is represented by science. It determines methodology. Professors are the carriers of knowledge, and can convey to the student how knowledge generation takes place. The student has to demonstrate to the professor that (s)he can learn these methods and that the professor can give the student a good grade for it.

'The second perspective is predominantly driven by a career motive. Students say that the MA thesis is the last component that they need to accomplish their studies. The student needs a good grade, but is trying to reduce the time needed for completing the thesis. Hence, the motivation is to get done with the thesis as quickly as possible, with minimal resources invested in it. The expectation of the student towards the supervisor is: Make my life easy!

'The third perspective is that a student comes and confesses that he doesn't yet quite understand what knowledge means. The student is searching, and the thesis helps to explore the question of what knowledge means for him/her. These are the students who enter the thesis process with a predominantly open mind.' (Urs Jäger)

Theory is there to help

Prior research is the launchpad for your ideas before you can provide your own evidence. It is there to enable your early advancement.

Metaphorically speaking

Research builds on prior knowledge. When you travel to the mountains, you need to build your excursion on maps, maybe field guides, the weather report, and review instructions on your climbing gear. Don't set off without building on those instructions that will make your life easier and safer.

Consequently, when planning your journey, carefully consider which insights to pack. Bring what will help you and leave behind unnecessary baggage. Of course, you will review prior findings in your subject area and compare how others have used the same methodology in comparable settings. Ideally, you take a closer look at more fundamental research, and maybe even some edge cases to familiarize yourself with what the fringes of your subject look like.

Research as a journey means to pack appropriately. For yourself and for your later reader: for efficient reading, do not integrate superfluous literature just to suggest that you've truly read everything that was to be read.

Rough coordinates

Theory—'The conceptual basis of a subject or area of study. Contrasted with practice. Abstract knowledge or principles, as opposed to practical experience or activity. An explanation of a phenomenon arrived at through examination and contemplation of the relevant facts; a statement of one or more laws or principles which are generally held as describing an essential property of something.'

Knowledge—'The fact or state of having a correct idea or understanding of something; the possession of information about something.'

The Student's Research Companion. Omid Aschari and Benjamin Berghaus, Oxford University Press.
© Omid Aschari and Benjamin Berghaus (2023). DOI: 10.1093/oso/9780192855312.003.0022

Abstract—'Existing in thought or as an idea but not having a physical or concrete existence; conceptual. Considered or understood without reference to particular instances or concrete examples; representing the intrinsic, general properties of something in isolation from the peculiar properties of any specific instance or example.'

Support—'To bear all or part of the weight of (something separate); to hold or prop up; to keep from falling or sinking.'

Train of thought

There are rather few fans of theory out there. If there were a superhero who went by the name of 'Captain Theory', people would likely not call on him even in the most dire situations. What is there to gain? Just a lot to read in technical jargon, at times illustrated by abstract simulations. However, what we criticize here is dealing more with the facade of theory and not at all with the core of theory: knowledge. You will agree that in most cases, you will not be able to do research without building on prior knowledge. Particularly with more fundamental research, the trick is only to pack what you actually need.

When you are planning to climb a mountain, don't bring your diving gear. When you plan to walk the beach, you really don't need much at all. For any journey, experienced travellers will advise you to pack as lightly as possible. Don't bring any stuff that will only weigh you down.

Theory will only be of service to you if you can actually use it in the context of your research project. Don't bring a sizeable bag of insights (particularly) into your final academic project document merely with the objective of impressing and of stuffing your bibliography. If you are contributing to establishing a field and feel that there are no particularly compatible theoretical fields to draw from, feel free to rely entirely on your methodological skills and your careful qualitative research design to explore. Don't feel committed to introducing theory if it does not appear to help you.

Even though theories are abstracts of knowledge, introducing a theory means also keeping in mind the scientific fields they spawned. If a theory is helpful to your project, this knowledge will be important to you. If a theory is not helpful to your project, this is a colossal waste of time and effort. Since undertaking a scientific project is hardly ever as well-founded as it deserves to be, your final academic project will also be an exercise in managing scarce resources. Thus, be sure that the theories you involve, discuss, and build upon in your project truly do provide a benefit to your project.

In essence

- Theory is here to help. Don't think of theory as convoluted and inaccessibly written litanies on obscure subjects. Instead, consider it the knowledge that has been accrued so far.
- The key to making theory useful is not to get overwhelmed by it. For your research to come together, include only what you need to gain an initial understanding of your subject. The less prior publications truly relate to your specific problem, the less attention you ought to spend on them.
- In most cases, investment into understanding the theory behind the methodology you are using to generate new insight in your project will be the most valuable. However, aim for a solid understanding of the fundamental mechanics of your methodology, rather than getting lost in the esoteric details. Give yourself licence to decide the cut-off point based on what appears appropriate in terms of your research goals.

To reflect

- What is my project truly about? On which specific insights do I need to understand the prior literature?
- How do I plan to generate new knowledge? What is the methodology? What is considered an up-to-date understanding of how I deploy this methodology?
- Does the amount of read and cited material come together well and usefully in my document? Am I over- or under-reporting and considering some areas of prior research in comparison to others?

Two travellers' tales

Victoria is not necessarily a bookworm. She loves to work and even to write, but she finds it hard to point to many things she likes less than the library building or literature search engine. Thus, she already knows that the theory part of her thesis will be the least fun. When she engages it, she feels that there is little else to do other than a broad and boring account of everything written about her subject. Yes, this will bore her to tears, but that seems to be the academic way of going about integrating theory. After reviewing her work, her supervisor congratulates her on her success—but also points out that focusing her theory section on those theoretical constructs she will actually be using later on would have helped her even further.

Ike likes to focus and to pack lightly, and that's what he does for his thesis. He considers his research to be also an exercise in bringing what you need, not more, not less. When approaching his project, he considers a few different ways of thinking about his project and settles on one particular theory that appears to be most useful to his case. He introduces this theoretical foundation and illustrates how this theory is settled in the context of other, competing theories. Then, he focuses on his perspective, and implements and documents his project. As part of his editing, he even revisits his theory section, and double-checks that he actually applied every bit of theoretical kit he introduced. His goal is to develop a lean project, where you can cut away nothing more. This focus also caught the eye of his appreciative supervisor.

How to tackle

First, consider whether your research design tends to be confirmatory or exploratory—does your field of research already provide ample, rigorously developed research for you to build on (rather confirmatory), or does your field not yet provide much ascertained insight into the subject you are interested in so that you need to scout the perimeter first (rather exploratory)?

Based on what your field provides you with, you will have more or less theory to work with, and you will probably also feel more or less compelled to work with this existing theory.

If you are pursuing a more exploratory approach, your use of theory might range from consciously avoiding previously published insight (make sure that you indicate and argue for a purposeful approach here); more usually, illustrate the research gap by introducing conceptually bordering, published insights. Try to strike a good balance on how much to report since, as your field is not yet very popular or well-developed, much of your theoretical reporting will be slightly off-topic in relation to your specific research question.

If you are pursuing a more confirmatory approach, much of your introduction and initial development of your research project will bank heavily on very specific insights won from previously published insight. In most cases, you simply cannot develop your hypotheses or your data acquisition, measurement, or analysis methodology without drawing from other people's work. In this case, it pays to be efficient and focused on those contributions that matter most to your development. Of course, you might also feather out your reporting on previously published insights, but as a general rule of thumb, the more confirmatory your research project will be, the more focused and purposeful to your research project your account of published insight will be.

Experienced peers' two cents

'There is a lot of political pressure to produce results. In political settings, people are looking for a faster bang for the buck. How can we produce more masters who know what they are doing, rather than making philosophers who care about "why?". I think this is a little short-sighted. If we start to take shortcuts in the theoretical underpinnings of why we do what we do, we're definitely going to be losing over the long run.

'As a finance professor, I could be teaching in class how an IPO is structured, how the leading investment banks do it, and the factors that shape the outcome. But rather than just doing that, I'd like to have my students explore and understand why we have IPOs and why we have investment banks, and the theories behind the shape and structures of the deals that we see. I think that will make their education more future-proof. Corona is a great example of an unexpected situation that makes you think harder about the Why instead of the How. We are living in a world where things happen pretty quickly and unexpectedly, so it increases the value of knowing the theories behind it a little better.' (Timo Korkeamäki)

'You have parts of the work that have to be focused and parts that have to be broad. For example, research questions have to be highly focused. The theoretical background of those questions needs to be broad enough to support them. One of the problems I had as an editor of *Journal of Management Studies* was that I would see papers coming from North America that ignored research papers from Europe. That is of course much less of a problem nowadays, when you have to be broad to support a research question. You can't answer a research question in North America any more that's already been answered in Europe.' (Steven Floyd)

Castle under siege

Expect your project to be criticized often and extensively. You will benefit from finding a productive way of processing this.

Metaphorically speaking

Research as a journey often feels like a trek up a hill in chilly and snowy weather. Every once in a while, you slide back down the hill, and you could have sworn that some hidden figures were launching snowballs in your direction. It will be a while until you reach a sunny patch with little incline.

Consequently, when you begin with your project, do not feel disheartened if the going gets tough and every possible way of progress appears to be up a snowy hill. But it's not only that progress is difficult: there will be plenty of instances when other excursionists will challenge the sense, mode, or intention of your exploration. What seems like bad manners will more likely be another instance of critical appraisal faced by your project. This critical distance will likely remain around you for as long as you work on your project—a critical way of testing and probing ideas is key in academia. Be prepared to calmly, courteously, and comprehensively answer questions as part of your progression. Being challenged—not only by the subject, but also by your social context—is part of the experience.

Research means opening yourself up to being challenged not only by goals you set yourself, but even more so by others' critical views. Once this is understood, it is easier to provision motivation and energy in the face of the inevitable challenges by many people—even by those who have much less insight into your topic than you do.

Rough coordinates

Criticize—'To play the critic; to pass judgement upon something with respect to its merits or faults. (Often connoting unfavourable judgement.)'

The Student's Research Companion. Omid Aschari and Benjamin Berghaus, Oxford University Press.
© Omid Aschari and Benjamin Berghaus (2023). DOI: 10.1093/oso/9780192855312.003.0023

Scrutinize/scrutiny—'To examine methodically and with close attention.' 'Investigation, critical inquiry.'

Headwind—'A circumstance or factor which inhibits progress, recovery, etc.'

Resilience—'The quality or fact of being able to recover quickly or easily from, or resist being affected by, a misfortune, shock, illness, etc.; robustness; adaptability.'

Train of thought

You might not have a clear impression of what pursuing your research project will feel like. It might be the colloquial walk in the park, it might be a ride from hell—or, more likely, anything in between. Probably, it will have its ups and downs. There is, however, something distinct about doing research that is a bit more informative and instructive: if you are engaging in a project that is focusing on a subject that many people are interested in, it will get challenged. Any research worth doing will come under scrutiny because people care. And any research under scrutiny will be under critical siege because the essence of research is that different approaches compete to be the most valid and the most reliable. Research is competition. If no one wants to compete with you, it's not a good sign: either your project is partially or entirely irrelevant, or you are so far ahead of your time that most people perceive it to be. Consequently, you are on the right track if the headwinds start to increase. Note that none of the above speaks to the advancement in your academic project and 'competing for completing'—we are speaking of the fiercely contested competition for the most valid, robust, objective explanations of phenomena.

The problem really is to differentiate among headwinds. Some headwinds should be heeded because you might, indeed, be on the wrong track—other headwinds should be a source of encouragement since they simply try to lure you away from leaving the path of righteousness as defined by the prevailing gospel in your field. Differentiating between the battles worth fighting and the battles best avoided is difficult. To make matters more complex, you might pursue a thoroughly innovative and worthwhile project and complete it successfully, only to find that your evaluation panel is composed of researchers who subscribe to a different school and don't take kindly to deviations from the established norms. You are more likely to get punished by evaluation for being innovative than you are for getting praise, since evaluations do not only have to do with your performance but also with your evaluators' scientific and academic convictions. They will have more experience than you, which means that they will find it easier to discover aspects of your research to nit-pick about if, for whatever reason, they dislike your findings. Of course, the rise of evaluation panels in particular is aimed at alleviating such skewed evaluations. At the same time, those academics who reject the existence of skewed evaluations most forcefully ought to be viewed with the greatest scepticism. Be aware, therefore, that leading the way to an innovative perspective comes with greater risk in terms of evaluation.

Headwinds are part of research. As a general rule of thumb, trust those headwinds that speak to details of your research more than these that focus on your overarching trajectory. Especially regarding the latter, the push-back you experience might be exerted to see how much you are willing to fight for your project. If you fall over at the first push, it's not a good sign. As research requires resilience, demonstrating it in the appropriate situation will not only help you stick to your plans, but also build confidence.

When approach your research project, be sure also to protect your personal motivation and energy with a tough shield. You are entering an environment that is built to test the resilience of your ideas. If there is truly nothing challenging about your research, you might need to consider whether you designed it to have enough energy to go beyond merely being a larger type of examination of your skills, and instead to be a true project geared to advance scientific insight. The latter will necessarily come with some intellectual and also emotional stress. Balance is important, but expect to be needing to find balance while being under siege.

In essence

- Scientific work means thinking critically. Consequently, encountering other scientists means being faced with their critical thinking and challenging of your ideas and approaches.
- Much of this will feel tiresome, and some of it will feel unwarranted to the untrained ear and mind. Rest assured: if you are working on an academic project and do not receive continuous critical feedback but instead continuous praise, your context might not be particularly academic to begin with.
- This leads to a set of key skills to develop: sorting, selecting, and converting critical thought to help you strengthen your project. And, among those intellectual capabilities, also the emotional capability to consider critical feedback a resource and not a way to stifle you.

To reflect

- Does your motivation easily bruise from critical feedback?
- If yes: how can you adopt a perspective that critical feedback is a resource in science, and that the greatest challenge is lack of such feedback? How can you insulate your motivation and your stamina from any (even the most fundamental) challenges to your project?
- Do you have a pragmatic approach in mind on how to sort, select, and convert critical thought on your project? What might that look like? How can you treat feedback as a scarce resource that needs refining and processing?

Two travellers' tales

Jack has taken being critical to heart. He loves to read himself into material, dissect it, carefully consider each component, and only then build on what he deems solid evidence. He's become excellent at comparing and contrasting research projects, insights, and methodologies, and he feels that his competencies to evaluate research increases with each week. This is also why he was so devastated by the experience of his first colloquium. After he presented his material, he was faced by a wall of tough questions, suggestions for improvements, and evaluative statements, each one feeling more threatening to his project than the one before. Jack knows he's quite apt at developing and passing on judgement—and he feels that this is an important capability to have picked up for research. But he also senses that he needs to develop his abilities to take blows to his project not with his body or his emotions, but with his analytical mind. He needs to become as quick and precise in processing critical feedback as he is in dealing it out.

Willow enjoys working on her research project. She is a rather careful person and tends to take those steps that she knows to lead to reliable results. Maybe because she tends to prefer the reliable route, she remains open-minded about continuously improving her project. Even though she knows that conducting her project means committing to a plan and carrying it out, she is open to picking up advice along the road. However, Willow is also keenly aware that she finds more than advice along the road. There's a wild assortment of positive and negative impressions one can pick up there. She decides that input along the way will be useful and important in helping to steer her project to success. Thus, she starts early to adopt techniques to sort the helpful from the mundane or from the harmful when considering comments during presentations of her project. She may have only encountered a handful of particularly helpful and inspiring thoughts while working on her project, but she is convinced that these few thoughts helped her turn her project into much more than what she could have done by herself.

Devil's advocate

While being challenged is part of research, it can take a toll on your motivation and energy. Plan accordingly: first, be prepared for most discussions of your work to yield little added insight (but be positively surprised when it does); second, plan some re-energizing after sessions that are full of critical attention and articulation.

How to tackle

While other chapters deal with ideas that make you roll up your sleeves and get to it, this chapter is intended to instead make you think about how to moderate your response to someone else challenging your project.

Try to develop your own technique of absorbing commentary and challenge on your work. This will be easier for statements truly intended as commentary, and harder for statements that truly attack one or several parts of your work. The twisted nature of this is, however, that you will likely be able to glean more useful insight from truly critical—and possibly sometimes even pointed and possibly harsh—comments than from mere pleasantries or vaguely related thoughts.

Whatever the quality of the comment, it pays to have developed a game face you can put on while taking in commentary. This is not advising you to do emotional labour—training emotional response as a disguise of what you truly feel—but it is advising you to try and train your mind to take whatever is being hurled at you or your project (the two might feel difficult to tell apart) as nothing other than what they are: utterances by the speaker. Remember to be as critical of comments as you are of others' publications or your own work: nothing can be simply taken as gospel. Everything requires a process of validation, possibly even refinement and qualification.

Thus, especially during critical situations like conference presentations or colloquiums, take the professional freedom to receive and accept input without requiring yourself to immediately evaluate and respond appropriately. Truly valued input does not require an immediate answer, defence, or rebuttal. Any comment on your performance has this strange duality of not mattering as much as your message (don't elevate comments to the level of your material) and of mattering so much that it will only be possible to appropriately respond after having thought about it for a while (don't relegate valuable comments to the level of friendly banter). Whoever is commenting will only have had very limited opportunity to think themselves into your project, and might simply be not particularly well versed in the field. Chances are that you may even have more expertise but less confidence, while they have less expertise and more confidence.

All in all: try to develop a professionally moderated response scheme to challenging questions and comments from your audience. Do so not to merely avoid a confrontational scene, but to take on comments and work through them in your own time and with enough analytical capacity—something that most people lack during rather high-stress and unfamiliar contexts.

The most positive attitude towards critical consideration of your work is that people care enough to follow your thoughts and are motivated to share theirs. Alright, alright—there are also plenty of people who simply love to hear themselves talk, too. Still, let's give them the benefit of the doubt. These comments are in any case the easiest to examine and cross off the list afterwards, anyway. Even though it does not always feel that way, critical feedback is valuable if you know how to handle it. Develop your own strategies in this domain to have this source of information at your disposal.

Experienced peers' two cents

'You may get very critical comments from your supervisor or during your defence. Those who have a positive, growth mindset and motivation for learning will take these comments as learning opportunities, and will be less impacted by them. If we as supervisors can enhance that kind of mindset, I feel that adopting this type of motivational insulating would be a life-long achievement.' (Madhu Neupane Bastola)

'You should have an open mind and question the world around you and the surrounding decisions, but you should also sort of focus that inward as well. This means that our project, our work or thesis or our decisions can be improved. Our own project, work, thesis, and decisions should receive the scrutiny that help them grow and evolve, too. If we take that open curiosity mindset seriously, then we also need to recognize that other people who have that same mindset stay directed towards us. That is not a bad thing. It's a good thing.' (Matt Farmer)

'Supervisors are part of this invisible debate by being part of academia. We have a thesis defence and I try to challenge my students and hope they challenge me as well. It is a matter of convincing each other. This is to be regarded a privilege. As a supervisor, I am as much a student as my student. This is the definition of good research because it involves people who are trying to learn together and from each other. I can only learn from them if they defend their work and put things in context and seeing the limitations of it. To be open to this kind of debate, to subject oneself to it, is crucial as one embarks on the thesis. I see too many students who ask the supervisor as to what they are writing is right. This is the wrong question to ask. They should write something that they are convinced about, based on the research they have done. And that must be so strong, that they can defend it.' (Ansgar Richter)

CONDUCT

Halfway through your journey, you will have made some headway, but there's also still plenty of ground to cover. In the midst of it, it can be difficult to retain your bearings and to keep being able to see the forest and not just the trees. Now is the time to keep some thoughts in your mind to make sure you'll reach your destination.

Growing into an expert

As you invest yourself into a topic, you will turn into an expert. Act accordingly. Seek and learn from those with even more expertise.

Metaphorically speaking

Research as a journey means that you will encounter many people who feel experienced enough to share expert opinion on most regions you might travel through. However, your travel success hinges on more than opinion—especially if you venture far off the beaten path.

Consequently, do not be surprised if you find yourself faced with not much more than (sometimes enthusiastically presented) opinions. Do not be surprised if you find yourself being the most knowledgeable person on a subject that you are researching. This can happen especially quickly if you chose to pursue a topic of your own interest and with only limited connection to supporting peers.

Research, to a degree, also means interaction among people. This interaction can be inspiring and fruitful, and it can be de-motivating and painful, and it can be anything in between. The quality of the interaction, however, does not only depend on either the researcher or their peer, but also on the collaboration they manage to strike up. A fit in styles can go a long way.

Rough coordinates

Expert—'A person regarded or consulted as an authority on account of special skill, training, or knowledge; a specialist.'

Title—'A designation given to a person as a mark of distinction or privilege on account of high social class or rank, or aristocratic status or heritage, or in recognition of service, attainment, etc. A name that denotes someone's status or profession, or role within an organization; a word such as

The Student's Research Companion. Omid Aschari and Benjamin Berghaus, Oxford University Press.
© Omid Aschari and Benjamin Berghaus (2023). DOI: 10.1093/oso/9780192855312.003.0024

Mr, Mrs, Dr, Professor, etc., that is used before someone's name to indicate status (esp. marital status) or profession.'

Comment—'A remark or note in explanation, exposition, or criticism of a literary passage; an annotation; a remark or criticism.'

Isolate—'To place or set apart or alone; to cause to stand alone, detached, separate, or unconnected with other things or persons; to insulate.'

Train of thought

As soon as you start working on your project, you will encounter few actual and many supposed experts in your field. Choose wisely whom you allow to have your ear when considering their judgement. While academics should share an obligation to be supportive, some experience in didactic behaviour, and generally a degree of humility in their assessment of their importance and insight, they are all mere humans, too. To the same extent, some are more professional than others. Try to detach yourself from those most detached from what you'd expect as reasonable and as supporting your learning experience.

When travelling, you will encounter more supportive spirits as well as those who you expect to be but who turn out not to be. Some fellow travellers are wiser, more well-meaning, and more able to facilitate a great journey for you than others. Some people are so pessimistic or narrow-minded that they will not be able to imagine you having a great experience if you do not adhere to their rules or perspectives. Keep in mind that 'expertise' is a relative term. Insecure people of higher rank may feel the need to strengthen their role by undermining the expertise of you or others, so that their own light is seen to shine more brightly. A fellow back-packer might possess better insight and be able to offer recommendations concerning your path than a tour guide who has done that route dozens of times and simply cannot imagine another path. It's not that simple, however: experienced travellers can be a great source for appropriate attitudes, perspectives, approaches—but they will also allow you to make your own way.

Titles are no reliable delineation to separate the helpful from those less so—indeed, some of the most dogmatic behaviour is reinforced by external certification of titles, positions, and status. This is not to imply that signs of experience and status will invariably compromise the capacity to be a good academic mentor: many highly decorated academics are also sage, supportive, and engaged peers. However, it is important to know that when you are on the road, you will encounter many people; establishing some critical distance from those who draw more energy than they provide is a fundamental survival tip.

Especially in situations where your performance and/or project are being evaluated by others who are not established in your project, be sure to be able to isolate yourself from opinions of higher-ranking academics who too readily speak on subjects that may be rather foreign to them. Expect misplaced confidence from your audience, and be ready to identify and possibly discard opinions that do not appear well-informed. However, this requires that you know your field well enough to make that kind of judgement.

Be aware, therefore, that this recommendation entails that you not only feel like, but truly try to be the person with the highest expertise in the room on your particular subject. This recommendation also entails that you should take on recommendations and insights from those whom you trust to be able and willing to provide solid guidance. When in doubt, be more suspicious of opinions on substance than on methodology—academics can usually transfer their knowledge on methodology more readily than on substance.

Now that we have discussed some of the shallower depths of expertise, let's consider how you would like to express, share, and use your expertise in the context of others. First, it will be important to accept that once you set your mind to work on a project for several months after having being trained in the subject for several years, there is very little doubt in our minds that you will turn into your personal version of an expert. How are you going to deal with possibly being the most informed person about your subject (and, certainly, project) in most rooms? To answer this question, you do not have to look far: at a university, you will be surrounded by many people who may serve as impressive—both positive and negative—examples of interpreting their role as experts. Consider growing into that interpretation of an expert that you will have found helpful and inspiring when you entered the field.

The academy is a place of expertise. But this expertise comes in many shapes and sizes. One of the most distinct traits of the academy is that people of high expertise but of different schools of thought come together to compare evidence and the validity of their individual perspectives. Given that expertise is both a central currency and a potent social agent, training, sharing, working with, and dealing with the malignant behavioural growths of expertise should be the subject of more explicit attention at university—alas, it is not. Expertise and its psychological and social implications might be one of the most impressive elephants in the academic room.

In essence

- It might seem implausible that you might actually be the expert in the room. However, that's precisely what happens to many more diligent and driven students during their final project.
- Titles and seniority are not always a good indication of expertise or particularly useful guidance.
- Observations of how academic leaders and subject experts act—both positively and negatively—are great sources of information on in which role as an expert you would like to grow into.

To reflect

- Are you the expert on your subject in the relevant comparison group (e.g. the doctoral seminar you are attending)?
- Which fields do you consider yourself to be an expert in? Where is this not yet true? Where do you want to increase your expertise, and which fields can you live with not being an expert in?
- How can you interpret your role as an expert? How do you want to behave towards others?

Two travellers' tales

Xena is generally a pretty confident woman. But presenting her research project before a room full of PhD students is not her favourite place in the world. She is simply not that sure how to deal with the stress the situation entails. She thinks there are plenty of ways to make a fool of herself, and even if she manages to present the most challenging bits of her work comprehensibly, there are still so many people in the audience probably smarter than her that it's just a matter of time before something or someone will make her look stupid by some brash comment. That's what she tries to avoid, most of all. In the end, university is for smart people, and losing your appearance of being smart means not fitting in. It's not surprising that she does not draw much from opportunities where she presents his work. She succeeds with this project, but it was a stressful affair.

Karl is generally a pretty confident guy. But presenting his research project before a room full of PhD students is not his favourite place in the world. It turns out that only very few people enjoy that—and only on select occasions.

So, Karl has already made his peace with the stress involved in being on stage. Beyond that, however, he's adopted a different attitude towards how to handle comments on his work. The bottom line of his thinking is: any comment you receive is an offer—but you are not obliged to take up these offers. The key capability in turning offered opinion into anything useful is to critically evaluate, select these opinions, and only then distil what they might signify. Karl knows that he's in a rather critical environment, surrounded with many smart people—albeit fallible, imperfect, and sometimes eccentric people. Yes, there's something to be won from heeding the opinions of those who spend the time to try to understand what he does. But heeding opinions requires evaluation, selection, and then reflection. Many opinions don't pass that test. Karl has discovered that considering opinions carefully and professionally has opened up the ability to look at his research from a number of vantage points. Yes, it means exposing his thoughts to an audience—but then, he feels that this is ultimately what research is about.

Devil's advocate

While the over-confident exceptions to this rule are more visible and seem greater in number, most students are rather under-confident about their competencies and insight into a topic. More introvert students especially tend to show greater attention to detail and stamina, but tend not to be too explicit and possibly even doubtful about their capabilities. It seems like a useful rule of thumb to encourage building expertise, noticing personal growth in expertise, and voicing expertise.

At the same time, well-developed expertise and a professionally academic humility go very well hand in hand. While expertise is knowing how to play even the more complex melodies on your instrument, finding the right way of phrasing, tempo, and intensity of delivery makes a good musician. So with building an expertise also comes building a sense of how to deploy it. Striking a balance between humility and confidence is key.

How to tackle

There is a simple two-step process here: Step one—especially if you tend to be nervous around people who either are or seem smarter or at least possess fancier titles than you do—try to consider becoming the expert not as the one who 'knows it all' about the subject but as the person who might be the most curious about it.

You might (rightfully) fear being put in your place for positioning yourself as a 'know-it-all' either by someone with more expertise or at least by someone of higher rank. There is little to be feared for someone who considers themselves, primarily, deeply and sustainably interested in the subject and secondarily—merely as a side effect of being interested—well-read and mentally invested. The effect, expertise, is the same, but your positioning hinges on a different motivation: you do not consider yourself arrived, but working towards arriving. This is commonly a useful and productive perspective (if you do not depend on convincing your audience that you have reached complete expertise).

Step two: repeat step one. There is no step two. Continue on the path, striving for understanding your subject better and better. For more stagnant subjects, this can become slightly old with time, but most subjects have such an inherent tendency to develop or to change through interaction with an ever-changing world that you cannot fully consider yourself a thorough expert anyway. Most of the time, you try to keep up or dig deeper. Expertise is a state of progress, not stagnation.

Certainly, there are professional situations in which the share of the knowledge you hold necessary to produce a contribution to an audience is so slim (e.g. the senior professor who teaches an entry-level course or the management consultant providing fundamental guidance to their client) that you can be considered, for all intents and purposes, the expert on all matters in that context. But even then, most driven minds will seek ways of looking at their subject through the eyes of the uninitiated, always wondering if there are ways to reconsider their subject—and delighted to find another perspective. Expertise is not only about the subject, but about being a professionally curious person.

Experienced peers' two cents

'We can help students sustain their will to learn if we take supervising students as the big responsibility that it is. We can choose to care about the student and his or her project. We can be mindful when we provide feedback. Not only that, but we can ask a student, encourage the student, motivate the student by saying, "Yes, this is a difficult job—but everyone before and after you faces these difficulties."

'It is not only about the students who benefit from a growth mindset, but also the supervisors. If we take an encouraging and mindful approach, maybe we can create a spark in the students. A kind of fire. Potentially that will energize him or her to go forward. I don't like to be pessimistic in a challenging situation. I'd rather like to say: "We can make a difference!" (Madhu Neupane Bastola)

Help others understand you

Allowing your audience to understand is key to presentations. Not your story, but their understanding of it is your goal. This helps with stage fright.

Metaphorically speaking

While some travellers are born storytellers, others do their utmost to avoid the opportunity to share their experiences. They doubt what they remember, they worry that they get ideas mixed up, and they are uncertain if what they have to share is even interesting enough to fare well with the audience. Then again, if they found part of their journey impressive, it can be useful for them not to try and tell a story, but rather try and make their audience understand why it seemed impressive to them—try and share what moved their minds.

Consequently, if giving presentations—to provide information—is not your forte, why not try and enable your audience's comprehension of your ideas—to help them succeed in understanding you? This approach works in the same way as the old saying, 'To truly learn something, you have to try and teach it.' Instead of performing a presentation, try and enable your audience to follow you. If you present and speak about material you only have limited insight into, it is easy to run into problems with it. If you aim to make an audience understand, on the other hand, you will have at least one additional level of quality assurance implemented—you will ask not only what you can speak about, but also how you can make your audience understand (which leads to testing your own understanding).

Research, to a degree, also means communicating with people. Often, this communication is too readily equated to 'speaking', and it is too seldom thought of instead as 'enabling others to comprehend and learn with you'. Not only that—it seems a more purposeful way of thinking about communication, and also slightly repositions and strengthens the role of the speaker—she is not just talking, she's actively trying to make sense to others.

The Student's Research Companion. Omid Aschari and Benjamin Berghaus, Oxford University Press.
© Omid Aschari and Benjamin Berghaus (2023). DOI: 10.1093/oso/9780192855312.003.0025

Rough coordinates

Presentation—'The action of presenting something to the mind or to mental perception; a description or statement; the setting forth of an idea, point of view, etc.'

Communication—'To impart (information, knowledge, or the like) (to a person; also formerly with); to impart the knowledge or idea of (something), to inform a person of; to convey, express; to give an impression of, put across.'

Comprehend—'To grasp with the mind, conceive fully or adequately, understand, "take in".'

Enable—'To impart to (a person or agent) power necessary or adequate for a given object; to make competent or capable.'

Train of thought

In some programmes, you will be asked to participate in and present your project to colloquium groups or at conferences. Depending on the environment and the experience of the moderators of these colloquiums, these formats can be very helpful—but they certainly do not have to be. In any case, successfully presenting half-developed projects does not come easily to everyone (to most, it does not). How to go about preparing for them, performing in a colloquium, and drawing insight from them?

A good foundational thought to keep in mind is that depending on how centrally structured the research efforts are in the group you will present in, people will be more or less knowledgeable about your topic. In general, you should assume that you have a considerable advantage in your own specific research project: no one in the room is as involved with it as you are. Consequently, many questions that may sound challenging or offensive to you might simply be honest attempts at understanding why you did what. Developing a research project predominantly means making a myriad of design decisions within the constraints of your context. Of course, many of those decisions will be shaped by these constraints—but these constraints will not be obvious, and likely to be (at least in part) different for your audience. Thus, asking why you chose to take one route and not the other can (but should not) feel like a challenge. People are merely trying to understand what you did and why.

There is one helpful technique to try, especially for the more shy presenters: given your advantage of insight into your project, try to turn the tables, at least in your mind. A colloquium presentation is not a test of your performance, but a test of your audience's performance of understanding you. Of course, you want your audience to succeed, which in turn asks you to be as clear, logical, and comprehensible as possible. By making it your aim that your audience comprehends you, you will shift your own efforts towards building a comprehensible and non-self-contradictory presentation. This technique helps you in three ways. First, you gear your whole effort towards minimizing friction in comprehending what you do; this greatly reduces your risk of frustrating your audience and inviting nagging questions that can—however unintended—throw you off. Second, you train your capability to communicate clearly. That is an important precursor to writing a good final academic project document. Finally, by training your capability to communicate clearly, you will be more apt at identifying those areas in your project that quite frankly are still in a mess that needs revision or restructuring. You cannot straighten out a messy project just by powering through it or increasing your personal resilience towards mess—you can only straighten it out by straightening out your thought processes, and learning how to communicate clearly is a great path to accomplish this.

Colloquiums are difficult, they can be painful, but they are also some of the most important teaching and learning tools to grow capabilities with. It is useful to try and isolate your person from your project to some extent before you enter a particularly challenging environment. Over-critical comments or questions can have quite an impact on motivation. One way to alleviate this effect is to see the colloquium as what it is: an exercise to communicate a complex set of decisions clearly and comprehensibly.

In essence

- In your final academic project, a key challenge is not only to create a sensible chain of ideas, but also to communicate this idea comprehensibly. Both challenges are equally demanding, but the communication challenge is often overlooked.
- Especially when trying to explain your ideas in presentation settings, it can be helpful to consider these presentation instances, not as examinations for your advancement, but as instances of examination for your audience.
- Considering your audience to be in a challenging situation—trying to understand your ideas—and you as trying to help them perform well—because you want them to succeed—can help you implicitly perform better and with more purpose: the presentation is no longer about you,

but about helping your audience understand. Wherever this appears to be challenging, your project might need adjustments. Revising the communication of your project can help you discover weaknesses in the project set-up that would benefit from adjustment.

To reflect

- What is it that you are trying to say, in a nutshell? Which parts of the story are strong and easy to follow? Which parts still lack support or integration? Which part seems too surprising?
- How can you help your audience to understand what you are trying to say? What is their position? What will be a problem for them to understand?
- Does your project and argumentation show weakness in the areas where it becomes hard to explain? Does your substance need revision?

Two travellers' tales

Lars sees presentations of his work as examinations for himself. He's commonly very nervous before any presentations and talks he gives. He feels that he needs to perform well in order not to fail at the particular challenge of his programme and his project. Since his nerves are usually occupied by worrying about his performance, he does not really benefit from many interesting questions raised or thoughts discussed. To him, it's simply a task of evading perceived attacks.

Yvie sees presentations predominantly as three things: an opportunity for her to sort her gathered insights, a challenge to communicate these ideas to her audience, and an examination of her audience's ability to comprehend her. As her goal, Yvie wants to enable every alert person in the audience to understand what she's going on about. While that may sound like a trivial goal to attempt, it can become quite a challenge when the subject gets complex. Thus, Yvie tries to self-evaluate all of her presentations and talks as much as possible with the goal to make her audience understand what she attempts to achieve. Often, this even rubs off on Yvie herself—after having drawn together her slides for the presentation, she feels more aware of what her project is working towards. This way, she separates her presentation from her project. She does not feel too nervous when delivering her talks and is more alert when taking part in the discussion. By following her approach, she has two opportunities to learn from colloquiums: first, by making sense of her material for her audience (and herself), and second, by being able to lead a more productive discussion on the subject.

Devil's advocate

While adopting an audience-focused and comprehension-supportive perspective is helpful to mitigate the possibly uncomfortable process of putting an act on stage, it requires ample amounts of insight and empathy for your audience. Reading the expectations of an audience and judging what helps them understand is not always easy. This is especially true if a format has produced its structures and conventions that everyone is most happy to see every speaker adhere to: imagine conference presentations that might be expected to adhere to certain conventions, even though these conventions may not at first sight seem particularly useful to you to make your audience follow you.

How to tackle

Two key components can help you make great contributions: first, knowing and adhering to established conventions, and second, attempting to embed this convention-following delivery into a frame that focuses on the idea of making your audience understand your project.

Conventions deal with the expected structure, granularity, and vocabulary of your contribution. There will be a common style of communicating ideas established in your field, and maybe even in the specific format of your talk. If this is rather classical and highly formalized, it will likely resemble the structure of a paper in your field. Identifying and following this structure will help your audience to follow efficiently and without needing to relearn your way of structuring your ideas. Enabling your audience to dive into your thoughts with their existing mental models generates an excellent foundation for allowing people to understand what you are trying to say.

Framing your contribution empathetically, with your audience in mind, focuses mostly on the introduction of your ideas—your first few minutes of setting up your premises. While conventions can help you keep the journey going, they do not provide much in terms of eliciting interest in what you have to say. This is achieved by the framing of your talk at the beginning. How can you convey what makes the positioning of your project interesting to you? Allow your audience to understand what makes the subject of your talk interesting to you and possibly to others. This mirrors what the introduction to a paper would attempt to create, but it is also represented—to a smaller degree—in the conclusion of your paper. Making your audience understand why a topic is interesting should not end with your presentation, but should echo long after you've stopped speaking.

Experienced peers' two cents

'During the process of writing or conducting their research, students will also develop their communication skills, e.g. collecting data, talking to people, seeking sources, seeking help from learning centres, academic advisors, utilizing their networks. So, communication skills become key. During the writing, they also need to present their thesis or their research multiple times. They may have to make a presentation when defending their proposal. Often, they need to defend their thesis several times. Communication skills and presentations skills are critical here.' (Madhu Neupane Bastola)

'When I was a doctoral student, we had one doctoral seminar, which was likely the most painful seminar I took as a student. There were five of us and we were assigned one paper at the very top of our field. Each week, we would meet and one of us would be assigned a paper to discuss, peel open, critique—but the expectation was that we would also read all the other four papers. So that we could discuss, contribute, ask questions that the person who was assigned to do it had missed and ask his understanding of what they thought about it. It was painful because these papers did not often open themselves on first sight. It required a bit of time to get into it—and you had to be able to discuss the merits and critique it. But that course has given me so much. There was only limited time, so you had to be efficient. The most valuable skill I took away was that I can read an academic text and on the first read get to the guts of it and comment on it. When I supervise, when I referee, when I do any of these tasks, this has been a huge time-saver. It was painful while it lasted, but it really paid dividends. When we get into academic jobs, a big part of that is reading other people's work and provide feedback on it.' (Timo Korkeamäki)

'When taking the role of co-reader or co-supervisor, I can pass on some encouragement to more junior supervisors. The way to get them into a different mindset is to expose ourselves with our own work. One practice that I fostered, was called "The Writing Workshop". In these writing workshops, we invited everyone to come and subject their papers to discussion. There were no presentations; the only ground rule was that whenever you attend a workshop, you must have read in advance the paper to be discussed. Second, you must come with your written comments on the paper. The author gives a few sentences of introduction and then it is open for discussion. Everyone contributes their comments and discusses the paper in a very honest way—obviously in the anticipation that their own paper may be next in line. Afterwards, all the workshop participants hand over their comments to the author of the paper discussed. So, as an author, you get a stack of papers with others' comments. Essentially, this is a frank review for the author. It doesn't matter who you are, what matters is the discussion. You step out of the role of an accomplished professor. You are just an author. This is very beneficial and motivating. And so, the writing workshop creates a huge boost of energy. It always involves doctoral students, and you can simulate it at the MA level as well by bringing together your mentees and letting them learn from each other. This is a way to create more opportunities at our institutions. We should take these opportunities, and we have the freedom to do this.' (Ansgar Richter)

Strange birds

Universities see their share of misconduct, regardless of rank. Train your ability to spot it, isolate from it, or, if need be, fight it skillfully.

Metaphorically speaking

While research can be a lonely journey, there is always a base camp somewhere. There's always a fireplace at which stories are told and opinions are shared. Some insightful comments can be heard, but also plenty of thoughts that are not necessarily intended to provide you (or capable of providing you) with anything but sound waves. Some are nothing other than downright mean.

Consequently, it is useful to train your ability to quickly identify useful and inspiring insights from those you encounter, and just as quickly identify and drop those thoughts that hold either little value or even harm. Especially on a long-haul trip, your motivation and drive will greatly depend on this ability to find value in (and sometimes even wring value out of) comments that might sound less helpful to an untrained ear. Of course, all of this hinges on your ability to derive constructive criticism from others' comments. A great deal of constructive criticism does not depend on what people say or how they intend it, but how you can perceive it and how much you can generate from even the driest and saltiest remarks.

Research means incorporating others' views to the advantage of your project. In some cases, this means just listening closely and appreciatively; in other cases, it means filtrating and upcycling waste material. Some things you will do best to just steer clear of. You will likely encounter all three types. The safest bet to keep hydrated is for you to bring filtering equipment that allows you to drink from more or less any source.

The Student's Research Companion. Omid Aschari and Benjamin Berghaus, Oxford University Press.
© Omid Aschari and Benjamin Berghaus (2023). DOI: 10.1093/oso/9780192855312.003.0026

Rough coordinates

Conduct—'Aptitude for leadership or management; good generalship; skill in managing affairs; practical tact and address; discretion. Manner of conducting oneself or one's life; behaviour; usually with more or less reference to its moral quality (good or bad).'

Misconduct—'Instances of unacceptable or improper conduct or behaviour. Bad management; mismanagement; (spec. with regard to official or professional duties) malpractice; culpable neglect.'

Harm—'Evil (physical or otherwise) as done to or suffered by some person or thing; hurt, injury, damage, mischief. Often in the set phrase "to do more harm than good".'

Ombudsperson—'A person appointed to investigate complaints against maladministration by a particular category of organization or in a particular area of public life, such as local authorities, hospitals, or pensions. A person who handles complaints, a mediator; a spokesperson for the rights of a particular individual or group.'

Train of thought

You're excited about your project, you've covered some ground, but you are still far from done. Indeed, you learn how much there is to learn about your subject, and that makes you considerably less confident, at least more humble if not somewhat ill-prepared. In comes a peer—more advanced or not, it really is not important whether it is simply a snobby Bachelor's student or an arrogant professor—and looks down her nose at you before she explains in exactly how many ways you are doing a disservice to the field, and how much better her own work is than yours. Needless to say that, if you are unprepared, your energy is depleted and your limited confidence goes right out of the window.

The best possible way to insulate against horrible people is, first, to know that they exist inside just as much as outside the scientific realm. Most vicious and unprovoked attacks on your project, your process, your insight, or even your own person commonly have the least to do with you and the most to do with those who launch the attacks. This is because in scientific social contexts, there is generally a substantial priority given to being kind to one another: everyone is keenly aware how quickly motivation can be killed, and that motivation is the foundation for any improvement. Furthermore, colleagues are just as keenly aware that they might be speaking after the person they attack, and might face the same dressing down. To speak a little more to the perspective of 'it's not you, it's them': experienced researchers are commonly not easily excited. There are few grounds for experienced researchers to become agitated except for three particularly potent reasons: first, they have identified you as being unbearably arrogant, and they see fit to put you in your place to retaliate; second, they feel insecure and threatened; or, third, they simply like to get worked up about something to feel alive.

First, while you should try to insulate yourself from scientific arrogance as much as possible, you need to invest the same care to avoid seeming arrogant yourself. The best strategy to avoid your own careless arrogance is to mitigate your own ignorance. Most arrogant behaviour is merely caused by people who don't know any better or who can judge the implications of their statements or actions. If you cultivate not only a humble and careful appearance but a factual state of mind, you will fare best with your peers. Second, there is very little you can do about an insecure, backlash audience. If you care about saving the relationship with the attackers, invest some energy in trying to understand what drove them up the wall. There are some spectacularly interesting revelations to be had from being empathetic with those who attack you—both in terms of how you conduct talks about your project and in terms of what you can learn about your project. Third, if you have a feeling that the person who is attacking you simply likes to explode and speak loudly both in volume and vocabulary, discard what you hear. Avoid paying too much attention to those who draw energy from you without enabling you to learn from their ideas. They are not much more than energy drains, and since a final academic project takes ample amounts of energy, you cannot afford to spend yours on those who waste it without return.

During your final academic project, you will likely meet as many strange people in strange moods as you do in any other phase of life. However, during your project, you will be more susceptible to losing energy and motivation, which you need to complete your project. This is not a recommendation to just stick with those people who are easy to have around because they agree with you. There is something to be said about the efficiency of clear and unmistakable criticism from experienced people. You will benefit from reviewing and working through those points of criticism that you feel hold a certain amount of truth and insight that you can draw from. However, you will not benefit from wasting time and risking motivation by taking to heart the tirades of someone who may simply have got out of bed on the wrong side. The most pragmatic recommendation is to treat immediate feedback thoroughly. In one crate of feedback, expect to receive countless worthless rocks, some truly valuable gold nuggets, and on a bad day, a de-motivational grenade or two. Be sure to sort before you appreciate.

In essence

- Demanding academic environments are often high-pressure environments. Some people thrive under pressure, but many show less favourable adaptation.
- People who adapt negatively to stress are probably as common in academia than outside academia. However, given the social and structured nature of universities, often you may not have the opportunity of avoiding them.
- Especially if you do not have the thickest of skins, make a habit of identifying and avoiding people who threaten your motivation in your project. If avoiding them is not an option, go into exchanges prepared to assess and discard their opinions at a moment's notice if need be. You have no time and energy to waste on them.

To reflect

- Do you find it easy to discard opinions that might be of questionable motivation or style?
- How can you heighten your awareness of those who don't mind damaging your motivation and energy levels?
- How do you optimize your ability to tell useful comments from detrimental ones to a degree that you do not discard possibly painfully phrased but appropriate and ultimately useful advice? How can you turn a stone hurled at you into something useful?

Two travellers' tales

Zoey has always been a diligent student. She knows that the university is a place of hierarchy. She's a student among students—and faculty are simply in a different rank. And there are ranks among faculty as well, with professors standing at the top of the academic food chain. Zoey assumes that professors are, with very little exception, simply smarter than most other people. They would not have got where they are if they were not. Consequently, Zoey is not surprised to experience professors as condescending at times. Some can even be quite mean. She wonders if they are intentionally behaving that way, or if stress and the university has shaped that sort of behaviour in them. During her thesis, she experiences a few instances in which professors overstep what she would call the rules of good behaviour. In her circle of friends, everyone has a couple of stories to share of professors abandoning the realm of courteous and professional conduct. Many of those accounts do indeed sound like rather unprovoked missteps of seemingly irritated and thoroughly stressed souls. Of course, there are also great and mediocre encounters with faculty—no doubt about that—but it remains interesting to note that some highly decorated academics can be difficult to be around. Zoey just chalks this up to 'facts of life', gets on with her thesis, weathers the odd storm, and comes out the other side.

Marco has always been a diligent student. But he also has a strong sense of good self-conduct—for himself and for others. During his time at university, he has seen some strange behaviour from many of the different groups of people assembled here. Be it students who kick over the traces while partying, lethargic administration staff, arrogant professors, or overly eager postdocs. It seems at times that this place is full of energy which surfaces in strange ways, some fun and exciting, others rather offensive and hurtful. Marco does not shy away from raising his voice when he witnesses overstepping gone too far, either towards himself or towards someone else. He figures the university to be a social place that claims for itself such high cultural and intellectual standards that it should go without saying that people owe each other a certain sense of professionalism and courtesy while working towards lofty goals. He tries to avoid those people at university who seem not to have a good grip on themselves. When he cannot, and he personally witnesses meaningful overstepping with or without someone getting hurt in the process, he discusses the instance with other witnesses and seeks to bring this overstepping to the attention of senior faculty in charge of managing the programme, or of faculty designated as university confidants, and to demand action against the overstepping party. He makes sure to do so together with the other witnesses. In a sense, he sees the university as a place that he himself can help develop and improve. When he graduates, he wants to wear his degree as a badge he can be proud of, and not the logo of a place where people are not treated particularly well. It's not only a matter of pride and sense of good self-conduct, in the end, but a matter of the value and reputation of his education in the job market: an institution that tolerates misconduct is always only a few instances away from a highly visible press scandal. Something he does not need when he applies to jobs. Better to try and help curb missteps as they happen.

Devil's advocate

Some comments cross ethical lines, and others can simply cross your personal boundary of what you feel is appropriate and what is not. If you feel that one of these boundaries has been crossed, do not be afraid to raise your concern; report this overreaching to the respective ombudsperson with your university. There is only so much that you can and should accept in the process of generating a useful input. You might think of it this way: you owe it to your own professionalism and that of your peers to put your hand up. Harmful transgressors need to be put in their place—end of story. You invest time into a degree from an institution that you require to have a good reputation. You risk your degree being worth less if it has been issued by an organization that has a bad reputation. If it helps to get the ball rolling, consider this not to be a matter of personally feeling hurt, but a matter of professional conduct in a professional relationship.

How to tackle

Your response to the stranger experiences in academic life will likely not be that 'one size fits all'. You may benefit from a staggered system of responses. There are two rather clear recommendations and a third, murky one.

For those missteps of others that you find negatively noticeable but not too harmful, consider chalking them up as a darker background against which lighter, appropriate behaviour can be clearly identified. Not all experiences in life or academia will be entirely pleasant—some might be neutral, less inspired, or less motivational. Against such backdrops, good behaviour can shine more brightly.

Those experiences that leave a lasting impression of risking harming you or others—unethical conduct, and lack of professionalism—ought not to go undiscussed and unreported. First, if you encounter such an experience, discuss it with friends or colleagues whom you trust to supply you with a more or less neutral second opinion of your account or maybe even their own witness experience. It is helpful to share a burdensome insight and seek another perspective to avoid feeling alienated by the experience. If you arrive at the assessment that you would not want to work in an institution in which what you experienced remains possible, there is very little opportunity other than reporting the incident to those individuals or organizations set up by your university to process such complaints. Try to learn about others' experiences with using these reporting structures. Depending on your experience and on local organizational structures, you might need to decide between handling your reporting within the university or immediately outside the university. When in doubt, you should consider leaning towards finding a solution inside the university since, for example, legally attacking a member of a university generates more of a push-back from the whole university than finding a way to adjust someone's future behaviour within the system. You may still want to discuss your case with an external and appropriately experienced lawyer, merely to gather additional information on which to base your decisions and next steps.

The third type of experience consists of skirting what still seems acceptable and what's over the line. Those who witness such experiences commonly are not all of the same opinion whether what happened was, for example, a joke or merely a roughly phrased statement, or someone overstepping to a degree that ought to be considered harmful and not to be tolerated. This third type of experience can easily throw a wrench into measures designed to punish bad behaviour on campus, since it divides witnesses and those possibly in harm's way. One way of judging such a situation is that if the experience led to a protracted discussion about what kind of behaviour is permissible and what kind of behaviour is not, that alone is distracting enough to draw an academic institution away from its mission. The mission of most academic institutions is not to find the lowest acceptable level of conduct, but to teach and to conduct research. These cases of doubt may be reported just as such: the encountered experience has distracted us from our primary mission. If that report reaches watchful eyes several times, a solid reporting structure will act appropriately.

We generally do not recommend that students directly seek confrontation with those at a higher level misbehaving if the confrontation does not seem likely to yield a productive outcome. It simply is not your job to teach behaviour to a higher-up. Instead, go through your university's ombudsman, student union, or any other segment of the institution that may advise you how to make your complaint effective.

Experienced peers' two cents

'A single phrase might hurt a student a lot. There is already a huge power gap between a supervisor and students—even if we are friendly with our students. They are being evaluated for their work. In this situation they already feel slightly awkward. In such a situation, if we are not mindful of the type of language that we use, we might unintentionally damage their confidence.

There is also a cultural difference here: what might be slightly more carefully phrased in some contexts can be very critically framed in other contexts. Even softening slightly—"this could have happened to me as well"—can already help. Then, combine with developmental feedback. Avoid a harsh tone. Be careful about your language.' (Madhu Neupane Bastola)

'Rather than from our comments, the students will also learn from who we are. How we conduct research. How we present ourselves. For that reason, we ourselves need to be active in our research. If we give priority to research, if we keep ourselves updated, students might learn from our behaviour, not only from our comments. "If my supervisor is careful, if my supervisor is meticulous, if my supervisor is hard-working, maybe somewhere inside I feel as if I want to become like her or him." If we can present ourselves as role models through our professional integrity, or the priority we give to research, and if we present ourselves as credible individuals, potentially that will also motivate our students. Conversely, if supervisors do not aim for high standards, it may be difficult to expect much from students.' (Madhu Neupane Bastola)

'Especially if you experience transgressions, if there isn't a structure allowing you to advocate for yourself, then try and create that structure. These things can be initiated from the grassroots at both undergraduate and postgraduate levels. There is always the possibility of advocating for change. And that in itself often seems like a really daunting thing. And students in particular doubt that that's something they can do. But getting involved with that process is of itself empowering, and often motivates and re-inspires you to continue doing your work. Because all of a sudden, you have a level of ownership of the journey, as well as the project. And I often think that these are two things that can be separated: the project that you are working on and the journey of getting that done in an institutional structure that's enabling that. Being involved actively in both can be really engaging, inspiring, and motivating.' (Kim Beasy)

'While I am a strong proponent of structural change for the better in universities, I want to emphasize the power and agency that students themselves can have within the system. This begins with recognizing the agency that you have to create change for yourself. And I think if we put students in a position of disempowerment and oppression through an academic system, that's not a very productive or a good feeling. Then they are just trapped and there is not much they can do.

'While I think the university structure needs to change, agency is equally important, and the student voice in advocating that change and leading some of it is not only important but is also one of the most effective ways to create change within institutions. We know that academic senates and academic committees and, you know, institutional managers tend not to listen to academic staff. But if the customers—that is, the students—have something to say and can rally around a particular issue with enough voice and enough impetus, then it is possible to create change that way. And I think in terms of how do you not get chewed up at the other end? It's about advocating for your rights and, where there is an issue, trying to ensure students don't feel powerless about whatever is happening.' (Kim Beasy)

Writing as modern architecture

Great academic writing not only facilitates but encourages compre-hension of complex material. It is intentional, clear, structured, and statically sound.

Metaphorically speaking

Especially as an explorer, your journey is only as good as your documentation thereof. In the end, you are exploring your destination not merely to travel, but also to record your findings and report them to others who can learn from you.

Consequently, writing becomes as important as exploring. Writing becomes a tool of communication to convey what you have learned. Certain conventions and types of structures have emerged as useful in efficiently communicating what you found, how you found it, and what you think about it. The better your writing, the more reading your report steps into the background and understanding what you did steps into the foreground.

Research means being able to clearly communicate the findings of your exploration. This favours a clear, well-balanced, and non-decorative style of writing.

Rough coordinates

Architecture—'The art or science of building or constructing edifices of any kind for human use. Construction or structure generally.'

Balance—'Stability or steadiness due to the equilibrium prevailing between all the forces of any system. An equality between the total of the two sides of an account, when added up, after making all entries on both sides.'

Clear—'Of words, statements, explanations, meaning: Easy to understand, fully intelligible, free from obscurity of sense, perspicuous.'

The Student's Research Companion. Omid Aschari and Benjamin Berghaus, Oxford University Press.
© Omid Aschari and Benjamin Berghaus (2023). DOI: 10.1093/oso/9780192855312.003.0027

Representation—'The action of putting forward an account of something discursively; a spoken or written statement, esp. one which conveys or intends to create a particular view or impression.'

Train of thought

In this phase of your final academic project, writing will slowly begin to take on a more important role. Especially if you did your research first and consider writing your report as a documentation of your work, you will have plenty to write about. Writing is particularly stressful if you don't know what to write about. A considerable amount of writer's block is easily overcome if authors put research before documentation. However, even if you adhered to a more logical order of producing your insight—research first, writing second—you will still have ample opportunity to get stuck at the beginning, in the middle, or the end of writing your text. The core problem is not what you write, but how.

When thinking about how you write your text, consider great texts to be very much alike to great modern architecture. Modern architecture is functional, clear, legible, transparent in some areas and opaque in others. Modern architecture is purposeful, balanced, structured, solid, and well-proportioned. Modern architecture is not ambivalent, it is not decorative or playful, it does not try to be impressive or sensible. Modern architecture is intelligent design minimalism that focuses on function. That's what your text should be, too.

If you consider research to be first a project and only a distant second a documentation of your project, then your text ought to be a clear window through which any interested person can look into your project. The clearer your window, the better for the person trying to understand what you have done. Another interesting similarity that great texts share with great modern architecture is their purposeful design. There is very little left to chance in a piece of modern architecture; it is much less led by decorative and pleasing aesthetics than by logic and consequence. Aesthetics are an outcome of most modern architecture, but it is commonly not the guiding thought that leads design decisions.

Likewise, great academic writing is not attempting to become the most beautiful poetry, but rather resembles an almost architectural structure of claims, relationships, and supports. The result can become thoroughly pleasing to read, but the guiding thought at the beginning was merely to become nothing more than the clearest of representations of your project.

If you can subscribe to this analogy, you make a whole toolkit available for yourself when writing—the toolkit of the architectural builder. Of course, you will quickly find that structure, support, and balance will be critical to generate a sense of completeness and confidence in your argument. Where you find two sides to an argument, you immediately get the sense of both sides needing comparable amounts of support for the argument to be balanced. Where you start a new development, you find that you can try breaking up the space into between three and seven elements, since most textual developments can be well-structured using somewhere between three and seven facets. If you have more, the thing becomes unwieldy; if you have less, you might need to invest in more detail.

You will find that planning your text can go far beyond the overarching chapters and down into the objectives of each paragraph. By planning whole books, you will find that you can reuse structures in similar places—for example, you will develop one mode of opening, consisting of four paragraphs, that you then reuse in every notable introduction to a chapter. Once you build your text architecturally, you start to find writing smaller elements of your book much easier. As you find that your book becomes less sequential and more hypertextual, you stop writing vertically and begin to write horizontally, for coherence in style, in similar sections such as introductions, conclusions.

Writing your text more like an architect and less like a lyricist will help you in a number of ways. First, it's the most efficient way to combat writer's block, as you first structure the text (ideally down to the paragraph) and then start writing. It is easier to be faced with 250 paragraphs of eight to ten lines than to be faced by 60 pages or even one book. You can write eight to ten lines on just about anything. If you plan to write ten paragraphs a day, your final academic project will be done in about a month of work. Second, it is safest to write something that your readers will be able to understand. If you adopt architectural writing skills, readers will benefit from you trying to achieve the clearest and most faithful representation you can generate on your project. Third, while any modern architecture can feel cold and industrial, it is the best place to make interesting contents come to life. Consider your research to be that interesting content that your text merely tries to capture.

In essence

- Writing will be among the biggest and maybe most intimidating chunks of work linked to your final academic project. Not only because it will probably be the longest text that you will write during your academic programme, but also because every step of the way confronts you with the freedom of another blank page which can be filled in countless different ways.

- Keeping in mind that you will need to write in a clear and well-structured way leads to the comparability of writing with modern architecture. Functional, transparent, well-weighted, smart, but also perfectly comprehensible.

- Trying to distance yourself from the idea that you will need to fill pages particularly creatively, and instead adopting the sense of constructing a building out of clearly laid-out information, also helps you to implicitly partition the challenge: you'll start trying to build one wall after the other—and not all walls at the same time. You can concentrate more easily and, rather than feeling the weight of writing dozens of pages in one document, you start breaking down larger portions into smaller segments. Before you know it, you are no longer writing one big book, but simply two handfuls of paragraphs each day.

To reflect

- How can you distance yourself from writing a document and embrace breaking down the document into individual chapters, subchapters, and sections?
- How can you write as in as clear and well-structured a way as possible? What helps you to simplify your thoughts and structure them in logical relations?
- What should you take into consideration when revising for structure and clarity?

Two travellers' tales

Nick likes storytelling, and he's good at it. His characters have depth, his story arcs have tension, his endings always contain an interesting twist. Since he's a talented writer, he tries to apply his talent to his thesis. He develops cliffhangers, finely chisels his unique headlines, and applies a way of writing that is somewhere between exciting to follow, quirky at times, but always sufficiently scientific. When handing in his text, he feels like he's given it everything.

His supervisor thinks differently. While he, too, gets hooked on the material, it's not for the right reasons.

Amanda likes the structure of projects. There's just something about breaking down a larger, complex piece of work into smaller, manageable tasks. Amanda thinks of this as something like a superpower she has. No challenge, she believes, will ever be too big, if she can break it down to work on it. With writing, it seems to be the same thing. It never scared her if someone asked of her a 10-page, 50-page, or 100-page manuscript. One hundred pages are just 10 chapters of 10 pages, each page is five to six paragraphs and each paragraph just four to five sentences. And Amanda loves to write sentences. Easy. It's all about breaking your material down, polishing each individual component, and then reassembling the components in one big text. Amanda is glad that it's the same technique which makes reading and comprehension easy that makes writing easier—breaking down the material, polishing it, and reassembling it according to the conventions that most papers in her field follow. Her supervisor is just as happy with the result: she's reading a text that she can quickly decompose, decode, and understand.

Devil's advocate

While clarity and structure are valuable in scientific writing, so is making your reader care and become captivated by what you have to say. In some instances, this is most effectively done by an introductory anecdote, an exemplary account, or some illustrative context.

How to tackle

The sense of architectural writing that we try to convey individually optimizes and then integrates structure and content.

The mission of the structure is predominantly one of efficiency and usability of your text. That is why the structure of your text ought to follow the conventions of your field. This simply increases the efficiency with which your ideas will be able to be scanned and understood. This leads to your first step: identify the conventions of your field or of publications like yours in terms of structuring and necessary elements. Take your available premises, the permitted number of pages, and begin a blueprint by assigning the necessary elements of your text a sensible amount of space on your manuscript's premises. Structure your document so that you end up with sections no longer than five pages, as if they were rooms in your emerging mental and textual building. Make sure that elements of equal importance and relationship are in a balanced correspondence with each other and connect to each other well. See to it that your largest segments, your parts or chapters, integrate as wings of a large mansion would be designed to do.

The mission of the content is to provide the motivational propulsion for your reader. Initially, the content you will write about informs structure in terms of its necessary dimensions, but then becomes confined to a statical structure. If the structure allots half a page to one specific piece of information, that will be it. Not too much more, not too much less. Content will have to be written efficiently or extensively enough to fill the spaces assigned to it. While it may seem that communicating more content in less space is always advisable, this is a mistake. Consider a reader's ability to take in information while reading the respective element of your text. They might benefit from particularly dense passages, but they might also be discouraged from reading on if the going gets to tough. The density (or otherwise) of your text needs attention when writing and when revising your text.

Great writing, in our mind, comes together when readers find a document easy and rewarding to navigate while being presented with an appropriately dosed degree of informational nutrition. Especially for academic writing, this might mean that there is no 'ounce of fat' you might choose to cut away—no bit of text that does not contribute to communicating your ideas.

Experienced peers' two cents

'Students need to report their thesis in language. This means that another critical skill employed is academic writing. This skill is discipline-specific. Each discipline has its own way of constructing knowledge, be it humanities, education, science, engineering, or any other discipline. Each discipline has its own way of constructing knowledge, and what is considered to be knowledge differs from discipline to discipline. Graduate students need to be able to communicate in that acceptable manner that is respected in their discipline.' (Madhu Neupane Bastola)

'We write with the goal of showing things. We write with the goal of showing what we know about the literature, describing a process that hasn't been described before, or just describing a theory as accurately or precisely as we can. However, those goals all differ from the goal of merely being understood. So being accurate or precise, for example, if that's your overriding goal, then that is going to lead you to use a lot more jargon. Jargon feels like a very precise way to write about our research. Instead of saying "the process through which countries develop a market system", you could just say "marketization". Speaking of "marketization" is more precise. It's denser and shorter, fitting, but it's also less accessible. It can only be understood if someone happens to know what "marketization" means. By distancing language from the common day-to-day language that even academics use, you just make it a lot harder for people to understand what you're saying. The best theory, the best thinking, the best contributions are not going to be seen or understood by most people unless you are writing about it in a clear way. I'm an advocate of that.' (Matt Farmer)

A magnetic introduction

If you want readers to explore your text, here is where to give them the reasons why. Keep it short in order not to put up a barrier to your ideas.

Metaphorically speaking

For others to follow your exploration report, you need to captivate your audience's attention as early and irreversibly as possible. There is a useful side effect to be found: the more you shape your text to illustrate what really matters and how your research can help understand answer any particular question better, the more you will expand your understanding of where it is you want to go and why.

Consequently, the introduction to your text will likely be the passage that you will revise most frequently. Don't think of this as redundant multiplication of work, but rather as a way for you to reflect on and refine your thinking about your project.

Research into a field means you would like to further your (and everyone else's) understanding about the subject. This is how you do it. Stating and then revising and refining your thoughts is a key tenet of scientific work.

Rough coordinates

Hook—'That by which anyone is attracted or ensnared and caught; a snare; a catch on the hook: (in various figurative uses, e.g.) ensnared, in the power (of someone); in one's grasp; attached to some occupation, habit, etc.'

Problem—'A difficult or demanding question; (now, more usually) a matter or situation regarded as unwelcome, harmful, or wrong and needing to be overcome; a difficulty.'

Solution—'A particular instance or method of solving or settling; an explanation, answer, or decision.'

The Student's Research Companion. Omid Aschari and Benjamin Berghaus, Oxford University Press.
© Omid Aschari and Benjamin Berghaus (2023). DOI: 10.1093/oso/9780192855312.003.0028

Trust—'Firm belief in the reliability, truth, or ability of someone or something; confidence or faith in a person or thing, or in an attribute of a person or thing.'

Train of thought

The introduction to your text will need to convince readers to read on. Here, you make the relevance of your work unmistakably clear. Don't mistake this as optional. It is vital for anyone reading your manuscript to get a sense of the purpose that drove you to do the project in the first place. Of course, that presupposes that you actually had a purpose that drove your efforts—be sure to build a clear sense of this either during framing your project or by developing this sense along the way.

In the world of our analogy, the thesis document resembles the ideal illustration of your journey. Very few people will be interested in your journey if you travelled between two entirely mundane locations. Very few people will be interested in your report if your journey has no remarkable features or cannot at least be seen from a perspective that makes it thought-provoking or insightful in some way. While, of course, content is king, there is also methodology to write more compelling introductions. Just like any good storyteller, you will introduce your story by starting with a hook.

The core text of good introductions is seldom longer than 500 words, or just over a page of text. See whether the following technique might work for you: split your roughly 500 words into six paragraphs. The first set of three paragraphs are dedicated to the hook. The second set of three paragraphs explain how you approached the topic. In the first paragraph, explain the element of your topic that everyone must agree with because it is generally accepted. In the second paragraph, introduce the complication, and link it to the inevitability of the first paragraph. In the third paragraph, illustrate the worst-case outcome of the complication down the road, if no solution to the problem is found. These three paragraphs will help readers understand what's at stake should there not be a solution found to the problem. As you introduced a hard-to-reject proposition in the first paragraph and a broadly accepted complication in your second, readers will find it difficult to reject the risk presented in the third. Given this introduction to the problem, it is time to illustrate your project as a contribution to solving the challenge: in the fourth paragraph, you illustrate how prior research has helped inform the environment of the problem, but failed to provide actionable answers—that's the research gap. In the fifth paragraph, you illustrate how you help fill the research gap by illustrating your project and methodology. Finally, in the sixth, you provide a brief teaser on the two to three key findings of your research, and where these findings will lead your readers in terms of actionable insight.

While this general script for an introduction hardly ever fails to provide a good overview of relevance and some idea of the contribution you make, it is important to keep a few key values in mind: first, 'storytelling' in scientific writing does not mean that you can take much creative licence—you cannot start making stuff up or be less precise on those facets that don't fit your story. In academic writing, 'storytelling' equates much more to a didactic method of teaching your readers about your project. It is a technique that deals more with making your content comprehensible and intellectually palatable. The big difference between storytelling in this domain and storytelling in other domains is that here, the authenticity and reliability of the information you share immediately builds or destroys the trust readers should experience when they read your material.

In essence

- The introduction determines whether any reader would like to read on. This will take the most condensed reasoning you can develop for why your research matters.
- This type of refined and distilled text usually only emerges after several revisions. Do not consider revisions a waste of your time. They are necessary to sharpen the edge of your story more and more.
- The introduction will require you, to a certain degree, to inspire your audience with a curiosity about the subject comparable to your own. To make this spark appear in your reader, consider how you would win the attention of a class you might teach about a subject.

To reflect

- What will motivate your readers to continue reading?
- What can you learn about your project when you read your introduction? Does your introduction raise interesting questions about your design? Are your project and your introduction fully aligned?
- How can you still increase the clarity of your alignment and the motivational element to continue reading?

Two travellers' tales

Bella is the biggest fan of her thesis topic. She loves every piece of it, its root in history, its potential for the future, and its relevance for today. Thus, of course, she starts her introduction at the very beginning—way back when her thesis topic first emerged, sometime in the 17th century. Where to start an introduction if not at the beginning?

Otto is the biggest fan of his thesis topic. That's why he wants to make sure that people will actually read his thesis. He is onto something big, he believes. But how to make sure that people get past the introduction? He reckons it would be best to divide up the limited space of just (half of?) a handful of pages and dedicate them to those questions that he expects to be on the reader's mind. However, he has a hunch that whatever he does, he should not develop the introduction into that insurmountable barricade between his readers and his insights.

Devil's advocate

Developing your introduction further and further may lead you towards overstating the excitement, importance, or relevance of your work. This requires you to find a careful balance between illustrating your text as interesting to the target audience, but at the same time not falling into the trap of impression management. Think of this process as cutting away anything that stands between your audience and an appropriate sense of the relevance of your work and the degree of your contribution. Don't fabricate, just make sure that the topic comes through with high-fidelity and appropriate amplification.

How to tackle

We generally recommend focusing on three missions in your introduction. First, enable your reader to follow why your research project deals with relevant questions; second, provide your reader with a broad overview of your project; and third, present an initial report of your findings. Consider the following six-paragraph approach.

First, explain the function and impact of your field or the field of your audience conceptually and possibly in a quantified way (some audiences are only convinced by numbers). Illustrate the benefit your (audience's) field generates when it operates ideally. Consider illustrating what would be lost if your field did not exist. Most readers should be able to agree: this (audience's) field is important!

Second, introduce the problem that you identified and that hinders your (audience's) field from working at its optimal level. Neutrally explain the mechanics of this problem and illustrate how it unfolds its detrimental effect. Most readers should understand the problem's basic mechanics.

Third, expand on the problem by illustrating and by providing depth to the weight of its detrimental effect. Make the pain this problem causes perceptible. Show how important it is to help this problem get solved. Most readers should get a clear sense of the detrimental effect.

Fourth, provide a brief overview of the research trying to help solve the problem. Show what has been done and how this does not yet help to solve the problem. Most readers should agree there is a gap that can be filled. Ideally, introduce the trajectory of your research project in terms of a broad first draft of a research question.

Fifth, explain what you did and how your contribution can help generate impact, and how it provides actionable insight to researchers and practitioners to help solve (part of) the problem. Most readers should find your approach suitable to help fill the gap and solve the problem. If it meets the conventions of your field, include your findings in the form of headlines here in your introduction.

Sixth, bring all the previous paragraphs together in one complete wrap-up which succinctly describes what your final academic project attempts. Provide an overview of your document. Most readers should clearly understand what to expect and why they should read on.

Experienced peers' two cents

'First of all, the worst thing to do is to look for a research gap. That's because maybe there are good reasons that there is a research gap: maybe there is simply no one interested in finding an answer to the so-called research gap. Often, people follow a research gap which is perhaps mentioned in the last paragraph of an article. That's what I'd never recommend following.' (Günter Müller-Stewens)

A contextualizing theory chapter

Use your theory chapter to take inventory of the ideas you build upon and to delineate the borderlines of the research gap you are trying to fill.

Metaphorically speaking

When exploring a certain region, you will likely have chosen it for a constellation of characteristics and your impression that this constellation might make for a place where something interesting happens. In the end, that's what drew you here. Explaining and helping your reader understand the characteristics that come together at your destination is the job of your theory section.

Consequently, set out to illustrate the key components that come together at the destination of your exploration. Explain how you'd expect them to interact in terms of what others have found about them, individually and in conjunction.

Often, research means exploring the conjuncture of components that are known individually and maybe in simple combinations—but not in that combination that your research design proposes to explore. Showing why this is interesting and what we already know is the point of your theory section.

Rough coordinates

Theory—'The conceptual basis of a subject or area of study. Contrasted with practice. Abstract knowledge or principles, as opposed to practical experience or activity. An explanation of a phenomenon arrived at through examination and contemplation of the relevant facts; a statement of one or more laws or principles which are generally held as describing an essential property of something.'

The Student's Research Companion. Omid Aschari and Benjamin Berghaus, Oxford University Press.
© Omid Aschari and Benjamin Berghaus (2023). DOI: 10.1093/oso/9780192855312.003.0029

Inventory—'A detailed list of articles, such as goods and chattels, or parcels of land, found to have been in the possession of a person at his decease or conviction, sometimes with a statement of the nature and value of each; hence any such detailed statement of the property of a person, of the goods or furniture in a house or messuage, or the like.'

Delineation—'The action or an act of tracing or marking out an object, feature, figure, etc., with lines, as on a map; the drawing of a diagram, geometrical figure, etc. The establishment or marking of a border or boundary. Also: a border or boundary. A distinction that exists or is made between things; a division, difference.'

Gap—'Any opening or breach in an otherwise continuous object; a chasm or hiatus. An unfilled space or interval; a blank or deficiency; a break in continuity. Also, a disparity, inequality or imbalance; a break in deductive continuity; a (usually undesirable) difference in development, condition, understanding, etc.'

Train of thought

Few words in academia appear to be as scary as 'theory'. Dry concepts, seemingly useless differentiations, endless historical debates on definitions and perspectives—would anyone please just tell me 'what's correct' in a way that I can understand? To be frank, most of the hostilities towards theory have more to do with lacklustre teaching. However, theory can feel more convoluted than useful at times. And you are supposed to write a theory chapter in your thesis? It might be easier than you may believe.

In the world of our analogy, you might link theoretical topics you'd like to illustrate in your thesis to waypoints of your journey. Don't speak of more destinations than you plan to actually visit—but be sure to introduce all places that you'd like your readers to follow you. As with planning and preparing the stops of your journey, keeping a sensible balance and structure is helpful: don't have your research run from one topic to another and back, but instead set out a simple structure of what you'd like to learn about a waypoint before you travel there. Follow this structure when preparing every semi-destination. The whole point of this is that if someone asks you where you're going, you will be able to introduce those asking to your path and explain why those areas are interesting.

A complete theory chapter usually offers four insights: first, introductions to the elements discussed; second, information concerning the relationships among those elements; third, a delineation of the gap; and fourth, the resulting detailed research question. Let us look at how you might set up a complete theory chapter: when doing research, projects usually become interesting because two to three topics intersect interestingly. Say you write a thesis on the role of retail furniture aesthetics in consumers' perceptions of brand. Your three topics are retail furniture aesthetics, consumer perception, and branding.

At first, your theory chapter should introduce the fundamental research on these concepts. Thus, your first three subchapters might simply be named according to these elements, and introduce each individual topic and past research in just a few pages. In these subchapters, you merely try to define what the terms stand for. You provide definitions to allow your readers to understand and share those definitions for the remainder of your thesis. However, the elements by themselves are not particularly interesting—the tension that makes your relevance arises from their combination.

Thus, your second step is to introduce research combining pairs of your three topics. In most cases, these combinations will already be established to some degree so that you will be able to find research on brand perceptions, the aesthetics of brands, and the perceptions of aesthetics. By introducing these neighbouring fields of research, you delineate your own research field. After you set the stage by introducing the individual topics, you now increase the tension between those topics by showing how their combinations create interesting perspectives.

Finally, after having introduced the neighbouring fields, you can advance to illustrate the prior research on your own field. Now, this field is clearly delineated, and either more or less devoid of prior research or filled with prior research that leads to specific questions that are still unanswered. Whatever space is left in this field can become the target of your research question.

By developing your research question from such a systematic approach to prior research, you will make sure of three things: first, you are knowledgeable about the environment in which you position your research; second, the risk you run that anyone might successfully attack the foundation of your research—your research trajectory—is decreasing. Third, merely for enthralling your readers with your project, you have ensured to explain why your research question is designed exactly as it is and not minutely differently.

Your theory part has some perfectly mundane functions (e.g. introducing the topics you work with), some storytelling functions (e.g. systematically building the tension among the parts), and functions of due diligence (to illustrate the reason for your choice of research question). It will only feel superfluous if you don't write it in a way that allows it to take on a distinct function. Finally, don't mistake the purpose of your theory chapter as necessarily pointing to one grand underlying theory that you will have to subscribe to. In some cases, your research goal may be to investigate a phenomenon in light of one distinct theory. However, at least in applied sciences, such as most fields related to business, your research trajectory will be driven by the phenomenon and not by theory. As theory is intended to help you understand or explain phenomena, introduce as much or as little of it as you feel comfortable with.

In essence

- Consider the theory chapter of your thesis as an inventory of the necessary topical building blocks required to make your research project come together.
- Aim for three goals: first, you introduce these components of your project; second, you illustrate their (potential) relations among each other; and third, you delineate and describe the research gap.
- The theory part of your thesis is just as useful to your audience in providing an introduction to the components of your project as it is helpful to you in accounting for the necessary components

To reflect

- What are the key components of your research project?
- What are the relations among these components?
- How can you delineate the research gap?

Two travellers' tales

Paul is not all that excited about the theory work in his thesis. Oh well, he thinks, best to put the blinkers on and simply power through. In terms of the entire document, allotting about 15 pages to discussing the theory seems sensible. So, Paul sets off and reiterates what others have written about his subject. The pages need to be filled.

Christine is not all that excited about the theory work in her thesis. She wonders what she really needs for her project in terms of theoretical underpinnings, and makes a list. That list branches out slightly while she is researching the theoretical foundation, but she finds that her theory chapter might be shorter than she thought. Better have a focused treatment of what she needs than adding much literature filler left and right.

How to tackle

There is a rather mechanistic but seemingly certain approach to developing your theory chapter. It seems to work most intuitively for projects that bring together three distinct fields as components—be they theoretical or practical in nature.

First, take inventory of your half-a-handful of—let's say three—components. Use a subchapter for each component to provide definitions and point to central research (some call these 'seminal publications') on the subject. Make sure your audience can understand what your terms mean.

Second, illustrate the relationships among pairs of the three components. Dedicate one subchapter to the relationship of A and B, of B and C, and of C and A. Some of these relationships will provide more material to work with, others will seem less well-travelled. This is fine. Simply try to illustrate how pairs of components interact with each other.

Third, take a look over the cliff and into the abyss of your research gap by bringing together all three components in one subchapter and reporting what has been done before in exactly the spot you are trying to help fill. If you are working on a novel combination of topics, you will find few if any publications. Here, qualitative research seems to be a sensible approach if you do not have a particularly interesting plan to transfer and apply insights from somewhere else. If you are working on a rather well-established combination of topics which has matured far enough for you to develop hypotheses, quantitative methodology will be more suitable, at least when judging by the state of your research field. Except if you expect to find interesting insights that can only be unearthed by applying qualitative methodology. You will be able to glean all of that from 'looking into the abyss' of your intended research gap.

Fourth and finally, take the description (contents) and delineation (borders between what is known and what is not) of the research gap you aim to work on and refine your original, broader research question into a set of more detailed research questions—improved by the help of an intensive and systematic review of the existing theory. Procedurally, this is the most important outcome of your theory section: a refined understanding and statement of what it is that you try to investigate. This also helps your readers to understand why you came up with your specific questions. Illustration 7 shows how to understand how the theoretical components come together to illustrate your research gap.

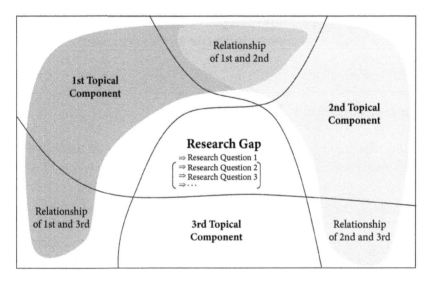

Illustration 7: The theory chapter delineates your research gap and refines research questions.

To mitigate the mechanistic nature of this approach, why not consider it a general, procedural recommendation that you can adjust to your specific

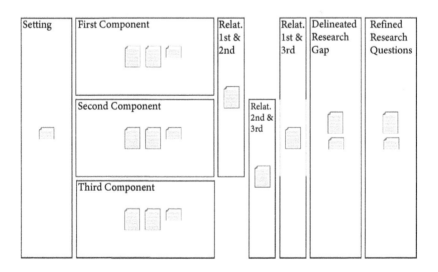

Illustration 8: Theory: work through components, relationships, gap, and refined questions.

case? Always take care to avoid simply removing meaningful, 'load-bearing' parts, as your line of argument might collapse. At the same time, do not feel obliged to keep material that, in your mind, has no role in this chapter.

To get a sense of how this conceptual consideration of a complete theory chapter might turn out in actual pages in your document, consider our illustration 8.

Experienced peers' two cents

'Finding papers can be daunting, especially if you're in a very crowded discipline because basically, you're trying to drink from a fire hose. And of course there are new papers being published every day. So, you've decades worth of papers to try to wrap your head around while also keeping up with current developments. It can be overwhelming. One useful tactic is to find others who have done an outstanding job of reading through that theory and attempt to use them as a starting-point. So instead of just diving into the deep end, you start with others who have plumbed those depths a lot, and use those as entry points. This way you can get your head around some of the initial ideas and topics. Textbook chapters are helpful for this kind of thing. And then you just go from there. And that way you're starting off at the most important parts and then branching out into the rest of the material. Just like a tree: you start with the trunk, and then you branch out, instead of just trying to take it all in at once.' (Matt Farmer)

'The problem with more abstract theoretical thinking is that it's all too easy for us as academics to stay in that world. But the problem with that is that you have to spend a lot of time at that level of abstract thinking to really be able to extract meaning. To be able to understand it, and for you to feel like it has any kind of relevance to your own life, too. Whereas, students don't usually have the luxury of having had many years speaking at this higher abstract level. Many of them don't have the chance to do that.' (Matt Farmer)

An instructive methodology chapter

Use your methodology chapter to explain what you did and why this seemed plausible. It will be useful even if things do not turn out the way you hoped.

Metaphorically speaking

Any excursion requires a mode of travel. Each mode of travel leads to different opportunities to discover and report—a plane ride has different advantages and disadvantages for exploring compared to a hike or most other modes of travel.

Consequently, describing your mode of travel will enable your audience to understand your findings appropriately in terms of the methodology of your advance. Only if you explain what you did can your audience understand how your results came to be. There is an added bonus: if you illustrate the mode of travel and the attention to detail you put into preparing your vehicle, you will benefit from a certain degree of insurance should things not go the way you intended. Especially if you carefully designed a technically flawless vehicle to conduct your exploration, your research might then circle an interesting reflection about how your (in theory) perfectly capable vehicle surprisingly did not in practice yield the results. Much can be learned by the next researcher who attempts what you tried.

Research in many ways means communicating what you did before communicating what you found. What you found can only be interpreted appropriately if your audience learns what you did to reach this.

Rough coordinates

Methodology—'Originally: the branch of knowledge that deals with method generally or with the methods of a particular discipline or field of study;

The Student's Research Companion. Omid Aschari and Benjamin Berghaus, Oxford University Press.
© Omid Aschari and Benjamin Berghaus (2023). DOI: 10.1093/oso/9780192855312.003.0030

(*archaic*) a treatise or dissertation on method; (*Botany*) †systematic clas-
sification (*obsolete rare*). Subsequently also: the study of the direction and
implications of empirical research, or of the suitability of the techniques
employed in it; (more generally) a method or body of methods used in a
particular field of study or activity.'

Configuration—'Arrangement of parts or elements in a particular form or
figure; the form, shape, figure, resulting from such arrangement; conforma-
tion; outline, contour (of geographical features, etc.).'

Limitation—'A limiting statement, rule, or circumstance; a provision. Point
or respect in which a thing, esp. a person's ability, is limited; a shortcoming
or weakness in capability or capacity; a defect or failing.'

Analysis—'A detailed examination or study of something so as to determine
its nature, structure, or essential features. Also: the result of this process; a
detailed examination or report; a particular interpretation or formulation
of the essential features of something. The action or method of proceeding
from effects to causes, or of inferring general laws or principles from particular instances; the tracing back of knowledge to its original or fundamental
principles. Frequently contrasted with synthesis.'

Train of thought

Doing your thesis means conducting a project. The difference between this
particular project and any other project is that you will adhere to scientific
standards. Part of those standards is that you will not only have a rudimentary
understanding of what others have learned about this subject (documented
in your theory part), but that you also adhered to a set of procedures when
adding your own insight to the prior knowledge: you will carry out your work
following an established methodology. Some might do case studies, others
may do a survey, yet others might do experiments, literature reviews, or any
other form of systematic generation of data for later perusal. The one thing
that is equal among all methodologies is that there are chances that they fail
to work, and that a small stand-alone chapter for methodologies may help
save the day: consider this chapter your safety net.

When travelling, your plan might be to get from A to B by bus, ferry, boat,
a short flight, and a canoe—in that order. While you cannot be sure whether
the ferry on that day was out of order, the flight had to return due to bad
weather, and the canoe leaked, you still need to make sure in advance that
you know how to use these modes of transportation. You need to know where

to buy the ticket for the bus, when the ferry will leave, how not to get seasick on the boat, not to pack too much for the little single-engine plane, and how not to fall into the stream when paddling. Just as when gathering data: life happens, and every so often your data-gathering does not go according to plan. When travelling, you might simply not get to the next destination— when writing a thesis, you sometimes only really have a chance to illustrate your capability to operate the methodology. In the end, your thesis is an examination form. Should your supervisor (who is often also your examiner) not get enough evidence that you are methodologically capable, you can build a safety net by illustrating the nature, function, fit, and best configuration of your methodology in light of the research trajectory.

Consequently, planning a small chapter on methodology is prudent when you are setting up your thesis document. In only a few pages, right after the theory, explain why your well-developed and delineated question is best researched using the methodology you chose. Explain what the strengths and general limitations of this methodology are, and how this methodology is most suitable. Explain what kind of results this methodology produces. Most importantly, methodologies require configuration: how did you set up the experiments and why? What was the strategy behind your interview guidelines for the management interviews, and why? Can you point to others who did the same, to provide support for your research design? All of this reasoning to support your choice of methodology will ensure three outcomes: you know what you are doing because you read into the literature on your methodology; you make appropriate decisions on how to design your research; if anything fails, you have a plausible foundation of experience to point to.

One of the most distinctive reflections you might encounter when working on your research project is that the project is one gigantic canvas, and you have all the paint and brushes in the world—but comparatively little experience in using them to create that painting of yours. This experience can be a little daunting. Common questions that flash before your inner eye concern not only what to do, but also where to begin, and how you will complete your project. You can make this experience less daunting, especially in the methodology department, by simply trying to aim for best practice. Commonly, best practice is rather brutally inefficient. Thus, you aim to strike a balance between the best possible practice and a realistic approach to tackle your research question methodologically. But before you arrive at a calculated decision, you will need to know what the best solution might look like. This is part of what you demonstrate in your methodology chapter.

In essence

- Your methodology chapter is intended to illustrate your approach to your audience—but it also helps you keep track of all decisions you made to explore your research question.
- The key to your methodology section is to demonstrate how your approach in all of its facets emerged as a logical conclusion and not as a result of mere happenstance or carelessness.
- While your methodological approach might feel like an abundance of degrees of freedom, you will find that critically questioning and continuously sharpening your methodological draft will make your decisions fall into place as a logical consequence rather than depending on your choice.

To reflect

- What are you trying to achieve with your research project?
- Which methodological approach appears most appropriate for the research question?
- What are the characteristics of this approach, and how can you determine their most appropriate design based on what you are trying to achieve?

Two travellers' tales

Dita likes working through her thesis project, but she does not see much purpose in the methodology chapter. She did interviews. That's it. Is she supposed to write a one-sentence chapter, 'I did interviews'? There's no real art to discussing a subject with people. Dita ends up almost duplicating the first few paragraphs of her findings as her methodology chapter, but something does feel off.

Quentin likes working through his thesis project. He sees the methodology chapter as something akin to a workbench on which he takes account of what he uses to generate and analyse his data, his procedures, and design decisions. In a sense, he considers his methodology section the documentation of what he plans to do and why he plans to do it—not only for his readership, but also for himself to remember. Critically, this is the place where he can double-check his plans with what others have done, reference procedures, or highlight conscious differences from previously published projects.

To Quentin, the methodology chapter feels a bit like his academic Swiss Army knife.

Devil's advocate

Granted, to the less intuitive researchers, developing your research design can sometimes feel like the biggest disappointment of the whole research process: how can something that sounds so much like a fun opportunity to finally decide what to do turn out to be such a locked-down, boringly logical, and nitpicky affair of planning to do what someone else did on some other project just to minimize the opportunity for others to challenge you on your design? That's not fun to most people.

And it is true: should you have ever considered your methodology part to be the most entertaining thing to work on, then it truly pays to set your mind into the mode you use to solve Sudokus. 'If there is a five over here, there cannot be a five over there'. Consider it a riddle or a puzzle in which there are only a few solutions (sometimes only one solution) that make considerably more sense than most others. There is a way to build an engine into a car, and it's not to mount it on the roof of your car, upside down, inside out.

It pays to understand the methodological mechanics of your field. If you do not yet fully understand the more complex methodologies (and most people don't understand most complex methodologies fully—these are specializations for a reason), then simply approach the challenge by selecting from the arsenal of methodology that you do feel comfortable with. Come back to the growth aspect of a thesis: don't shy away from approaching and learning a methodology that seems reasonably within your grasp to learn. You have the best opportunity to learn a technique if you have a concrete project for applying what you learn. Lean into it. If you did not find that you positively need to learn and apply the most horribly difficult and occult methodology, you will likely succeed in adopting it to a degree allowing you to complete a not too complexly designed project. Keep things simpler and more robust rather than borderline complex and catastrophic. You can rest assured that complexity will enter projects all by itself.

How to tackle

A suitable research methodology depends not only on what you would like to find out (even though it seems so temptingly obvious), but primarily on the state of research in the field that you are working on. A different way of putting this is: 'Don't reinvent the wheel.' Reinventing the wheel simply suggests that you did not dive deeply enough into your wheel-related literature beforehand, and did not let the state of the field inform your research design decisions.

This is why it is generally recommended to start your methodology chapter by building a solid bridge to your theory chapter. One bridgehead is the refined (set of) research question(s) at the end of your theory chapter formulated as a conclusion; the other is the reiteration of this refined (set of) research question(s) at the beginning of your methodology chapter as a starting point for your considerations. (You might argue that this is all too repetitive—but then you may remember that sometimes only parts, possibly chapters, of your thesis will be read. Each chapter should be complete in and by itself. Moreover, the factually repetitive part is limited to the wording of the questions, since the framing will be different: in the former chapter as a result to your theory review and in the latter chapter as a starting point to your considerations on methodology).

After your research question as a starting point to your methodology, a common and useful approach would be to first deduce the general research approach, often called research design, as a logical conclusion based on your research questions. Use a subchapter for that. It should become irrefutable that the trajectory of your question suggests your chose general research approach. Make sure that the reasoning behind your choice becomes clear and difficult to challenge. This choice is based, not on personal preference, but on what is called for. You would not suggest going scuba diving if the question you are interested in can only be answered on top of a mountain. Typically, there is one general approach that feels most easily defensible. Only if you are comfortable enough to defend competing approaches can you can take your pick—and even then, you will enjoy your pick more if you select it based on how easily it is defensible against challengers who propose another approach. Especially for PhD projects, you might decide to conduct a multi- or mixed-methods approach to balance the advantages of one methodology against the weaknesses of the other and vice versa. For BA and MA projects, your methodology will likely remain focused on one project, with a more uniform overarching general research approach.

After you have illustrated your general research approach, take another subchapter to explain your specific research approach. Which specific methodologies are you going to apply to gather and analyse your data? What seemed prudent in the general research approach remains recommended here, too: explain why you choose what you choose. Do not take the liberty of picking and choosing methods based on mere preference—draw a logical line between your mission and your methodology. If you plan to combine multiple methodologies: how do they help each other?

To go into greater detail on the specific research approach, it is common to explain the specific process of your data-gathering and possibly even your analysis. Try to explain why you designed the process this way, or whose practices you are following. Here, building on established procedures that you understand and feel comfortable in applying is commonly the most robust and defensible approach. Furthermore, explain the source of data and sampling (if applicable). The same recommendation returns: explain your choices. Make your methodological decisions make sense to the reader. Finally, explain your use of measurements (if applicable). By now, you will be muttering along with us when we say: explain your choices. The more this becomes a mantra in your methodology chapter, the better.

Finally, invest another subchapter in discussing the possible challenges, risks, and limitations of your research design, and develop mitigation strategies. This is not to adopt an overly defensive perspective, but rather to be open about how you consciously tried to make your research methodology as robust as possible.

A resolving findings chapter

Report your findings in accordance with your field's conventions. Answer your questions. Structure your findings to ease the later discussion.

Metaphorically speaking

As an explorer, much of the point of your expedition is to report what you found. While we are convinced that travelling itself is the reward for those who set out to explore, it is difficult to argue that travelling without aim is not a waste of energy. Exploration needs intent—ideally, a discerning intent: your journey ought to serve a purpose that matters to others. Reporting your findings is the initial part of satisfying this purpose.

Consequently, reporting your findings generates the foundation of making your research functional—to inform others of your results. Just as with your methodology, reporting your findings ought to be carried out as neutrally and transparently as possible. This is the final part of the process, during which you can considerably harm the integrity of your work.

Research means making a contribution. Here is where you make a big part of this contribution.

Rough coordinates

Finding—'Something which is found or discovered. Also: a find, a discovery. The action of coming across or discovering something or someone by chance or as the result of searching or enquiry; an instance of this.'

Convention—'General agreement or consent, deliberate or implicit, as constituting the origin and foundation of any custom, institution, opinion, etc., or as embodied in any accepted usage, standard of behaviour, method of artistic treatment, or the like. A rule or practice based upon general consent, or accepted and upheld by society at large; an arbitrary rule or practice recognized as valid in any particular art or study; a conventionalism.'

The Student's Research Companion. Omid Aschari and Benjamin Berghaus, Oxford University Press.
© Omid Aschari and Benjamin Berghaus (2023). DOI: 10.1093/oso/9780192855312.003.0031

Structure—'The arrangement and organization of mutually connected and dependent elements in a system or construct. The quality or fact of being organized in a particular manner; definite or purposeful arrangement of parts within a whole.'

Concrete—'Hence, generally, Combined with, or embodied in matter, actual practice, or a particular example; existing in a material form or as an actual reality, or pertaining to that which so exists. Opposed to abstract. Applied by the early logicians and grammarians to a quality viewed (as it is actually found) concreted or adherent to a substance, and so to the word expressing a quality so considered, viz. the adjective, in contradistinction to the quality as mentally abstracted or withdrawn from substance and expressed by an abstract noun: thus white (paper, hat, horse) is the concrete quality or quality in the concrete, whiteness, the abstract quality or quality in the abstract; seven (men, days, etc.) is a concrete number, as opposed to the number 7 in the abstract.'

Train of thought

It will come at no surprise to you that the chapter on the findings of your research project is important. However, given that most research projects do not yield thoroughly clear-cut answers, the most substantial design decision becomes: how do I structure what I've learned from my project?

When you are telling someone about a journey you made, you will probably choose the chronological way of recounting most of the significant steps from when you left home until you returned. That commonly makes for a personable and relatable story, but it does not really get across efficiently the most essential findings that you encountered. Explaining to friends what your trip was like by showing them a long slide-show and making them follow every one of your steps and experiences is commonly seen as rather dreadful and boring. Not that you necessarily need to make every experience spicy to your readers, but trying to write an accessible and comprehensible findings chapter is, indeed, a sign of great scientific writing. Don't give us the slide-show of all of your experiences; instead, describe a well-structured set of relevant experiences that are genuinely interesting and that are set in an architecture that feels complete and integrated.

When planning your chapter on insights, take inventory of what you have found. Some findings will feel more substantial, others less so. Some findings will feel more surprising, others less so. Some findings will lead to more questions, others less so. Try to sort your findings by an aggregate of such characteristics to get a well-balanced idea of what the kernel of your insight might be and which other findings might be more tangential. If you arrive at quite a large number of individual little findings that you gathered enough support for to warrant their reporting, try to group your findings into facets of an answer to the research question. Do not forget that your research question from the beginning is the actual reason to set off towards these insights, so make sure you will provide an answer to your research question. A plausible answer to your research question may be a careful elaboration on 'it depends'.

When presenting your findings, the traditional problem enemy is that your findings might simply not be interesting: your research may simply have produced the plausible, expected outcome. That can seem a bit bland at first sight. The plausible solution came from your research. The other common issue with findings is that you could not find support for hypotheses you were testing. Both findings are less problematic if you do not decide to consider them a problem. If you arrive at an answer that appeared plausible from the beginning: great, everything went more or less according to plan, and you found evidence for results that previously were intriguing but not available. Congratulations! Conversely, if you arrive at an answer that previously appeared implausible, since you found considerable support for your hypotheses: great, something went differently from what careful reasoning would have suggested. You found something new. Congratulations as well! Whatever the findings are: if you have a good grasp of the prior knowledge of the field (that entails that you picked a question worth asking), and if you have implemented your methodology appropriately (that entails you did not influence the result inadvertently), your findings will be valuable because they can be deemed as support for future research.

Make sure that you answer your research questions. You carefully developed them for this moment. Do not skip over explicitly answering the questions that guided you here. The likely statistically supported, confirmatory evaluations of hypotheses will likely be much shorter than those to more open-ended research questions that produced complex, qualitative findings. However, both types of answers commonly have some complexity to them, so that a short yes or no will likely not be telling all that you have to say to answer your questions. Provide a balanced and well-weighted answer to your research questions.

In essence

- Your findings are the collection of concrete insights that you unearthed by conducting and completing your methodology.
- This may feel a bit like reporting a rather low-level inventory of data.
- Keep in mind that this is the first time your audience has read about your findings. Keep close to the data you have gathered, to leave enough room to interpret, contrast, and contextualize in your discussion.

To reflect

- What is new in your inventory of palpable and concrete insights, having completed your research?
- How can you arrange your findings meaningfully so that your arrangement helps you initiate a synthesis of the material but does not go too far (and leave too little space for discussion)?
- What should you hold back from your findings because it is too much a matter of interpretation?

Two travellers' tales

Fanny is excited about her findings. However, she finds the discussion of her findings difficult. Is she supposed simply to repeat the findings? Everything seems so repetitive. She settles on splitting her findings in two, reporting some here and others there, repeating parts of both. Even though this seems profoundly odd, she simply does not get a sense that she is splitting her report into two.

Simon is excited about his findings. He gives a complete account of his results in the findings chapter, and takes great care to structure his findings in a way that it will be easy for him to pick up his findings again in the discussion. For the discussion, he plans to take a closer look and contextualize what he found. He knows this will take more of his own thinking, interpretation, and integration than the mere reporting of findings. He is looking forward to this—finally some more thinking about the findings instead of mere reporting.

How to tackle

Reporting your findings largely depends on the conventions of your field. Beyond these conventions, the two sizable research design domains, qualitative and quantitative, are going to influence the amount of work and freedom you will have. As a general rule of thumb, reporting quantitative research findings is almost thoroughly standardized in terms of briefly reporting and evaluating your findings, while reporting qualitative research findings is much more extensive, and is influenced by your interpretation of your data and the consequent reporting structure.

Just as before, begin the findings chapter by building a bridge to the previous (methodology) chapter. It is useful to lead into your findings by recapping the general set-up of your data acquisition structure so that people who are new to the findings immediately find a basic orientation in the first paragraph. If you choose to let your research questions help structure the presentation of your findings—a good default idea for structuring—then also make sure you offer a suitable, brief overview even ahead of your link to the methodology chapter. This overview will be a lead-in to your findings chapter, just as your questions lead-in to your methodology, which became the source of your data: your text then structurally and logically resembles the emergence of the main subject of your chapter.

If no other structure is more commonly adopted in your field, consider structuring your work to be as thoroughly aligned as possible with your prior development. This means recalling the structure of your research questions and considering how far they can help you structure your findings. Especially when testing hypotheses, it is plausible to work yourself through your findings by reporting one hypothesis after the other. Use the conventional way of reporting within the structure of your investigation. As for qualitative work, the degree of reporting conventions is generally lower. Your research questions will not only provide you with a suitable structure to explore your data, but will also increase the cohesion of your overall text. Use subchapters to report on individual research questions and sub-questions.

In your findings, make sure to consciously distinguish expected from unexpected insights. There are countless ways of doing this; picking an approach that works regarding your specific case is, as always, your duty. We merely intend to make you aware that you can to a great extent steer the impressions of your findings by working mindfully with expected, interesting, and counterintuitive findings.

Once you have reported your findings in a structure that feels most sensible to you in relation to your field and your data, devote another subchapter to sum up findings in relation to your research questions. The final few paragraphs should provide a useful bottom-line overview of your findings which provides the reader with a high-level account of what you found, ideally structured by the set-up of your research questions or hypotheses.

Your findings chapter must include explicit answers to your research questions or hypotheses to the degree that your findings allow. Make sure the answers are visually easy to identify, and that the pinnacle of your findings—your answers—are not easily overlooked.

Experienced peers' two cents

'Think of it as if it were a ladder where you are first describing the concrete, real world, what actually happened. What did these participants or subjects do when you did this manipulation? What was their response to it? These are your results. Then, you are taking a step back, to ask what these results mean on their own? You're still just in the context. You're standing there, the participants have just left the room, and you wonder what does that actually mean, what you just witnessed? What does this gathered insight, this data mean? How do I interpret that result? How do I translate that into the language that I'm using in the paper? Instead of recounting what happened, you use the more abstract terminology for it.' (Matt Farmer)

A progressive discussion

Take a few steps back and put your findings into perspective. This will require more synthesis, more conscious and active sense-making.

Metaphorically speaking

A journey is not just about getting from A to B and reporting what's at B. The slightly less obvious part is: how did it change your (by now well-informed) perspective on things? How did what you found during your journey relate to what you expected? Where were the deviations? How well did your experience integrate with what was to be expected? What turned out interesting?

Discussing your findings and building a synthesis of what was known before, what you found, and how these two sets of information converge or diverge is key to making your audience understand the value of your expedition. If everything ran like clockwork, and you can confirm what was expected, your discussion will feel like a celebratory victory lap. But the project is usually one in which—while the methodology was aptly chosen and worked according to plan—the results were not predicted. That is when things typically get exciting. The key requirement is, however, that things did not get exciting because of any intended or unintended influence by you.

Research means reflection and synthesis into an existing set of theoretical constructs. The discussion section in your report is the place for this synthesis.

Rough coordinates

Discussion—'Treatment of a subject, in speech or writing, in which the various facts, opinions, and issues relating to it are considered; the action or process of talking about something in order to reach a decision or to exchange ideas.'

The Student's Research Companion. Omid Aschari and Benjamin Berghaus, Oxford University Press.
© Omid Aschari and Benjamin Berghaus (2023). DOI: 10.1093/oso/9780192855312.003.0032

Sense-making—'The action or process of making sense of or giving meaning to something, esp. new developments and experiences.'

Synthesis—'In wider philosophical use and *gen.* The putting together of parts or elements so as to make up a complex whole; the combination of immaterial or abstract things, or of elements into an ideal or abstract whole.'

Interpret—'To expound the meaning of (something abstruse or mysterious); to render (words, writings, an author, etc.) clear or explicit; to elucidate; to explain.'

Train of thought

The discussion chapter is commonly among the most obscure parts of any thesis—for both the writer and the reader. After having discussed the topical setting, prior insights, methodology, and findings—what on earth could be left to discuss?

It's a bit like when you tell someone about your journey: you are being quite systematic and detailed about it. You describe your preparations, illustrate your experiences, and report the weather at your destination. While you report everything that comes to mind, it's easy to forget to bring everything to the point about how the journey changed your perspective on things: the answer to how the journey shaped your view of the subject. You might venture in this direction by describing what you were surprised to find, how your experience differed from the experience of those who went somewhere similar, how it made you appreciate one and reject another experience, what you took away from it for your future travels, and so on.

A great discussion does not just reiterate the findings, but also qualifies them in light of different contrasts. Much of this means reflecting on your findings and developing what is particularly interesting about them. Since you've developed a useful account of the prior knowledge in the context of your research topic in the theory section, this is the place to start. Contrast your findings with those of others, and ask yourself three questions: Where do they match? Where do they diverge? And if they match sporadically, and other times they diverge, what might cause the divergence of your findings from those of your peers? This will provide a solid foundation for generating a feeling of the tension within your findings. The more tension you discover, the more intriguing your findings and the more attention you should pay to making sure that it was not you who introduced this tension by your research design. The less tension you discover, the more conventional your findings and the more reflection you might invest into how irrevocable the expectations are in this field. What would need to change for the relationships you investigated to change their behaviour? In applied sciences, you commonly come across at least two different contrasts: practice and theory. In the former, you illustrate what your findings may mean to practitioners in the field; in the latter, you illustrate what your findings imply for other researchers. Thus, it is common to have two subchapters titled 'Practical implications' and 'Theoretical implications'. Finally, even though your research gap, question, methodology, and findings may have been carefully developed, they will show limitations: for example, you may have chosen to try to contribute to only part of the research gap by formulating the question carefully. Your methodology will likely have been limited by the resources you have. There are simply natural limitations to any research project. These need to be illustrated transparently.

Even though the discussion chapter appears the most obscure to many junior scientists, this really is a place where you can illustrate how your research project shaped and advanced your thinking. If you consider your thesis to be a process of maturing, this is the place in your document to illustrate this maturing. While the thesis serves to demonstrate a whole host of qualifications (e.g. working with prior research, configuring and applying methodology, developing findings), the discussion chapter is where you demonstrate your capability to learn and (to a degree) your ability to teach others the key insights from your own research process.

In essence

- Writing the discussion means taking a step back and looking at your findings in context.
- The discussion requires you to add a noticeable amount of interpretation and contextualization. You are now at the gradient between your local project and the greater, published (looking towards theory) or observable (looking towards practitioners) context.
- Do not underestimate how much this synthesis contributes to your own understanding of what you have found, and how this relates to other insights you knew before. Writing a discussion takes thinking about what you found, realizing or even creating the broad patterns of generated insight, and then reporting them. You cannot write a discussion without having thought and integrated your findings before. If your

discussion feels as though it is merely repeating the findings, then you may not have made that step yet.

To reflect

- How do your findings relate to what others have found? How does it relate to what you observe in practice?
- Where did your findings converge with what was to be expected? Where did they diverge?
- What did you learn from your findings?

Two travellers' tales

Steven is excited to finally see some palpable process in his project: he collected his data, analysed it, and reported the findings in a way that provides him with a good sense of accomplishment. Some insights are more mundane and others are more exciting. In his discussion, he thrives on this mixture: he presents the predictable findings in context of the extant literature in a way to underscore how his research set-up replicated reliable, predictable findings. Building on this foundation, he introduces the findings that do not fit the previous insight in the literature and discusses how his contribution of novel insight fit with the findings of others and what this contrast suggests. Wrapping up his discussion, he elaborates on implications for research and practice, as well as the limitations of his work.

Francine is excited to finally see some palpable process in her project: her data is collected, analysed, and the findings have been written. But what now? Simply repeat the findings, writing it slightly differently? Francine remembers vaguely that it is good form to state the limitations of her work, so that's what she gets done first. She knows that her projects has many shortcomings, and she carefully confesses to each one of them, overlooking that any project will have some sort of, often resource-determined, limitations. In doing so, she undermines even appropriate parts of the project, thinking up ways they could have been done much better. The discussion of her limitations draws her mood down. This, in turn, makes the actual discussion of the findings in contrast to the literature much more difficult. Francine doubts her findings and adopts a very defensive and vague style of writing, selling her findings short. She finishes her discussion chapter, but to her, it resembles more of a reckoning.

How to tackle

Discussing your findings is frequently overlooked, since it can be easily mistaken as a repetition of those findings. Discussing findings means putting them into context with previously published insights, reflecting on the contribution the findings deliver to solve your questions, and considering how your insights allow for a new view of the subject.

This chapter requires much synthesis on your part. After having spent so much time working with other people's insights (in the theory section), discussing the methodology that you will likely have drawn from other people's work (in the methodology section), and reporting objective data (in your findings chapter), it is easy to lose most of your appetite for weighing in yourself. It is not uncommon that, at this time, you might find it difficult to give yourself licence to apply your insight to the subject in order to critically but also creatively bring together these different sets of impressions. However, that is precisely what is asked of you here.

The discussion chapter demands your personal integration of all findings. These few pages are a slightly different animal from all the others—they will probably feel different to write. In a way, this chapter does not report what you or others did and which data you found. It is instead the essay within your paper that only becomes accessible when you have achieved what you have achieved: reviewing the literature, conducting a sensible project, and reflecting on the findings.

Once again, it is useful to introduce this chapter by linking back to the previous one(s). Begin your discussion by providing a brief 'headline' account of the findings—possibly your collection of research questions and answers reported in the findings.

Beyond that, there is (can be?) no generic structure that always works well enough to recommend as a starting point. This choice is simply too much influenced by your specific topic.

What always works, however, is to consider the premises you have available for this piece of your manuscript, and split them up according to the number of perspectives and points you wish to develop. Try to bring the depth of your individual thoughts into balance with each other, and consider how complex your thoughts can become to work in their individual spaces. There is only so much that can go on in one passage of your text for readers still to follow it. Think about whether you consider a sequential development of your thoughts, one building onto the next, or whether instead you go for a broader multi-perspective approach in which you develop a handful of observations and reflections next to each other.

Whichever design and development you implement, be sure to frame your discussion not only with a connected lead-in but also a (few) suitably integrating wrap-up paragraph(s). Distil and state the most interesting considerations and reflections, but possibly include open or newly emerged questions in relation to your research trajectory.

Experienced peers' two cents

'The discussion is where you're taking a further step back. And now you are looking at your results as a single piece of evidence in full detail. Now, taken together with the other findings, how does it fit into the larger group of studies or pieces of evidence of what you're writing? You are ultimately writing for a critical audience that you are trying to convince. You are constantly moving up and down what we call the ladder of abstraction. Having those levels of abstraction along the way of explaining your ideas, it helps your audience. And it helps yourself to clarify your own thinking, too.' (Matt Farmer)

A consolidating conclusion

Integrate the key components of your text and outline its implications to research and practice. What are the limitations of your project?

Metaphorically speaking

Any meaningfully long journey will contain so many impressions and details that its report will benefit from a summary. Sure, this summary will sound somewhat similar to the introduction. But now, you place a bigger emphasis on the findings and your reflections thereon. Now would also be the time to think about how you could have travelled and explored differently, and what you really could not fit into your travel plan: the limitations of your journey.

Consequently, writing your conclusion means taking a third step back (with your findings being the first step and the discussion being the second) from your project, and looking at it to write the in-a-nutshell account. Here is the place to tell your audience which other promising destinations you saw on your journey, but only from a distance, and could not cover. Here is also where you would delineate which areas you could not cover during your exploration.

Research means being able to provide an abbreviated, reflective, and integrated account of what you have found, but also to explain where others could take things further.

Rough coordinates

Integration—'The making up or composition of a whole by adding together or combining the separate parts or elements; combination into an integral whole: a making whole or entire.'

Reflection—'The action or process of thinking carefully or deeply about a particular subject, typically involving influence from one's past life and experiences; contemplation, deep or serious thought or consideration, esp. of

The Student's Research Companion. Omid Aschari and Benjamin Berghaus, Oxford University Press.
© Omid Aschari and Benjamin Berghaus (2023). DOI: 10.1093/oso/9780192855312.003.0033

a spiritual nature. A thought that is expressed in words, esp. one written down; a considered remark made after devoting careful thought to a subject; a philosophical observation.'

Implication—'The action of involving, entwining, or entangling; the condition of being involved, entangled, twisted together, intimately connected or combined. A relationship between propositions such that the one implies the other; also, a proposition asserting such a relationship.'

Limitation—'A limiting statement, rule, or circumstance; a provision. Point or respect in which a thing, esp. a person's ability, is limited; a shortcoming or weakness in capability or capacity; a defect or failing.'

Train of thought

Especially after a detailed discussion, the conclusion can feel somewhat superfluous and repetitive. To be honest, the conclusion has more of a literary than a scientific function. That said, however, the documentation of your thesis is a literary product, and it would not be particularly wise to shrug off designing the part that some call the most important. After all, this is one form of the destination you are trying to reach.

When you tell someone about a journey, your audience will be interested in the destination. In your thesis document, that destination will roughly equate to the findings. However, to learn how this journey has shaped your perspective, your audience will look to the discussion. To reach a final sense of integration, your readers will look for a few pages on which you close the brackets that envelope your entire document. Telling someone about a journey and not having a final, closing statement that sums up your experience merely feels unfinished.

If you consider the discussion a reflection on the findings, you might consider the conclusion a final reflection and extract of the whole project. In that sense, it mirrors the function of the introduction. While the introduction is written to lead your audience into the project by highlighting its relevance, the conclusion is written in a way to ensure that readers know what to take away. Both introduction and conclusion generally avoid introducing new content, but instead provide literary functionality, so that people will be willing to invest the time in reading the chapters on theory, methodology, findings, and discussion at the beginning, and will be able to comprehend and take away the key things to be learned from the text. As a good test whether your introduction and conclusion work as a pair, take both texts back to back and have them read as an extended abstract by someone not familiar with the matter. Given their function, introduction, and conclusion should each be no longer than two pages.

In essence

- The conclusion is the final integration and reflection on what you have learned and deem worthy of reporting to your audience. Ideally, it starts by illustrating your project in a nutshell, including your questions and findings.
- As well as offering an even higher degree of reflection on your findings and your discussion, this is also the place to do some housekeeping. What were the limitations of your study? What are the implications for scientists or practitioners? What does your research suggest in terms of future research?
- The conclusion is short, but do not underestimate its role in orienting readers: many turn to the conclusion first to get the most efficient overview of your project.

To reflect

- What is the most distilled way of illustrating your project?
- What delineates your project? (Limitations, further research opportunities.)
- What should readers take away, even if they only read your conclusion and nothing else?

Two travellers' tales

Tim is getting close to finishing his thesis. Just the conclusion (and some revising) is standing between him and submitting. But what to write in the conclusion? The discussion has already felt like a rehashing of the findings—must he now repeat everything again? Tim is not sure why that would be useful. However, it seems like what every one of his colleagues has been doing, so he does the same. If he just uses some slightly different but interchangeable terms, it will cover the repetitions, he thinks. Still rather strange.

Guinevere is getting close to finishing her thesis. Just the conclusion (and some revising) stands between her and submitting. Guinevere is happy to take another step back from the insights generated and her way of looking at things in the discussion. Now, it's time to take an even broader look at her project, considering what it was designed to do and what it was not designed to do, what academics and practitioners can take away from it, and where her vein of research leads next, in her opinion. Of course, everything needs a quick wrap-up, too, just in case her supervisor jumps to the conclusion first to familiarize himself before reading the whole text. Then, it's finally done.

How to tackle

To many, the conclusion seems like a painfully repetitive rehashing of what has been reported and reflected upon. Still, this short chapter has its role. In a sense, your conclusion mirrors the function (and possibly the dimensions) of your introduction. While your introduction provides a compressed preview of the project, your conclusion provides a reflection and adds some information and direction for use.

Once again, you lead into your chapter by presenting the previous one(s) in the first paragraph. It may be helpful to review your introduction to identify a theme that you would like to pick up on here, to make your conclusion generate a slight echo of your introduction.

Beyond this recapitulation, it is customary in many fields to provide specific subchapters that discuss how your project helps further academic understanding of the subject—implications for research—and how your project's contribution can become effective to practitioners—implications for practice.

As if a natural balance to your illustration of how you see your work unfold its use, the conclusion is also home to the limitations section. Here, discuss in what ways the practical constraints of your project limit the power of your contribution. The idea is to make your audience aware of how far the insights generated can provide a sure footing, and where your work ceases to provide evidential lift.

Finally, some researchers enjoy outlining where they see potential for future researchers. While we tend to view these recommendations for future research projects with mixed feelings—the reader will not necessarily share the motives of the author and thus may evaluate differently what's worth pursuing further—they can serve as interesting perspectives on how the field might progress.

COMPLETE

Now that you are coming close to your destination, much of the journey lies behind you—but the going tends to get more difficult. Your energy reserves will likely have dwindled. Every step appears to take additional effort. Keep these thoughts in mind to make sure you'll reach your destination in a stride and not a limp.

Revise frequently

Developing a text and the thought behind it means revising and rewriting. It may seem repetitive, but this is the motion that propels you forward.

Metaphorically speaking

The story of your research journey is a complex one. It does not necessarily unfold in a way that it can be told efficiently—you will experience hold-ups, walk in circles a few times, and encounter one or two locked gates. All of those dead ends, the initial disorientation, and the occasional randomness hinder those who are keen to learn about your journey.

Consequently, reporting and writing down this story efficiently and purposefully will likely not happen at the very first go. You will need a few rounds of drafting what happened until you get at the core of what's worthy reporting. The key here, in every iteration of refining your account of the project, is to trim away those bits that do not add to the report and keep only the passages that cannot be made more efficient in appropriately communicating what the idea was, what others wrote, what you did, what you found, and how you thought about all of it thereafter.

Research means communicating your ideas, procedures, and findings efficiently and transparently. The best way of achieving efficiency and transparency is to draft, revise a few times, have other people read or listen to your report, and work with the responses to revise a few more times. Revising, presenting to others, allowing others to read, and working with their feedback is the central tool for many academic writers.

Rough coordinates

Revise—'To look or read carefully over (written or printed matter), with a view to improvement or correction; to improve or alter (text) as a result of examination or re-examination.'

The Student's Research Companion. Omid Aschari and Benjamin Berghaus, Oxford University Press.
© Omid Aschari and Benjamin Berghaus (2023). DOI: 10.1093/oso/9780192855312.003.0034

Editing—'To prepare an edition of written work by (an author) for publication, by selecting and arranging the contents, adding commentary, etc.; to prepare (an edition of written work by one or more authors) in this manner; to prepare an edition of (such work) in this manner.'

Restructure—'To give a new structure to; to organize differently; to rebuild, rearrange.'

Distil—'To subject to the process of distillation; to vaporize a substance by means of heat, and then condense the vapour by exposing it to cold, so as to obtain the substance or one of its constituents in a state of concentration or purity. Primarily said of a liquid, the vapour of which when condensed is again deposited in minute drops of pure liquid. To extract the essence of (a plant, etc.) by distillation; to obtain an extract of. To extract the quintessence of; to concentrate, purify.'

Train of thought

When you write any longer document—when you fight your way through every page of it—it seems entirely implausible to, every once in a while, delete a whole page, section, or even chapter and start over. The effort simply appears too substantial, the loss too painful. However, many texts benefit greatly from radical revisions. Especially if you do not plan your writing in advance, the chances are that your text is so close to your thinking that it does not read particularly clear or convincing. It is considerably harder to revise a large and sufficiently convoluted piece of text than to redo it from scratch. Don't consider what you've written as being lost, but as a stepping stone to get yourself to the destination that you are trying to reach.

A pragmatic way of revising your text is, every once in a while, to start a fresh document and only transfer those parts you are particularly happy with. The other parts remain in the old working version and serve as a basis to restructure your thinking so that you have a leg up for rewriting the respective passage in the new working version. For a larger piece, you might do this every once in a while, for a sense of quality assurance. Beyond this continuous revising and refinement, you may benefit from the sense of clarity from having continued with a document that builds on your strongest material and not on a selection of stronger and weaker passages. Any text will have imperfections—but following this approach, you automatically distil your document toward a robust text.

Finally, brevity is bliss. Any first draft will likely be longer than a refined final manuscript. Cutting away the superfluous from the essential will improve every manuscript. Focusing on less vocabulary rather than more decorations will help the reader focus on what is essential to you as the author. Don't be dismayed over the need to revise—rather, embrace revising as a great source to improve your text. Remember that, in the long term, your aim is not to hand in quickly, but to hand in something that you can look back on for a few years to come.

In essence

- Revising is a key technique in writing. It relieves the stress of getting it right at the first go. Still, it supports your goal of developing a useful and well-developed text.
- Don't consider revision as fixing something broken or as the mark of a newcomer. Instead, consider it a necessary and useful step to approach to your ideal outcome. Consider revising a smoothing of the edges. This is hardly ever sufficiently done in one run, instead requiring many.
- An important component of revising is not to keep adding new information. Rather, try to identify the key facets and make those come out more and more clearly with each revision run.

To reflect

- Which parts of your text need the greatest attention and should be revised most carefully and likely frequently?
- What can you cut away from your current text, and what must remain?
- Is it more useful to work on your current text, or is it time to start with a clean slate, transferring the key passages and ideas and redoing the passages you feel least comfortable with?

Two travellers' tales

Hailey has worked through her project diligently and is truly looking forward to finally writing it all down, submitting, and being done with the thesis. She feels that she is slowly running low on energy and motivation for a project that has accompanied her for the past five months. She has planned to write everything in more or less one go—the material is all there, the memories are still fresh, what could go wrong? And it did not go wrong. It just went differently from what she expected: her final text turned out to be more complex, stubborn, detailed, and less streamlined than she thought. This also shows if she tries telling someone about her project: then, Hailey goes off on details and hardly ever has a clear, short, and to-the-point answer. If she just had a few more weeks to revise …

Ulrich is rather humble when it comes to his writing skills. He has read many excellent papers during his time at university and even more during his thesis, and he can tell a wonderfully lean and clear text apart from one that is still rough around the edges. He allocates the time needed for revision and feedback rounds with a few friends. Some underlying themes and chains of logic he started drafting as soon as he started working on his project. In the end, he finds his document closer to the exceptional papers than to those which feel as though they'd need one (or a few) more revisions. A great side effect is that he has now refined those key trajectories of his research, so that answering questions about his project is usually a matter of one sentence.

Devil's advocate

While there seems to be hardly any argument against revising your work, there is something to be said for keeping your revisions—especially your initial draft—to evaluate your own advancement. This means that an earlier revision should not be considered entirely obsolete, symbolically standing between you and finally getting done, but rather as part of your path to a more matured mindset about a subject. Keep old versions can also be a good motivator to see how far you have come. Furthermore, they can help you determine whether your changes actually constitute improvements for the text or mere alterations. When you find that working on your text makes it different rather than truly better, it is typically a sign that you are done with it.

How to tackle

When planning to write your text, consider each passage of your text as going through four stages. Some passages might come to you more easily, others will take those four steps or even more.

The first stage is the creative outline stage, in which you openly and freely collect your ideas and try to form first logical chains among the individual observations, concepts, elements. Try to avoid being judgemental at this stage—just collect your ideas and document an initial account of what you want a chapter or subchapter to be speaking about. Consider this a construction site, where you collect your material and set up the general scaffolding for the construction you are attempting to build.

The second stage is about taking inventory of your creative outlining. Identify the elements that you speak about, the relationships that you try to illustrate, the processes you explain, the chains of reasoning that you hypothesize about. During this stage, set out to achieve a sense of whether your current inventory feels balanced and plausible. Where is your inventory of ideas and evidence lacking? Where is it already quite solid?

In the third stage, you complete your inventory by improving those passages that seem missing or underdeveloped, to generate a balance among the components of your text. Bring the components of individual (sub)chapters back together into larger and larger pieces, finishing by putting all larger parts together to form a complete document. Do the components feel in balance and appropriately weighed against each other? What do you need to adjust?

Finally, working through the entire document, revise the text for flow and a clear sense of development. Since you have mostly worked on components until now, making these components connect well with each other becomes key. Do you write your chapters so that they lead on to how the generated insight will be used in the later chapters? Do you introduce chapters by connecting them to their intellectual foundation? In the end, the document ought to read as one elaborate and extensive answer to a single question, held together by a sense of cohesion—not as a collection of distinct chapters and subchapters.

While research takes a thoroughly objective, analytical, and neutral approach, writing about research requires a greater engagement in synthesis and a willingness to consciously shape a text that appears appropriate to the subject. This sense of appropriateness and balance cannot be delegated to anyone (as the procedure of an analytical methodology can be delegated to other researchers' prior methodology recommendation). It remains in your hands. The best way to support it will be to test the appropriateness of your text by having a friendly but critical mind read it and provide feedback.

Experienced peers' two cents

'When a student hands us their draft, we can consciously decide to read their text with a sense of interest. To a large degree, it is our own choice with how much interest we put into reading our students' papers. It is also our choice what kind of emotion and what kind of attitude we adopt in trying to phrase our answer. If we carelessly convey negative energy, the student will be discouraged rather than encouraged.

'If we read their thoughts with a sense of interest, we will find some areas where he or she has done well, and we will find some areas where he or she can improve. So, we can give directive comments—not in the sense of giving instruction, but in the sense of developmental feedback. During my research, I analysed comments provided by supervisors. In numerous instances, these comments identify what's wrong with the student's writing. But they fail to suggest avenues for improvement—what can the student do?

'A growth mindset helps the student to invest long hours without getting tired, to face challenges without getting frustrated; they will produce multiple drafts while understanding that those tasks are there to benefit themselves. It is easy to identify which students have the growth mindset, since those who have it see revisions of drafts as learning opportunities and don't ask themselves why they should do it.' (Madhu Neupane Bastola)

'I really abused my supervisor in a mean way because he must have read between 50 and 100 drafts. They were not full drafts of the dissertation, but I'd write something, have him read it, and the next morning, the piece of paper would be waiting for me on my desk all red. The world's best supervisor. I really abused his kindness. He is the benchmark for me. He's the model I try to go after.' (Timo Korkeamäki)

'You don't know what ideas will be the most effective to use until you start writing. And you may find after you've written a few pages: "this sort of line of logic that I thought was going to work is not right." I hit a dead end—this doesn't work. "I guess I wasn't thinking it through all the way." Our minds are very limited in what they envision in one go. Most people cannot envision a fully fleshed out argument. Just start to write it. It can break you free of that writing anxiety that I think we often get.' (Matt Farmer)

Core motivator, key critic

Optimism and criticism are strangely interlinked when working on challenging research projects. One of the many paradoxes to reconcile.

Metaphorically speaking

Everyone who has set off on a long and demanding journey knows the ups and downs of being excited and eager to make some miles on one hand and on the other worrying why on earth one would ever try to attempt what you are about to attempt. Setting yourself off on an unusually demanding challenge both exhilarates you and makes you feel slightly foolish at the same time.

Both impressions are emotional responses to being challenged. Neither is more helpful than the other—they just work in different ways. Your motivation will help you move forwards. Excessive motivation may, however, lead you to assess your situation too optimistically and make you overly confident. Worrying and being overly critical about your own performance or seemingly foolish plans, on the other hand, can make you nervous, but it also keeps your adrenaline up and your attention sharp enough to solve problems along the way.

Research requires you to work through several obstacles. Both motivation and self-criticism can be employed in a way to help you propel yourself forward. Depending on your personality, you may find it difficult to push away the emotional texture that comes with challenging and stressful settings. If that's the case, why not try to put these emotional responses to good use?

Rough coordinates

Motivator—'Something which acts as a stimulus to action or behaviour. A person whose role is to motivate others to take a particular course of action; a person who has the ability to motivate or enthuse others.'

The Student's Research Companion. Omid Aschari and Benjamin Berghaus, Oxford University Press.
© Omid Aschari and Benjamin Berghaus (2023). DOI: 10.1093/oso/9780192855312.003.0035

Critic—'One who pronounces judgement on any thing or person; esp. one who passes severe or unfavourable judgement; a censurer, fault-finder, caviller. One skilful in judging of the qualities and merits of literary or artistic works; one who writes upon the qualities of such works; a professional reviewer of books, pictures, plays, and the like; also one skilled in textual or biblical criticism.'

Work—'The product of the purposive labour or operation of a specified person or other agent; things made, considered collectively; creation, handiwork. Also more generally: the result of (one's) labour, something accomplished. A literary or musical composition, esp. as considered in relation to its author or composer.'

Continue—'To carry on, keep up, maintain, go on with, persist in (an action, usage, etc.). To cause to last or endure; to prolong, keep up (something external to the agent). To carry on in space; to prolong, produce. To remain in existence or in its present condition; to last, endure, persist in being. To persist in action, persevere; to go on, keep on. To proceed in one's discourse; to resume or go on after pause or interruption.'

Train of thought

One particularly noteworthy experience of conducting your own project is that you will need to be your own primary motivator and more or less automatically become your own sharpest critic at the same time. You know every shortcoming of your project, but you still need to mobilize your strength to keep on pushing, try to straighten out what you can, and build as solidly as possible, going forward.

There is really only one way of combining the goals of your role as your own motivator and key critic: build a motivation from generating the most solid results that you can. Not from the reality of having generated the most robust results, but from engaging in the process of improving your research. Try to adopt a positive sense towards straightening out crooked bits; enjoy the sensation of having made something clearer and eliminated ambiguity; generate satisfaction from working on your project and not from merely finishing it.

Certainly, some projects feel as if they have gone on for too long. At times, projects appear to be helplessly lost simply due to one shortcoming or mishap. If your project is not graced with particularly good fortune, you will find yourself in one of those experiences. The best possible way to turn around a seemingly deeply demotivating state of affairs into something more productive is changing your perspective to try to generate motivation merely by working on the project.

This approach leads you to just one complication: what to work on next? Certainly, there are just as many exhausted situations imaginable where you cannot even identify where to start, and yet you will find some sort of ranking of whether it is more plausible to work on revising your data or taking a crack at the theory part. It does not matter much at this point what you continue with. The most important thing is to continue with something and try to work on that for one to two hours. After this session, sit back, relax: things are going forward. Yes, you have not solved everything, yes, much work lies ahead, but rest assured: you can work on it. Draw from this ability to work on your project. Simply because, 98% of the time, all you do is work on it. 1% you start it, 1% you finish it—the rest is working on it. It's the point of the project. The only threat comes from not working on it. If you work on it, it's just a matter of time until something useful comes out of it. Even though today, some differentiate between working smart and working hard, we spend too much time breaking our heads on how to work smarter and not simply doing the work itself. Another word for it is procrastination.

In essence

- You will likely find yourself needing to be both your chief motivator and your chief critic.
- The most productive way of integrating both hard-to-reconcile roles may be to gradually calibrate the expectations you have about the results you will accept as passable.
- This requires learning to understand what determines the quality of your research, at what cost this quality can be achieved, and whether you have the resources to reach the level of quality that the critic in you expects to see. In short: you'll learn if the standards you set for yourself are actually achievable. Don't be distraught if you find that your critic is more powerful than your motivator—this is not uncommon.

To reflect

- Can you identify both perspectives—the internal motivator and the internal critic—within your mind? If one is missing, how can you nurture the missing voice?
- Do you find both perspectives in a constructive balance with each other? If not: how can you help both perspectives to balance out better?

- Can you see a critical side in your motivation? Would you not agree that there is something motivating in criticism?

Two travellers' tales

Victor is feeling the stress of his thesis. On one day, he is ever the optimist and sees his project as some of the best work he has ever produced; another day, he is down in the dumps and finds nothing positive about his material. Victor finds it hard to balance both assessments, even though he has a feeling that both extreme accounts are likely exaggerated by the fact that he is running low on energy. He decides to take a week off from his project to cool down and get his head into a more useful place. His starting place after the few days is to think of his project as middle-of-the-road—some things are actually good, others could be better. Nothing to lose sleep about. He realizes that even once he hands in the thesis, there will be strengths and weaknesses. Just like every other person's thesis around him.

Ida is keenly aware that she can be her own hardest critic since her youth. She finds herself prepared that during such a prolonged and demanding project, 'horribly critical Ida' will show up every time she runs low on energy. It's the stress talking. Not that she cannot handle or cope with productive criticism—this is her way of handling and coping with criticism—it's just that she learned that if she feels like digging herself into a ditch, her actual performance may have little to do with it. She tries to listen to the signals of stress and exhaustion, and makes arrangements to regain some of her energy as soon as they show up. That does not mean that every once in a while, the weaker parts of her project don't become obvious to her. It's just that she can help improve them much more easily when being energized by her motivation to improve her project and not being pulled down by her fear of not screwing up.

Devil's advocate

While you cannot reach your destination if you get tangled up in emotional responses to your work, there may also be a certain limitation on how far you can reach, how demanding you can be with a project that leaves you perfectly calm. To go through a final academic project utterly unmoved might sound like a pleasant experience—but it is meant to be a challenge, and the very definition of a challenge is that it will not go unnoticed. It seems to be all about the balancing of demand and challenge on one side, and coping well enough to sustain the required effort on the other.

In a way, completing any project means reconciling your inner motivation to progress and your ambition to improve with the constraints of resources, especially the time and energy left to work on the project. More often than not, a project becomes mature when thoroughly overgrown ambitions are being cut back to size to roughly fit the reality of a project a few weeks or even days before its submission. Especially for demanding and non-routinely conducted projects, maturing does not necessarily mean reaching a defined goal; it also means finding out where, precisely, this goal was located.

How to tackle

Being critical and motivated about a project requires an efficient methodology of integrating two different perspectives onto the same subject side by side (and not losing your mind in the process).

Consider implementing a regular review of your project. Choose a frequency that provides you with enough time to perceive changes—possibly every (other) month. This review aims at integrating these two perspectives. On one side, reflect and write down what you enjoy most about your project and why you are motivated to pursue it further. Focus on the substantial aspects of your project, not merely its rewards. Try to put a good handful of reasons, from most to least productive, in terms of motivating you. Do the same with those aspects of your project that you are not happy with yet, that you see the need to improve.

Focus on your top three motivators and drill a little deeper: why do you enjoy these characteristics of your project? Focus on your top three critical observations: why is it worth improving these characteristics of your project? Try to allow both your sense of a motivating 'reason for being' for your project and your feeling of why your project should even be better to generate energy and focus for your next steps.

Consider listing how you ideally—given unlimited resources—would go about implementing your improvements. It is useful to think broadly here, since you will come out of this exercise with a greater sense of closure due to having considered a larger range of options instead of just one or two. You might come up with a handful of (possibly multiple-step) remedies for each of your leading criticism. Evaluate every one of the remedies in terms of how realistic they are to implement, given your current resources like time and energy remaining. Are those remedies that seem unattainable truly, thoroughly unattainable? Are those remedies that seem attainable truly effective enough to solve the issue? Discard those unattainable remedies, as well as those which you don't see as sufficiently effective to improve your project (rather than just making it different). When in doubt, conserve time and energy when considering adding to a project (thus making it more complex and spreading your effectiveness even more thinly); instead, invest energy in improving and strengthening those fields that are central to your project.

Experienced peers' two cents

'I would come back to social supports. Social supports, and also whatever it is that research students need to do to make themselves feel good and cutting themselves a break. A thesis means months worth of work—but actually this is a part of the process. And interestingly, you're not expected to get it right. In fact, that's what the journey is about. It's about getting it wrong, learning from your mistakes, and being able to go on from there. So again, that's a growth mindset. But actually the mindset itself is a way of processing and getting through that experience or whatever negative experience that happens to be; hence why I think it's so important for an environment to foster that and build that person up to be able to have and take the perspective that actually it's okay for them to make mistakes. They are expected to do that. This is a journey in which mistakes make the greatest learning.' (Kim Beasy)

Frustration is a fuzzy teacher

*Some frustrations suggest trying another approach. Others indicate
low energy or just a boring task. Telling them apart means learning
from them.*

Metaphorically speaking

Any demanding research project is a trek fraught with odd hurdles, momen-
tary disorientation, bad weather, and increasingly sore feet and mind. Of
course, you toy with the idea of simply leaving it be, calling a taxicab, rid-
ing home, taking a shower, and sleeping in your own bed for the first time in
weeks. But then again, the wilderness won't explore itself.

Consequently, some discomfort during your thesis is to be expected. Two
of the key capabilities to keep in mind here are, first, to tell discomfort you
can live with from discomfort that is wearing you down, and second, how to
cope with the discomfort or adjust what causes it. Mere unreflective enduring of discomfort risks allowing the sensation grow into a pain and possibly
into immobilization. Something you don't need during an exploration. Be
mindful of what bugs you, set it in the context of your goals, evaluate the discomfort, and find ways to adjust to endure or alleviate the sensation before
you get stuck.

Research, to a degree, also means maintaining your ability to perform on
long-term projects. This might be the most meta-level capability trained by
actively conducting research: in most cases, it's an endurance test for your
mind. If you consider it as such, make provisions, and remain attentive to the
sensations you experience along the way, you will fare better.

Rough coordinates

Frustrate—'To balk (to stop short as at an obstacle), disappoint (a person).
To deprive of effect, render ineffectual; to neutralize, counteract (an effort or
effect).'

The Student's Research Companion. Omid Aschari and Benjamin Berghaus, Oxford University Press.
© Omid Aschari and Benjamin Berghaus (2023). DOI: 10.1093/oso/9780192855312.003.0036

Irritation—'To excite to impatient or angry feeling; to exasperate, provoke; to vex, fret, annoy, ruffle the feelings of.'

Perspective—'The relation or proportion in which the parts of a subject are viewed by the mind; the aspect of a subject or matter, as perceived from a particular mental point of view. Now only: a particular attitude towards or way of regarding something; an individual point of view.'

Change—'The action of substituting one thing for another, esp. something of the same type; succession of one thing in place of another. The action or process of making or becoming different; alteration, variation. Also: an instance of this; an alteration in the state or quality of something; a modification.'

Train of thought

Who would ever say that an irritation is useful? Irritations are annoying, and everyone who experiences one wants it to go away. When working on your final academic project, irritations are plentiful—some can be quite distracting, and others last almost as long as the whole project. Annoying? Certainly—but helpful, too: creative tension is part of good work. It entails enduring a certain amount of ambiguity.

When hiking particularly long paths, a few blisters are not necessarily avoidable. For some, carrying the backpack becomes painful. Others experience problems with their knees or hips or shoulders or any other limb. For some of those, you may have simply overstressed the respective joint or ligament. For others, pain means you are doing something wrong.

When you encounter frustrations during your thesis—and it seems almost inevitable that you will, at some time—there are several possible sources for frustrations to check for. Let's discuss some of them:

First, your frustration may be a sign of you doing something in an awkward or overdone manner. You might consider them micro-level frustrations—those that deal with activities and their implementation. Are you trying to tackle that countless-references-theory-chapter? Attempting to get thousands of people to complete your survey? Working through a never-ending findings chapter, discovering more and more different perspectives you should write about? All these are instances of you following ideals of appropriate outcomes that feel convincing to you but might simply not be efficient or realistic to achieve. It might simply not need as much. The reason it feels frustrating to do might be because you are attempting to do it in a frustrating way—not because the activity itself necessarily is a nuisance. Some frustrations emerge from design decisions that set you up for failure. The safest way to avoid a continuous sensation of frustrations is to consider them, not as a necessary fact of life, but as a reminder to reconsider whether you are attempting something worthwhile for your project and employing a suitable set-up. When reconsidering the bit of your project you feel frustrated about, try to evaluate your current attempt in light of whether the scope you are attempting is valuable to your project, and whether the approach you chose is the most efficient way to carry out your approach without risking lower quality. Frustrations should not be mistaken as pointing you towards shortcuts, but should be seen as prompting you to rectify those unsuitable decisions that lead you to experience the process as painfully inefficient or unlikely to succeed.

Another source of frustrations might be not in the detail, but rather your overarching perspective on the project. You might consider them meso- or even macro-level frustrations—those that deal with part or all of your project, resources, and experiences. Maybe your project encountered a few setbacks, perhaps you could not follow the original path, perhaps you simply screwed something up—yes, that happens too. Hardly any projects worth doing come easy and without risk. Sometimes, risks don't generate much return, but merely represent sunk costs. That's simply life. Sure, those experiences can frustrate you. But they are only unavoidable if you don't risk anything. Often, what it takes is a different perspective on the situation to understand the value in not finding confirmation of your hypotheses, of not finding your qualitative research yielding conclusive results. Research produces results in many shapes and sizes, and sometimes it takes several looks to find their value. Consequently, the best path to work through these frustrations is simply to try to change your perspective on your project and its results: focus on its strengths, on the steps you've already completed, the results you did generate. Sure, there will always be more steps to take and more work to be done. However, you can be certain that the steps that you need to take will be easier if you count your project's advances than if you count your misfortunes.

Finally, there are plenty of frustrating activities associated with research and its many tedious and at times monotonous tasks in relation to handling and processing data, reviewing papers, writing text, etc. There are many mind tricks you can apply—from trying to involve gaming elements to mixing up tedious with exciting tasks—but the essence of it will remain the same: frustrations may be inevitable. You can almost count on them to haunt your project from time to time.

Be it an awkward set-up of your operations, a sneaking weariness with your project, or simply the twenty-fifth transcript of an expert interview that drives you up the wall: frustrations will likely be part of the final academic project experience. The idea is not to evade any chance of frustration from the start, but rather to notice frustrations, try to understand what they want to teach you, and turn them into a lesson.

In essence

- Frustration with any facet of your work is inevitable for all but the most balanced people.
- However, the frustrations in your work and you learning to endure and overcome them may be the most potent sources of maturing within your project. If it's all just a walk in the park, you'll come out the other side much as you went in. If it's quite the ride, you'll come out a different person.
- In many instances, frustrations can occur from continuous stress. It's not your project, but your passing inability to see anything positive about it. Try to get some distance between yourself and your project. Give yourself licence to take time off by realizing that you will not advance any more quickly if you just keep blocking your advancement.

To reflect

- If you feel frustrated with part of your project: are you certain that you are trying to follow a plausible approach in this part of your project? Are your expectations realistic?
- If you feel frustrated with your overall project: can you point to specific sources of your frustration? Are you in a position to change these sources of frustrations?
- Should the sources of frustration be numerous and diffuse: are you sure that you are not simply exhausted, and that your frustration is a symptom of running low on energy? How soon can you replenish your energy?

Two travellers' tales

Jane loves working, 'being in the zone', and feeling the sensation of flowing through tasks. The early stages of her thesis went by quickly and productively, since many of the tasks were clear-cut and ready to be done. That's when Jane excels: ploughing through a pile of work. Now, coming closer to the end of her project, it starts to show that she will not be able to tuck in all the ends of the project and make everything fit perfectly. Working on stubborn issues that simply do not seem to be resolvable irritates Jane to a degree that she loses much of her energy on frustration rather than actually working through— and maybe even accepting some of—the issues. It was only after she took a few steps back from her project that she was able to switch from 'tearing through the tasks to be done' into 'bringing everything to the best possible end', also accepting that some questions will remain unanswered, and some data will simply not fit her hypotheses and propositions. You have to leave some questions for others to answer, she thinks.

Warren knows how stuck he can get in challenging projects. He has adopted a routine of listening closely to frustrations, irritations, and other types of reaction that he has come to expect when stress levels rise and solutions appear to move further away. He takes these sensations as valuable pointers to areas in his projects that need his attention, but will not subdue him for longer periods of time. That's why he takes frustrations that impact his work as signs to make a physical note, step away from work, clear his head, and re-engage the issue when his mind is calmer, and he can consciously rather than unconsciously react to whatever bothers him. This way he tries to judo his way out of frustrations. Works quite well. It's pretty difficult to get Warren on edge.

Devil's advocate

Surely, there are also final academic projects that run like clock-work and cause very little wear and tear on the researcher's mind. Then, there are excellently organized, particularly talented, and mentally resilient researchers who soak up experience just by reading about the dead ends and missteps but never truly experience them. For the rest of us, frustration will remain a companion that will occasionally show up and need some attention.

How to tackle

In academic research, there are countless potential sources of frustration— from getting stuck while deciding on a topic to getting rejected after several revisions of your close-to-perfect publication. There is no simple and standardized way of tackling these frustrations. Indeed, no simple and standardized way of dealing with frustrations—avoiding them, fleeing them, fighting them, and so on—seems to be productive.

Consider frustration a negative emotional response to an experience, not the experience itself. You might try to change the experience to generate less negative response to it. Often, that will be the more comfortable and effectively resolving path to take. In other cases, you will not be able to change the experience, so the only alternative to tolerating the frustration is to find a way to decouple your response from the experience. One way of achieving this might be reconsidering your and others' roles within the experience, reconsidering the task as a game, shifting the experience into the domain of curiosity by exploring why it is that this experience frustrates you and what might unlock your ability to disconnect the link between itself and your response.

When you sense a frustration, consider whether you can change what frustrates you or not. If you cannot change it, explore how you can change your response to the frustrating experience. Consider discussing the experience with peers. Do they understand your frustration? If both strategies fail and no one seems to see your point: that's pretty frustrating, indeed. Maybe take a break to take your mind off things—it might simply be exhaustion.

Just try not to expect never to be frustrated, or expect to be able to evade every sense of frustration. Frustrations are great to learn from about your motives, your ways of working, and about how you can try to shape your emotional responses to external stimuli. Frustrations can be a great teacher.

Experienced peers' two cents

'At least on the doctoral level, it is quite common that people can get pretty frustrated with the bureaucracy in the end. Until you reach the final stretch, you will feel like you're changing the world and that you're working on something really meaningful. Then comes the lady and puts the little plastic form on every page of your thesis to check if your margins are correct and sends you back to reprint. You have to do certain things to have your thesis in revision, and then you have to wait forever. That's when reality hits.

'Many people enjoy the part of independent research and thrive on the sense of independence. But then you have to return and conform to the rules, you adjust to the forms, the institution, the country, the professor. This is necessary, but frustrating.

'Some people have unusual approaches to supervising. Some people may say: go to the mountains and come back when you have a finished thesis and I will look at it. Based on my experience—the first time someone works on a research project, they really don't know what to do. Especially what to do when they hit the wall. About the language of the field, from data to methods to actually putting it on paper writing—you need a lot of help. Obviously, you can get done with your thesis by figuring it out on your own, but this is where supervisors can give giant value added by holding their hand and providing feedback.' (Timo Korkeamäki)

Relaxation as a research methodology

Research is demanding and tiring. Without relaxation and distraction, you may not sustain your energy levels on a long journey.

Metaphorically speaking

Research means stress to your 'mental muscles'. Stretch, and you avoid cramps. Don't stretch, and you quickly find walking down the next hill more painful than it would have to be.

Consequently, consider maintaining the well-being and health of your mind as part of your challenge. Remember that it's your mind that is doing all the work on this journey. You will, in the past, have had a range of experiences of your mind working at lowest and up to its peak performance. Since you will be interested in conducting your final academic project as efficiently as possible, your best bet will be to try to make your mind perform at its best.

Research, to a degree, also means helping your mind to develop and deliver a great performance. Taking breaks and finding ways to take your mind off the project is key to refreshing and refocusing on those bits of your project you have stared at for too long. To see the forest for the trees again, have a nap at the lake.

Rough coordinates

Tire—'To become weak or exhausted from exertion; to have one's strength reduced or worn out by toil or labour; to become fatigued.'

Relaxation—'Recreation or rest, esp. after a period of work; respite from mental or physical stress. Also as a count noun: a relaxing activity or pastime. Abatement of intensity, vigour, or energy; an instance of this. Chiefly Physics. The gradual return of a system towards equilibrium or a steady state; spec. the reduction of stress caused by gradual plastic deformation in material held at constant strain.'

The Student's Research Companion. Omid Aschari and Benjamin Berghaus, Oxford University Press.
© Omid Aschari and Benjamin Berghaus (2023). DOI: 10.1093/oso/9780192855312.003.0037

Distraction—'The drawing away (of the mind or thoughts) from one point or course to another; diversion of the mind or attention. Usually in adverse sense; less commonly = diversion, relaxation (as in French).'

Stimulate—'To excite (an organ) to increased activity, to quicken the action or function of.'

Train of thought

Innately, science is a thoroughly rational process. However, don't be mistaken: it will not turn you into a robot. Most people who undertake scientific projects—especially those less experienced—also encounter a rather distinct set of emotional responses to scientific projects. We are not only talking about the frustrations of a seemingly failing experimental set-up or the elated sense of achievement. We are also talking about the wide field of emotional responses that people might experience when they involve themselves fully in a challenging project that hardly any people (besides themselves) care deeply about: uncertainty, self-doubt, panic, embarrassment, and in conclusion different facets of depression. Those experiences are not uncommon, and we are convinced that emotional responses to demanding projects are much more constructively captured when they are discussed than when they are ignored.

Travelling takes energy. People respond differently to investing energy. Some regenerate quickly, others take time to regenerate, and yet others find it difficult to avoid drawing more and more power from their depleting reserves, getting more and more frustrated in the process. Some can ignore it when their feet hurt, others will be driven somewhat mad by it. Taking enough breaks, putting your feet up, and travelling with an appropriate mindset is key to alleviating the most pressing signs of fatigue and hopefully avoiding fatigue fractures altogether.

The best reason—even for a diligent person—to take a break is that you can rest assured: your mind will not really completely abstain from working on the problem. While you take a few days off, your mind will keep the project cooking, even though on a lower and maybe a different flame. There is a curious relationship between working through your project and the need to take breaks. Not only will you need to rest from time to time, but your mind will work more creatively on the problem than when you use it to carry out distinct processes. You might encounter the situation that you work diligently and tiring on one particular area of the project, apparently with little advancement. Not only that: your tiring shows that you need to refresh your energy, but also that you might be working less efficiently, since your potentially diligent work still doesn't suffice for the problem at hand. Taking a few days off and allowing your mind to reconsider the problem at hand from a few different angles will likely provide you with a slightly different evaluation of your options and, by extension, a more efficient, alternative way of tackling the problem that felt tiring before. Taking a break from work to allow your mind to focus on all alternatives is, consequently, not only an approach to regaining your energy but a way of to assessing the best angle of attack.

Taking a few steps back from your project can feel most rewarding if you keep your mind occupied with something else. A great way of taking a productive break from your thesis is a weekend trip to explore a city you don't know yet. New impressions will jog your mind, entirely manageable challenges of finding your way around and exploring the town will give you a sense of accomplishment, of something easily done. Merely immersing yourself in another environment will help take yourself away from your thesis and recharge, and generate a sense of having created a little indulgence. Introducing oneself to an environment that is made up of simple and rewarding problem-solving helps many people stimulate their mind to juggle with their current project challenges. Don't be discouraged if you return and the challenge still seems difficult—it still is. But generating new impressions of solvable problems will be the best ground for your further advancement in the thesis.

In essence

- Even though scientific work is highly rational, there is no arguing that the considerable challenge involved can cause considerable emotional stress to most researchers.
- A good way of thinking about the emotional stress that you subject yourself is to consider your emotional energy level.
- The key to arriving at a long-term and continuously productive way of working is to take phases of relaxation seriously. Every so often you can plan them. Other times, you might simply find that you'll need a moment away from the desk today (or at least tomorrow). Don't worry about being productive. If you are involved with your project, your mind will take your project along and gnaw on the toughest challenges automatically, at the back of your mind.

To reflect

- Are you an emotionally sensible and responsible person? Do you take good care of yourself? If you are not sure about this: how can you increase your attentiveness to your own needs for emotional balance?
- What's your stance on performance and relaxation? Do you see the link between them?
- Can you accept that, to progress, you might need to let go of the most challenging problems of your work for a few days?

Two travellers' tales

Xavier went through his programme like a breeze. Most tasks could be solved by simply throwing his entire mind and energy against them. There were not many instances where he felt that his straightforward approach to overcoming obstacles was not the most efficient way of tackling things. This changed during his thesis. He worked with a rather laissez-faire supervisor who clarified it for him that a good supervision is close to a zero-contact supervision, and that this would also pay out in grades. Xavier set up a demanding project and the going got tougher and tougher. Since he knew from experience that the project would start to crumble if he did not invest more and more energy into it, Xavier tapped deep into his energy reserves. Soon thereafter, he found these reserves exhausted. No matter how close he came to powering through, this project was simply not going to be powered through. Xavier took several weeks off to cool down and refocus. He regained some strength and completed his project, limping over the finish line rather than crushing challenges. But he made it.

Kerstin tends to look at challenges like she looks at walls in the climbing hall—with a mixture of respect, an analytical mind of efficient paths, and a keen sense of where she might become more and more tired, constantly seeking spots where she can catch her breath. She applies this way of carefully planning out her path and energy levels to the thesis as well. Where others set aside six months of intense work for their thesis, Kerstin starts planning three phases of working on the thesis, separated by two brief vacations away from the desk. During the week, she makes sure to keep up her engagement in two recreational sports, and consciously sets aside time to go to concerts or galleries. She considers all of these activities as necessary counterbalances that will help her climb this vertical wall that is her thesis.

Carefully and respectfully considering the challenge ahead of her turned her into a pro when provisioning her mental and motivational energy.

Devil's advocate

Adding periods of relaxation to your work routine serves the purpose of increasing and renewing your focus and performance on the project. It is not intended to change the nature of your project from challenge to leisure cruise. However, if the contextual motivations of completing your thesis are largely intact (i.e. you wanting to complete your programme and start a career), you do not have to fear that taking a break will be an undue indulgence and draw you too far away from your project. To most, the bigger risk is to underestimate the beneficial effects a good balance between performance and recreation has on their creativity and productivity. In many projects, the will to endure is higher than the skill to reach particularly high performance by continuously replenishing energy.

How to tackle

Either you already know great ways to unwind, or you should try to find a few of those. Thereafter, make sure to plan time for and actually do these things that clear your mind and loosen up your muscles. Do this regularly and in a variation that suits you.

Be sure to also have some ideas for the situations when relaxation becomes a necessary semi-emergency: what are great ways to combat those medium-stress experiences when you simply need a reset? There will be 'happy places' you like to visit or activities you truly cherish. This can also mean factually to put some distance between yourself and your workplace: get out of your work space, out of the house, possibly out of town, and the region. Go some place else for a few days, see something different, and return with some renewed energy and adjusted perspective.

None of this is unduly spoiling yourself. All of it is intended to functionally serve the maintenance of your motivation and energy. Any energy thoroughly depleted and motivation entirely snuffed out will come at such a premium of cost that most of us cannot afford to run that low and still keep going.

Finding and pursuing great ways to unwind is one of the unsung heroes of productivity. It's the ultimate research methodology. Just as many races are won not only by driving fast but by making regular, smart, and efficient pit stops.

Experienced peers' two cents

'Sometimes you get these jumps forward, and occasionally you just don't move at all. It can be quite difficult if you're in quicksand anyway, and you feel the pressure from society, from family, from peers if you are ever going to get done. What has worked for me was working on multiple fronts at the same time. You hit the wall somewhere, you let that mull and take on one of your other battles. At least psychologically, it is good for you, since you get a sense of moving forward. Maybe not on all things, possibly not even on the most important things, but at least you are moving forward.

'It is so important for you that you stay mentally healthy through the process. A big part of this mental health is the feeling that you are moving forward. So, you have to feed that.' (Timo Korkeamäki)

Fear of writing

When too much depends on one activity to proceed, this activity can become inaccessible. Unblock by taking tiny steps and shift your perspective.

Metaphorically speaking

Research is pathfinding. Pathfinding takes inspiration, creativity, and keen observation skills. Sure, you can also try to thrash your way through the underbrush, but how long will your stamina last? Especially with an expedition as sizeable as your thesis, managing your energy reserves smartly is key. Particularly if you feel your energy reserves dwindling, don't waste them. Relax for a bit, calm down, observe your surroundings, carefully judge your options to proceed, and then test your options.

Consequently, When you feel an onset of writer's block, consider carefully if trying to power through is really the sensible path to take in your situation. It might be—it might not. In most cases we observed, attempting to power through and discipline yourself out of a situation where you could not immediately find your path led to more exhaustion and less advancement than what a few days of stepping away from the project and then a careful consideration of the options to proceed might have yielded.

Research, to a degree, also means mind over muscle. It is an easy mistake to think that work is work and that discipline helps the builder to build his cathedral. It might help some. It does not help those, however, who do not see the path to follow next. For creative work—and research is a variant of creative work—seeing the path to be followed (or at least to be created) is crucial to avoid diligently taking steps to nowhere.

Rough coordinates

Writer's block—'a (usually temporary) inability of a writer, esp. a professional writer, to produce or continue working on a piece of writing.'

The Student's Research Companion. Omid Aschari and Benjamin Berghaus, Oxford University Press.
© Omid Aschari and Benjamin Berghaus (2023). DOI: 10.1093/oso/9780192855312.003.0038

Confidence—'The mental attitude of trusting in or relying on a person or thing; firm trust, reliance, faith. Assurance, boldness, fearlessness, arising from reliance (on oneself, on circumstances, on divine support, etc.). In a bad sense: Assurance based on insufficient or improper grounds; excess of assurance, overboldness, hardihood, presumption, impudence.'

Anxiety—'Worry over the future or about something with an uncertain outcome; uneasy concern about a person, situation, etc.; a troubled state of mind arising from such worry or concern.'

Overwhelm—'To overcome or overpower (a person, the mind, etc.) with emotion. To bring to sudden ruin or destruction; to engulf; to crush; to defeat utterly or conclusively. Also: to overcome or overpower with excess of work, responsibility, etc.'

Train of thought

Especially when faced with a white piece of paper and plan to take a typing excursion over the next 100 pages, it's not unheard of for authors, both junior and experienced, to get stuck in writer's block. But it's not only at the beginning that the block might hit you; it might just as easily be somewhere in the middle or even near the end of your manuscript. Seemingly losing the ability to express yourself in written form can come at any point. While an acute case of writer's block feels like the most incurable condition ever experienced, it is, however, a much more mundane situation than you may feel.

First, writer's block usually has a reason. In most cases, writer's block does not have much to do with you being unable to comprise words or losing the ability to write. Instead, many cases of writer's block relate to a counterproductive impression of the author's current situation. This impression may come from a distinct sense of fear that captivates your mind to the degree that it immobilizes you when you are trying to write. And there is much you might be fearful about concerning your thesis: 'What an embarrassment if I write something wrong!' 'What a disappointment if the statistics don't turn out in my favour!' 'Surely, I don't know enough about that topic to write!' 'I might not be clever enough to do this.' 'I might not be informed enough to do this.' 'My ideas are simply not worth putting on paper'.

These are plenty of reasons not to continue and finish your journey. Given your impression that your thoughts are simply better not being put down on paper, writer's block does not appear as the problem, but as the solution to prevent whatever you fear happening from become real. Writer's block often presents itself as a self-fulfilling prophecy aimed at the concept, 'If you don't move, nothing bad will happen.' Of course, that's a false sense of security because the clock keeps ticking and your deadline inches towards you. While there are more reasons for writer's block than this immobilization-by-fear—for example still being fuzzy as to what exactly to write about or where to begin—this less rational and more emotional mechanism is both common and painfully powerful, as it is one of the forms of writer's block that is self-reinforcing: the better you block, the safer you seem.

If you count yourself among those immobilized by a fear of failure or inadequacy, there are two polar opposite ways of getting out of that ditch: first, steely and sometimes painful discipline, and second, relaxation, mindfulness, and not taking things too seriously. While the former approach appears more logical to many and the second rather counterintuitive, there is considerable risk involved in the former: you are trying to force your way through a wall of which you don't know the thickness or material. It might be just a slight obstacle that you can push through (and you will encounter many of those). If you are experiencing writer's block to a degree that you feel this to be detrimental to your well-being, however, chances are that only the second approach, relaxation, can help you get your text done without painfully blowing a mental fuse on the way. Remember that following the 'steely resolve' strategy requires going against your gut, your sense of emotional well-being—something that seems to us too risky to recommend to most people in most situations.

Let's explore the second avenue: relax yourself, be mindful, and don't take things too seriously. Chances are that your expectations of yourself and what you can reasonably accomplish during your thesis are exaggerated. Consider for a moment that you've completed the bulk of an academic programme and have been confirmed to engage in your thesis. The educators at your institution believe that you can do this. Otherwise, you'd not have made your way here. Furthermore, regardless of what you may have been led to believe about your thesis—even your doctoral thesis—it is not important to the degree that you allow yourself to lose your mind over it. A thesis is an academic project used in part to examine your scientific proficiency. If you've seen what we've seen, 'scientific proficiency' is to be seen in sometimes substantial air quotes. The reason for those air quotes is that scientific proficiency has much more to do with intellectual attitude and commitment than what is sometimes seen as scientifically relevant and rigorous. That leads us to our next point: consider what other, less prepared, less bright, and less creative people have got away with and graduated. And you mean to tell us that it's you who is going to limbo even below that performance? We don't know every one of you, but in most cases that requires a medal for lowest self-esteem. And that's precisely what you try to counter here: a sensation of low self-esteem and self-confidence. You need some self-confidence to write. Otherwise, you will not trust yourself to have something to say. And you do. In fact, you must, to continue. There is, consequently, little to do except to build up some steam.

There is another element of the second avenue (one that eerily looks like the first): once you've built some self-esteem, there is little else to do than slowly and gradually pick up your pace and get that text done. Once you've built a positive attitude toward your project, remind yourself that the same educators that green-lit your project proposal in the first place want to see you succeed, since they want to graduate you. Your family is rooting for you on the sidelines. Your siblings are excited about the graduation buffet. Your friends are crossing their fingers for you. So many people are rooting for you to completing your project that you can decide to write, not for you, but rather for them. Do your best, do your worst, just do it. But don't try to force your way against your personal convictions, and write if it still feels that you are taking steps in the wrong direction. Instead, take another break and re-adjust. Put your mind in the mode that aligns 'completing your thesis' with 'good', and try to give the whole process of being allowed to write your thesis as a positive connotation—not only because it helps you, but because that's what it is: quite a luxury of a pastime. Even though it does not always feel that way.

In essence

- Writer's block is among the most common challenges to anyone who writes. Lack of confidence and fear of detrimental outcomes can be one of the reasons that prevents someone from writing the next sentence.
- There is the path of steely resolve, of trying to discipline yourself over the finish line—but does that really work? We have come to find that it can work if you need to rather mechanically report material and not be particularly creative. Going against your emotional grain, however, comes with considerable risk.
- The more reliable alternative is to try to relax your probably very high expectations and simply try to take the first step. Here, you need to relax and give yourself licence to first draft material, maybe only headlines, that you will later revise into a text whose quality will suffice. Do not aim for perfection, go for as much polish as is reasonably possible. But first, you need something to polish.

To reflect

- Do you suffer from writer's block? What seems to be the root cause of it?
- Do you need to write more of a mechanical report of material you already have, or do you instead need to creatively develop a text?
- In the case of a mechanical report: do you think you can use your discipline to get going again? In the case of creative writing: what seems to be the best way to calm your fears? Can you discuss them with friends, colleagues, or even an academic mentor?

Two travellers' tales

Lana is known as 'Captain Determination' among her friends. Most of the challenges she encountered in the past, she managed to tackle and overcome by discipline and steely resolve. Maybe her training as a promising competitive athlete before she came to university has something to do with it. There is little better than discipline to put mind over matter. However, she has found out that determination works best if applied to a stack of tasks, to a training routine, to something that needs to be done but not necessarily questioned or thought about. During her thesis, this turns into an issue. The project itself, Lana was able to outline and work through diligently—she aced data collection and coding—but the writing process, the long, wide plains of white pages—felt impossibly difficult for Lana to fill. The urge to move forward made trying to be disciplined even harder. There were just not enough ideas there, yet, to really get going. This only happened after she did something new: tried to step away from the disciplined approach and instead allowing herself to sort her ideas, put them in a sensible and well-balanced order, outline the structure, and then start writing. That's when her strength in following discipline helped her again.

Yoel is not the most disciplined person on earth, but he tends to get his stuff done. What Yoel thrives on is a white piece of paper. He loves sketching and drafting ideas, chaining them together, structuring and sub-structuring his material down to the most detailed level. Thus, he does not find it particularly challenging to get going on his thesis document—but he does lose interest as soon as the central ideas are drawn up. That's when he has to switch from an openly creative and eager-to-discover mindset to a more disciplined, more production-minded way of working. Yoel reminds himself that none of his thesis will be particularly useful to anyone if he does not manage to complete the development of his ideas and wrap everything up into a well-presented and structured document. He completes his thesis by instead maintaining a continuous output, writing a few hours each day, rather than risking his progress and coming to a complete halt by working in sprints. He finds it easier to negotiate with his inner sloth to take small, continuous steps than to put a large bet on that one big sprint to the finish line. After all, that's how sloths survive—small steps, every day.

Devil's advocate

Occasionally, you simply 'don't feel it'—you cannot make a good mental connection to the ideas that you are trying to capture in text. That's perfectly fine if it has not gone on for too many weeks and does not conflict with your factual or perceived schedule.

If you 'don't feel it', consider not writing for a few days. Texts written from a clear idea are commonly more structured and easier to revise and extend. Trying to write when everything tells you that you do not want to or are not sure what to write about has a tendency to generate the most hodgepodge material possible. This is often very difficult to revise and improve upon.

Avoid going against the grain and trying to write when you don't know what to write about. Instead, don't write, but collect and structure your ideas. The time will come.

How to tackle

If you find yourself unable to produce text but in need of doing so, be mindful that the mere notion of your having to carry out one activity to complete a stressful project might make just that activity unavailable, as if that particular productive muscle is painfully strained—how ironic! Three angles of attack come to mind.

Regarding writing as an activity, you cannot change the fact that you will eventually need to write. There is no way around that. However, you can change your perception of agency, from being compelled to write to viewing the activity of writing as less emotionally charged—or, in a full reversal, to see it as a cathartic release of finally bringing what you have in mind to paper. It appears that you're not going to get done without this release of ideas onto paper, so this mental model is not even that far off. If you accept that you cannot get around it, sooner or later, you will come around to the view that going through it is the only path forward, and that you don't want to be stuck in front of your final opponent forever. It's a slightly bland place to be stuck.

Regarding your project, you will likely have passed your honeymoon phase. You are looking forward to getting done some time soon. There is very little standing between you and your goal of reaching your destination. Every day you make a little headway, you get a bit closer to your goal. If you are at all interested in advancing from your current position, there is very little standing between you and your finishing line if you merely stroll a few metres every day. Once you manage to cover those few metres every day, the scenery will change, and you will find more solid footing. Your ability to take greater strides will increase. All of a sudden, you will pick up some speed; the final leg of your journey will not feel impossible to finish, but simply a matter of days or weeks. Your mood will have lightened up.

Regarding what has happened in your programme until now and what will happen after you submit your text, your final academic project is merely another project. Certainly, it's a great project, with ample potential and quite heavy in terms of credits, too, but it's really not the be-all and end-all of your academic or professional career. It is one milestone. It is highly unlikely that it is this milestone that everything depends upon. It's a marker that you pass by, an experience that you take in to the best of your abilities, but that's it. Just as with every other challenging experience, your thesis will feel anticlimactically unimportant and unchallenging as soon as you submit it. Just like the final exams of your school time or most challenges ahead of you, similarly to when climbing hills, the next peak always look more insurmountable when you scale it, but laughably insignificant from higher up. Especially when trying to adjust your emotional responses to free yourself from writer's block, it might be useful to keep in mind that this will appear insignificant in a couple of months. The question today is: what to do to get from here to there. Maybe just to start dialling down the impression of an excruciating load—it can help.

You are writing a research report. One text of many you've written before and one of many you will write hereafter. For getting unstuck: this is not as important as it sometimes seems.

Experienced peers' two cents

'As far as approaching the paper more generally, I've benefited from not starting with the introduction, but rather starting with writing out whatever arguments you're going to make—your storyline. For me, it has always been helpful to just start writing. Writing is so hard, you have all these ideas, especially if you have a decent idea of what you're going to write. Are you reading a lot of literature instead of trying to create a perfect outline of everything you're going to do? It can be helpful to just start writing about the topic, just getting your ideas on the page because often-times you don't know what arguments are going to work.' (Matt Farmer)

'I think it is helpful to divide the work into chunks, especially PhD thesis work. Concretely, structuring the thesis as individual papers, where each is a journey in its own right. This is helpful. With BA/MA thesis work, you don't have that luxury. However, a MA thesis should be structured as a paper. As a supervisor, you can provide that structure.' (Ansgar Richter)

Mitigating mental overload

Your project is most likely too large to keep in your mind at any one time. Focus your mind on the individual problems and challenges to be solved.

Metaphorically speaking

Just like a very long journey, your project will be too complex to try to keep every turn, every place, every path in your mind at the same time. You will be aware of certain impressions, of critical decisions, but there will also be long passages of literature or data analysis that you cannot keep in mind. You will encounter seemingly brand-new ideas that you will, discouragingly, rediscover in your old notebooks and find you simply forgot them.

Consequently, try not to require yourself to become fully aware of your entire project before you can work on it. Sure, get a sense of the whole journey to retain a sense of orientation, but then train and use your ability to more and more quickly focus on individual packages—theory, data acquisition, analysis, discussion, etc.—of your work. Learning to switch from scene to scene, zooming out to your project overview to see the relations among all components, and zooming in to fine-tune decisions is one of those hidden mental capabilities trained by the thesis.

Research, to a degree, also means training the agility of your mind to 'pan and zoom' in, out, and around your project. At no time will you be able to have your entire project in your mind in full detail, but your mind will adapt to zoom into individual passages quickly, switch between them, provide detail and overview—just not everything at once.

Rough coordinates

Cognition—'The action or faculty of knowing taken in its widest sense, including sensation, perception, conception, etc., as distinguished from

The Student's Research Companion. Omid Aschari and Benjamin Berghaus, Oxford University Press.
© Omid Aschari and Benjamin Berghaus (2023). DOI: 10.1093/oso/9780192855312.003.0039

feeling and volition; also, more specifically, the action of cognizing an object in perception proper.'

Process—'A continuous and regular action or succession of actions occurring or performed in a definite manner, and having a particular result or outcome; a sustained operation or series of operations.'

Granularity—'Consisting of grains or granules (a small grain; a small compact particle; a pellet); existing in the condition of grains or granules.'

Focus—'The location at which an object must be situated such that a given lens or combination of lenses will produce a sharply defined image of it. The sustained or intense concentration of interest and attention on a particular thing; an instance of this. Also: the ability to sustain such concentration.'

Train of thought

Your final academic project focuses on a central question and maybe a few sub-questions. There is reasoning for these questions, a foundational argument of relevance that rightfully motivates you to ask and to try to answer them. Your answers rest on many dozen, if not hundreds of other research projects and their findings. Your own project likely generates and builds insights from large amounts of data—be it quantitative or qualitative—based on a more or less rigorous methodology of acquisition and analysis, which in turn builds upon several other projects' findings and recommendations. Then there are your thoughts discussing your findings and putting everything into perspective, and your considerations on who should care and why, and what your project could not possibly also include. In other words: your final academic project produces the proverbial metric tonne of mental material, and all you have to juggle it is your magnificent but wheelbarrow-sized brain. No wonder that overloading your mental limits is a real problem when working through your final academic project.

Most final academic projects will present you with the opportunity to substantially overload your mind if you try to call up every aspect and instance to think it through from A to Z at any one time. Even if you do not try to bring up the big picture, you will find yourself commonly forgetting about great ideas that you had a few days, weeks, or months ago. It is not uncommon to leaf through old notebooks and find perfectly interesting ideas that you either thought you had just come up with recently or that you never thought you had. The immediate experience and evidence of becoming forgetful due to the high load on your mind can be unsettling.

The best way of avoiding the common circumstance of mental overload—and, quite possibly, the only way to complete a final academic project—is not only to focus but also to develop sufficient mental agility to quickly pan and zoom through your project's current mind map.

While focusing on one particular aspect and substructure of your project seems so utterly banal and basic that it might not even warrant a discussion, actually mastering focused work on an individual but interconnected component of your project while not severing this component from its logical neighbours is a difficult task. It does not come easy to most people to avoid getting side-tracked by other tasks within the project or the document. It is difficult to avoid getting carried away with one component and neglecting the others, leading to an imbalance among the individual elements. Focusing on elements of a larger, complex project successfully requires the second ability foreshadowed above:

Developing mental agility to quickly pan (shift your focus) and zoom (change the level of detail) through your project might be the ultimate skill to avoid mentally overloading yourself when working through your project. Much of this entails becoming more and more at home and immersed in your research project, but there is also a cognitive capability linked to this skill. Quickly calling up the complex setting of your theory discussion to make a link to an equally complex discussion of why you designed your data acquisition process as you did requires that you feel at home in the individual mental spaces of your thesis, but also that you accept that you have to move from one mental space to another in order not to overlay, obfuscate, and effectively confound your focus.

While working on a text produces something tangible and working on a project consists of many individual components and tasks, there is a much more abstract and too rarely discussed aspect of conducting research: the way we think about our projects, the way we mentally handle complex systems from the largest structures to the smallest ideas, procedural implementation, self-evaluation, and improvement. Even though our academic projects unfold most comprehensively in our minds, this is the state we least consider for closer examination or training.

In essence

- Your thesis will be too complex for you to keep in your mind as if it were one indivisible unit.
- To think more productively about your thesis, try to modularize and compartmentalize your thinking about it.

- Consciously train your ability to either focus, pan, or zoom through your thoughts about your project in order not to succumb to its complexity.

To reflect

- Can you clearly make out the components of your thesis project, as well as the connections that integrate these components?
- Are you apt at focusing your attention on one component without too commonly sidestepping to another field of attention?
- Do you feel comfortable navigating your project's components and changing the detail level from the overarching structures to minute details?

Two travellers' tales

Zayd is a smart guy. Impressively smart, indeed. He has breezed through most of his exams with exceptional grades. His colleagues like to call him Ze Brain. Now, stuck in the middle of his thesis, however, he does not feel too smart: for several weeks now, he has found it difficult to move even an inch forward. Working on his project went well—but writing it all down, making sense of it all, is overwhelming him. He is trying to keep everything in mind at once. Zayd feels that he can only write one comprehensive and cohesive account of his project if he can keep every aspect of it in his mind at the same time. Only if he can think it can he write it, he believes. Clearly, that does not seem to work particularly well.

Marie is a smart woman. Impressively smart, indeed. Marie tends not to simply 'do' tasks. She analyses them, develops solution strategies, and then usually comes out the other end more relaxed, and sometimes even more successful than others. Never sidestepping the challenge, merely accepting the task on her terms and using her techniques. One of those techniques is to try to avoid getting overloaded by any number of challenges at the same time. Marie has developed a rather sensible impression of the load on her mind—and if that load increases too far, she stops and reconsiders her approach. When writing her thesis, it became immediately obvious to her that the task itself would overload her if kept in mind all at once. So, she broke down her writing, as she broke down her project, into smaller chunks that she could then focus on and work through. This also made shifting attention from one chunk to another easier. There was always something to do—until she was done.

Devil's advocate

With time, your ability to mentally switch between the components of your project, to regain an overview, to see the relationships among the components, and to drill down into the details, will grow, and will at some point feel indistinguishable from keeping your whole project in mind.

How to tackle

If you find yourself unable to produce text but in need of doing so, decrease the load of obligation you experience by structuring the material you have to write until you have a fairly clear understanding of which idea goes where. Capture your ideas, sort them, put them into a systematic structure, and try to write your text, not 'top down', as a whole or chapter by chapter, but rather 'bottom up', paragraph by paragraph. You can write six- to ten-line paragraphs, possibly a hundred words. Write a good, clear paragraph and outline the next five or six paragraphs to complete the section, rather than writing six or seven paragraphs when you are not entirely sure what to write about. You will have a difficult time revising this text, and might end up needing to discard and rewrite it entirely. If you are on a tight schedule, aim instead to produce something you can revise instead of something you are certain to have to rewrite. Take a look at illustration 9 to get a sense of the difference between one sample document, six chapters, 60 pages, and 300 paragraphs—the entire work does not look so menacing if you divide it up and continue work on one of the small paragraph steps.

Experienced peers' two cents

'I really like the tactic of reverse-outlining: getting your ideas out first and then see which of these work, which don't, and then make an outline from there. Once you've written out some core arguments or ideas that you want to make, not even in any order necessarily.

'I think this has just always been difficult for me. And I've noticed that other people can find it difficult to do an outline without having written anything. You just don't necessarily know what a good logical order for the ideas would be. You don't always know from the start which points you want to make.

'For example, when you're writing a literature review, you don't need to cite every single study or paper that's ever been done on the topic. You just

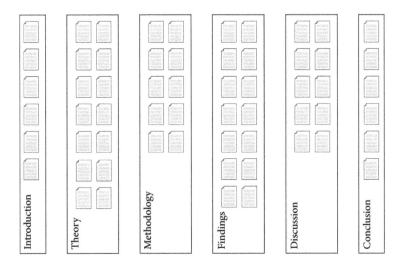

Illustration 9: Writing your thesis can seem impossible, but writing a paragraph is not.

need to cite the ones that are most relevant to what you're writing about. And that can be difficult to know until you've written some reviews out and see.' (Matt Farmer)

'It is very difficult—even for us more established and experienced writers—when we need to write something new. We know it will be difficult. We don't know where to start. If we just have a kind of example or a structure we can go through, we can understand and learn from that how to develop such a document, ourselves. Therefore, we can help our students to follow that process and try to adopt key characteristics of the writing.

'I still remember, while I was doing my Master's thesis at the University of Sydney, I handed in my draft, and my supervisor said: "This kind of methodology isn't good enough, and the project is not going well—I was expecting more from you! Please read my paper." So, he sent me a paper that was somewhat related to my research. When I went through his methodology section, I realized how much detail I needed to include in mine. I realized that I had missed out a lot of information—e.g. details about participants, details about instruments that I was using, information about how I constructed instruments—so many things. Then I realized the value of good guidelines. That's how examples can reveal their value.' (Madhu Neupane Bastola)

Write like a journey

Determine a healthy work rhythm and go at your own pace. Be mindful of individual impressions and pay attention to detail. Enjoy the journey.

Metaphorically speaking

Just like a good hike, research means taking one step after another many times over. There are several ways of trying to ignore this basic insight, but the fact of the matter is that the journey is in every step—not just the lovely spots, the impressive lookouts, or the destination.

Consequently, do not make your project harder than it has to be by lumping together parts of the challenge that will invariably become too big to work on. Two key ideas are of importance. First, break down your tasks into smaller bits and pieces; second, work on your individual, smaller bits and pieces to advance through your project. If you feel like you are discussing and discussing and planning and planning, but you do not seem to make any progress, you are doing it exactly the other way around. Planning does not make you progress—progress happens when you implement the plan. During implementation, you need to take one step after another.

Research, to a degree, also means telling planning apart from implementation. Only planning instead depends on your ability to achieve an overview of your project and the interconnections among its components. But implementation requires watching your two feet taking many, many small steps. Telling apart the two modes of thinking of and working on your project provides you with a much better sense of why you are progressing or why you are not.

Rough coordinates

Structure—'The arrangement and organization of mutually connected and dependent elements in a system or construct. The quality or fact of being

The Student's Research Companion. Omid Aschari and Benjamin Berghaus, Oxford University Press.
© Omid Aschari and Benjamin Berghaus (2023). DOI: 10.1093/oso/9780192855312.003.0040

organized in a particular manner; definite or purposeful arrangement of parts within a whole.'

Component—'A constituent element or part. Each of the constituents of a system which are not necessarily identified individually but are defined as equal in number to the minimum number of species required to define the composition of the system.'

Detail—'The dealing with matters item by item; detailed treatment; attention to particulars. Esp. in phrase in (the) detail, item by item; part by part; minutely; circumstantially. So to go into detail, i.e. to deal with or treat a thing in its individual particulars.'

Paragraph—'A distinct passage or section of a text, usually composed of several sentences, dealing with a particular point, a short episode in a narrative, a single piece of direct speech, etc.'

Train of thought

Especially when starting to write, the critical source of doubt and avoidance is that you are facing the stack of blank pages that will need to be filled. Writing a thesis also means writing a little book on a subject—to many, a displeasing idea. There is, however, a neat technique that allows you to conquer even the largest stack of papers: consciously outlining and structuring your path before you try to walk on it.

Among the most clichéd notions related to travelling is the saying that any journey is a series of countless steps. While completing a whole journey feels overwhelming to many, it is easy to take individual steps. Even though this idea is not wrong, to many, it is not helpful—there is seemingly little connection between the small scope of the steps and the seemingly gigantic distance covered by the journey. However, what immediately feels more useful is to consider any journey as a series of passages that follow one another: take the bus to the train, take the train to the airport, take the plane to the other city, take the subway, and so on. While the journey from one continent to another seems almost insurmountable when thought of in one continuous mode of travel, it becomes perfectly easy to implement when broken into its constituent pieces.

For writing, your journey may be represented by the 60 pages of your thesis or 200 pages of your dissertation—thoroughly impossible when you try, in one go, to think through each of the (say) 30,000 or even 100,000 words. You will not be able to concentrate enough or muster up enough mental capabilities to formulate a thought that long and then write it down in one go.

Writers have chapters, subchapters, sections, and paragraphs with which to structure their products. When breaking down your project into chapters, you will end up with five to eight smaller chunks. Still, they are too big to think and write out in one go. So, you plan out your subchapters. After this phase of structuring, you may find yourself with subchapters that are a couple of pages long. Those few pages are the segments of your journey. They have dimensions that allow you to think through each as an integrated argument made up of multiple statements. Consequently, you can plan out your argument based on these statements, and assign paragraphs to each statement. Depending on your personal style, the subject you describe, and the chapter you are working on, you will have between two (say, for convoluted theory fields that would suggest presenting one field in one paragraph) and five paragraphs (say, for a quick succession of specific and focused supports of a statement) on one page.

Following this idea of structuring your entire document before you write requires you to lay out a first draft of your general thought process before you start writing. To a certain degree, this disentangles the creative process of thinking through your ideas from the more mechanical process of writing it all down. While writing can help your thinking, and thinking certainly helps when writing, each task require a different trajectory for your attention: one is directed at creating solid reasoning, and the other is directed at communicating this reasoning. Furthermore, the result of your initial thought process can be messy. Writing a mess is as painful as it sounds. It does not get you closer to your goal, but further away. Finally, consider your thesis less of a document and more of a written argument. Constructing the argument before writing is helpful to focus your resources on the dominant thought process first, only later focusing on how to make that thought process as transparent as possible.

Breaking down your challenge into many smaller, more manageable pieces, is not only one of the most powerful tools to combat writer's block—it is also a meaningful support to help you think your way through your project once it has become so large that you can no longer keep it all in your mind.

In essence

- If you find yourself having problems writing your thesis in one sequential attempt, consider drafting a preliminary structure of your text.

- Carry this pre-structure through, from chapters across subchapters to sections and paragraphs, to the level of detail and determination that appears appropriate to your state of mind.
- Once you have this, notice the opportunity to quickly pan and zoom across your project to focus on those challenges that suit what you feel like accomplishing today.

To reflect

- What is a useful breakdown of the overall text you are trying to write?
- What are you already certain about, and which parts of your pre-structure still seem more of a draft today?
- Today, would you rather write a few paragraphs or work on something larger?

Two travellers' tales

Nadja is close to completing her thesis project and now mostly has writing left to do. Since she does not particularly like writing, she put it off to more or less the last moment. Now, she finds it incredibly difficult to get going. 'If I just get going and then don't stop, I can bang out the text in a few weeks. I know what I need to write, anyhow. Just long days of intense writing,' she thinks. Having this mountain of work she does not truly appreciate in front of her does not help.

Andrew is close to completing her thesis project and now mostly has writing left to do. He knows himself: trying to tackle the entire writing project head-on will likely not work. He would simply get tangled in the complexity and size of the task. Rather, he splits up his text into chapters, those into subchapters, sections, and, eventually, paragraphs. He is certain of the chapters' contents, has a sense about the subchapters, but gets a feeling that he can only decide which contents will be covered in which sections, but not fully flesh out the material just yet. As for the paragraphs, he just needs them to get a sense of how many building blocks he feels are appropriate for each section. Dimensions and balance matters, he thinks. Each day, he tries to complete one section of somewhere between five and ten paragraphs. A thoroughly doable daily task. Every so often he manages more, sometimes less, but he writes at least a few paragraphs each day. This way, he feels as though he gets into a good rhythm and makes progress.

Devil's advocate

Even though progression largely depends on your focused working on individual components of your project, it does help to have a sense of the degree of advancement in your mind. Even if just to throttle the energy you invest and control for you being able to reach your goal with the time and energy you have at your disposal. Conversely, planning requires an understanding of the details involved in the steps to be planned.

How to tackle

Your text of 60 pages may break down to 6 chapters, 30 subchapters, 50 sections, and 210 paragraphs. Depending on how you want to think about your text, you can motivate yourself by merely writing a paragraph of which you already know the trajectory. Or you might choose to work on an interesting topic in a wonderfully focused little section of about half a dozen paragraphs. Or you might use the broader brush to bring together multiple topics to form a meaningful component of your project as a subchapter. Maybe it's time to finalize one of the building-like chapters that you finally know how to finish. Or you just want to get an idea of how far your project is and check how many pages remain left to be filled. Now, you have a structure and, with that, the ability to use your text to pan and zoom at will at what catches your interest on that particular day.

Experienced peers' two cents

'One of the best pieces of advice that I've ever got when it comes to writer's block is to sit down with the sole intention to write a single paragraph. That is my current goal.

'If I sit down, and then I write the paragraph and I feel like writing more, that is bonus writing that you are getting. But if you sit down, and you write that paragraph, and you decide that you don't want to, you can walk away. And nine times out of 10, when I sit down and write the first paragraph, I would rather not stop. It doesn't even have to be the first paragraph.' (Matt Farmer)

Be kind to yourself

While being critical with your project is useful, getting cross with your-self is not. You are asking a lot from yourself. Be just as merciful.

Metaphorically speaking

Just like an extensive excursion, your research project will from time to time put you on edge. However, pressing on with a grudge may easily cloud your decision-making capabilities. You'll be looking for those shortcuts, elect not to visit the areas that sound particularly promising—you just want the journey to be over with. Particularly in tricky terrain, taking the shortcut might not only be a pity, but could leave important and particularly valuable bits of your journey untouched.

Consequently, before you commit to any rash decisions, wind down, calm your mind, be kind to yourself, and only then take substantial decisions. You are on a long-haul trip—try to be merciful to yourself. If you think about it (and if it helps you to think about the situation this way), the project does not matter that much. Realistically, hardly any people are going to take note of your project. And if it does not matter that much, why not just try to enjoy it somehow? You will only be able to make your project matter to others if you yourself can at least partially enjoy it.

Research, to a degree, also means finding a good balance between ambition and relaxation. This balance can be hard to find, and it's likely more useful to think of this balance as oscillating rather than static. At times, you will push harder, at other times you will need more slack.

Rough coordinates

Mercy—'Clemency and compassion shown to a person who is in a position of powerlessness or subjection, or to a person with no right or claim to receive kindness; kind and compassionate treatment in a case where severity is merited or expected.'

The Student's Research Companion. Omid Aschari and Benjamin Berghaus, Oxford University Press.
© Omid Aschari and Benjamin Berghaus (2023). DOI: 10.1093/oso/9780192855312.003.0041

Critical—'Given to judging; esp. given to adverse or unfavourable criticism; fault-finding, censorious.'

Dissatisfaction—'Act of feeling deprived of satisfaction; displeased; disquieted by the feeling of the insufficiency or inadequacy of something.'

Encouragement—To inspire with courage sufficient for any undertaking; to embolden, make confident. To stimulate (persons or personal efforts) by assistance, reward, or expressions of favour or approval; to countenance, patronize; also, in bad sense, to abet. To allow or promote the continuance or development of (a natural growth, an industry, a sentiment, etc.); to cherish, foster.

Train of thought

A common sensation among students—particularly PhD students—is the fleeting individual notion, 'Maybe I am simply not smart enough?'. People find themselves surrounded with other bright people who appear to be advancing more quickly, reading faster, writing better, learning with less effort. The environment in which you are graduating is the most challenging you have ever experienced. This bears both some truth and some illusion.

Say you set out on a competitive expedition. You know of other expeditions, but you can only check their Instagram posts of their recent discoveries. Certainly, everyone's beach will look more beautiful, everyone's mountain looks taller, everyone's sky looks more blue. It's not entirely impossible to get a bit discouraged by this.

A little discouragement is not the end of the world. In the end, there is some truth to it: you are undertaking likely the most challenging academic project you ever attempted. Your peers are good. But they also predominantly share what works and don't necessarily share what does not. Consequently, a bunch of smart people appear brilliant due to selective reporting. The closer you are to your peers, the more you will learn about their problems, shortcomings, and challenges. After some wasted time fearing that everyone else is quicker, faster, smarter, you will realize that the only concern really is that you lost a couple of days by obsessing with investigating your supposed sense of competition. You don't have any.

However, there is also an inward-facing and maybe more challenging outcome of the notion that you are way behind: dissatisfaction with your own advancement often gives rise to self-directed measures of discipline. Some people respond well to self-chastisement and become productive—others lock up altogether and get stuck over longer periods of time. If you know yourself to respond well to self-discipline, go right ahead. But if you don't, the solution to your locking-up will simply be to take a few steps back and get some perspective.

Especially if you are usually a rather diligent person, you will likely have involved yourself far too much in your project and have lost a well-balanced sense of working performance and quality of life. This is especially true if you feel that you are being stuck or perceived as lacking in performance drags down your motivation, mood, or even energy for other activities over weeks. Take a step back, find a bench in the park, cool down, and realize that whatever the project, it's really not worth losing your mind over it. Take a few days or even weeks off from your project and return to it with regenerated energy. If you feel like you're a severe case, walk away from the project. You will return by yourself if it's worth it. If not—it might not be worth it.

In essence

- It's not unlikely that you will experience instances during work on your project in which your optimism and hope for a good outcome will fade, and your central experience will be that of discouragement—be it for a certain reason or because you are just exhausted.
- If you already feel slightly tattered, you might feel like looking left and right at your colleagues and see how they are doing. But comparison often leads to feeling worse, not better. A combination of your own discouragement and a lack of complete information on your peers' existing state of affairs is to blame.
- So, you feel down and everyone else seems ahead. The final stick for your back is that you are simply not that sure any more about what you can and cannot accomplish. If you experience any or all of these three symptoms, it is time to take a few days off and be merciful with yourself. At the very least, your thesis will otherwise be a pain to complete—and it does not have to be. Find your balance and return when you have found it.

To reflect

- Do you experience discouragement, penalizing comparison behaviour, and nagging uncertainty?
- What does it take for you to realize that these are emotional and not rational responses?

- Can we persuade you to step back from your thesis for a few days, calm your nerves, and return when you feel more balanced?

Two travellers' tales

Ben is a resourceful person. He's a diligent worker, and his ample resources of energy have been the source of some pride in the past. During his thesis, however, he feels that even his resources appear limited, all of a sudden. Since he is used to powering through, whatever the current challenge may be, he tries to push on, only to find himself in a deeper and deeper ditch from which it seems difficult to get himself unstuck. After only a few weeks of time out from the thesis, he regains his energy and finally finds his path to submitting his material.

Ophelia is a resourceful person. She's diligent, but has also seen her share of exhaustion due to excessive workloads. She has decided to see her diligence and her sense of self-protection as a pair of capabilities that require each other for her to move forward. When she feels rested and relaxed, she works diligently. When she feels exhaustion setting in and relaxation fading, she makes sure she takes generous breaks—enough not only to halt the exhaustion, but also to replenish the energy, she has expended. It does not make sense merely to retain a level of exhaustion—exhaustion has to give way before further productivity can set in. That conviction is what carried her through to submitting her thesis with no meaningful breakdowns.

Devil's advocate

On one hand, there is acting consciously to protect your productivity and energy levels; and then there is detaching and distancing yourself too far from the motivations to complete your thesis. Especially when you feel a high workload threatening to exhaust you, take a few (maybe many) steps back. But if you are already in a state of relaxation, don't leave your project so far behind so that you may never come back and finish it. Try to find your boundary between 'far enough away to recharge' and 'too far away to return'.

How to tackle

Being kind to yourself in exchange for being demanding takes many forms. You will know best how to treat yourself. What is often overlooked, however, is that being a friend to yourself goes further than merely granting yourself a treat every once in a while if you feel that you performed up to your own expectations.

Try not to consider your working self merely as owing you results and advancement. Sometimes things work out well, and you make advances, sometimes not. Try not to consider your recreational self merely as owing you relaxation and replenished energy. Occasionally you can take full advantage of taking a few days off and return energized, sometimes you can't.

Especially if you pursue demanding plans—conduct a challenging research project, try to relax on a long weekend while your head keeps spinning work-related ideas—you will only succeed part of the time. You will fail the other part of the time.

You will certainly have heard about productive and detrimental cultures of failure. Establishing a productive culture of failure is not only something that organizations and teams benefit from; it is a crucial and complex self-regulatory skill you can and should learn to apply for yourself, especially if you tend to attempt demanding projects.

The more demanding your projects become, the greater the likeliness that you might not succeed completely, thoroughly, or at all. You are conducting experiments which sometimes carry a high risk of failure. Do not subject yourself to high-risk environments without the necessary mental, emotional, and procedural padding.

Explore what a productive culture of failure might mean to you. Now is the time to explore this; after university, the challenges you will face will become less and less certain to be designed to be achievable.

Experienced peers' two cents

'I was talking about my research to a supervisee and it made me remember the time while I was writing my own thesis. If we as supervisors go back and remember how difficult it was for us, we can be sympathetic to the students. We need to see thesis writing from the students' perspective, not from our perspective.' (Madhu Neupane Bastola)

'It is good to take distance for a while, days, or weeks or months, I don't know. If I let it be for a while, it gets significantly better. When you are finally through finishing your study, taking all the bureaucratic steps, and everything is off your desk, it's a bit of relief for many of us. Especially for a paper. I have sometimes returned to my own work and thought—Who wrote this? This is really good! That happens almost universally.

'I've had some experiences that every other day, it looks great, and every other day I am ready to throw it into the rubbish can. When we get so involved with our own work, it becomes difficult to look at it objectively. That gets better with time. I've seen this happen to my students, too. When they go back to the earlier work, it starts to look much better.' (Timo Korkeamäki)

'There are roadblocks on the way. Students may have trouble finding the right data. There are setbacks. At a later stage, there may be trouble with submission deadlines. Students need to realize that this is a natural part of the process and the experience, e.g. data finding should create despair. Data will always have its own limitations, this is natural. The supervisor should give some reassurance and help the student to reflect on that. It's important to start early with the process, e.g. defining a good research question by going through a process of iteration, testing the question, modifying it. One has to make sure it doesn't lead to frustration, given that MA programs, for instance, are typically rather short and compressed in terms of actual time to work on a thesis.' (Ansgar Richter)

'A person undertaking research needs to cradle themselves in things that make them feel good. They need to be able to step away and recognize that leaving their project for a couple of days actually does make the world a better place. I think it takes quite a while for that to sink in. I think I'm still learning to do that.

'Research can be an isolating journey, especially to novice researchers. It takes a helpful social context, a friendly environment that nudges student researchers to recognize that taking breaks is indispensable. That this text might take three hours to write at night and will take 30 minutes to write after a good night's sleep on the next morning. The institutions at which we learn and teach should take a more proactive role in fostering these environments that instruct students to be mindful and smart about how they invest their energy and solve challenges. Otherwise, research can turn out to be just not very healthy. Students should not be facing the possibly most challenging project of their academic careers and face down every individual problem, challenge, and nuisance in perfect isolation. That's not what we have educational institutions for.' (Kim Beasy)

Necessity of ownership

Your thesis is part of your study experience. It results in your grade. Your name will be on the cover. It requires your ownership, your decisions.

Metaphorically speaking

Your journey is your journey. Not your tour guide's journey, your friends' journey, or the journey of the person who wrote the travel guide. You will likely fare better if you take full ownership of your trip, arriving at the key decisions and walking the talk. In the end, you want to look back on your voyage and get a distinct sense of this being something that you achieved, and not that you were merely a passenger along for the ride.

Consequently, we encourage you to take ownership of your project in the most complete sense of the term possible. Sure—in some instances, your project might be part of a larger research project which then defines part of what you do, but still: there ought to be left enough space for you to define, design, and fill with life. Your final academic project is part of your academic programme, and as such holds the potential to provide a great learning opportunity in independently engaging a problem. If your final academic project seems to be set up too differently from this general idea, try to win back some autonomy.

Research, to a degree, also means independence. This independence shows itself in the (at least relative) freedom to pick your topic, in your approach to help shed light onto what is not yet known, and in all the little design choices that shape your work ahead. The 'relative' nature of your freedom to pick and design your project points to the necessity of integrating within your context—your field's state of the art and also, possibly, your supervisor's project landscape if you are working on a project that he or she suggested to you. Still: try to capture a large bit of autonomy within your project so that you can rightfully claim that this was truly your final academic project.

The Student's Research Companion. Omid Aschari and Benjamin Berghaus, Oxford University Press.
© Omid Aschari and Benjamin Berghaus (2023). DOI: 10.1093/oso/9780192855312.003.0042

Rough coordinates

Ownership—'The fact or state of being or feeling responsible for solving a problem, addressing an issue, etc.'

Decision—'The action, fact, or process of arriving at a conclusion regarding a matter under consideration; the action or fact of making up one's mind as to an opinion, course of action. The result of this action or process; that which has been decided; a conclusion, a judgement, a resolution; a choice.'

Responsibility—'Capability of fulfilling an obligation or duty; the quality of being reliable or trustworthy. The state or fact of being accountable; liability, accountability for something. The state or fact of being the cause or originator of something; the credit or blame for something.'

Reins—'A means of guiding, controlling, or governing; a curb, check, or restraint of any kind. Control; the capacity to direct or govern.'

Train of thought

One of the continuous themes throughout this book is that when we talk about 'your final academic project', we consider the first word in this term among the most important: it will be your—and no one else's—project. You need to build motivation, you need to follow your interest, you must carry it out, steer it yourself, and make the decisions. Especially now, close to completing your thesis, it becomes essential again to remember that you get to call the shots on your thesis. While supervisors, experts, lecturers, colleagues, and friends may voice their opinions, you are the one who is setting their signature under the text.

When you are embarking on a journey to a country that you have not been to before, you will likely encounter many experts who will tell you what to do and how to do it. Many will truly know a thing or two about your destination, and many will share their opinion to your advantage. But then again, you will need to make the decision yourself, which path to take and which sights to see. Everything will need to fit your journey, from your perspective. Nothing has to suit anyone else. The goal is to make your own ambitions for your journey as rigorous as you see appropriate—no one else's.

By now, you will have subscribed to the idea of your final academic project being a canvas that holds ample opportunity for you to design, compose, and combine. In essence, this creative process is both your opportunity and your obligation, both your experience and your examination. While some voices appear more eminent in terms of steering your behaviour—your supervisor or your examiners—they can merely voice recommendations. You are in a position to accept or reject those recommendations. Since you are the only person who is as deeply involved with your particular project, don't expect anyone else to be able to make a recommendation that ought to be blindly implemented. Be aware, however, that fully taking on the reins of your own project reinforces the requirements your project imposes on you: you will need to be able to argue and support your choices—not to defend, but to explain your decisions. Certainly, you can play it safer and easier by instead clinging to your supervisor's every recommendation and asking for orientation at every intersection—but then you are rather working on her project than on your own. Keep in mind that supervisory cooperation is not a zero-sum game. Balancing ownership of your project with integrating and interfacing with your supervisor's interests and suggestions means not to feverishly look for the extremes, but to seek a consolidation of interests. If you are interested in collaboration, you will also likely be interested to find this balance. You might consider your performance in doing so part of your project and part of your learning opportunity.

Completing your thesis, to a degree, also means accepting responsibility for your own choices. For that to work out, you will need to have made some choices—regardless of recommendations. This does not imply that you should ignore guidance; rather, you should never take it without reflection and unquestioned. If you feel that you agree with most of the guidance you receive, it might be time to take the next few decisions on your own and minimize your resistance to those critical points that will make or break your project and that you really cannot decide on your own. The final academic project is a great opportunity to try to walk on your own two feet. The potential implications of your not succeeding are not so critical or irreversible that you cannot make course corrections or recover from them. On the other hand, you will likely want to steer a project that you can rightly call your own.

In essence

- For better or for worse, your final academic project is *your* final academic project.
- While there will be many people around you with an opinion on what to do and how to do it, you will be the one making the decisions.

- Taking ownership of your project will be an important basis for motivation throughout the process. While shying away from the responsibility sometimes feels more comfortable, you will find that most benefit occurs when you lean into your project and consciously take the reins.

To reflect

- Do you agree that your thesis will require your personal ownership of the project? What does that mean to you?
- Do you feel fully in charge of your project? What encourages and enables you to do so? What hinders you? Can you tone down what hinders you taking full charge of your project?
- Whose support do you want to invite to your project? How much of that support? Which support is available and which support is not?

Two travellers' tales

Paula likes to reach her goals. Checking off particularly juicy items, often long-term projects, on her to-do list is a particularly satisfying thing to do for her. However, for goals to be reached, they need to be well-defined. In terms of her thesis, Paula has accepted that the person who is defining where the finish line is will be her supervisor. Thus, Paula wrestled a goal definition from her supervisor that is second to none: he patiently answered each and every question that Paula asked about so that she developed a crystal clear understanding of what it was that he wanted to see in her thesis project. This made the project much easier for her—but it also changed the nature of the project to a certain degree. No doubt that she handed in a thesis manuscript that resembled exactly what her supervisor expected from her. But was it truly *her* thesis?

Chad likes to reach his goals. He is a pretty uniquely and independently thinking person. He tends to make sure that the goals he follows are actually his goals and not anyone else's. In his thesis, Chad outlined and defined the character and the outcome of his thesis according to his own understanding of an optimal design. He is aware that outlining your own path and defining your own goals can be more risky than following the instructed path and goals of a supervisor, so he tries to be as attentive and accommodating as possible to the perspectives of his supervisor. During his work on his project, he comes across the opportunity to collaborate on gathering data with a professional association active in his field. He benefits from the access of that association, but also learns that he has to trade off some freedoms when phrasing the survey. Since Chad knows where he wants to go with his project, it was easier to judge how much influence he could trade off according to his partner's preferences in exchange for access. Having this clear understanding of being responsible for his project also helped him carefully consider and choose the proposals and suggestions by his supervisor. Chad always knew that without a clear understanding of what his goal was, he would have a hard time reaching it. During his project, he picked up first-hand experience on the importance of navigating and integrating external opportunities into his project. These opportunities often come at the expense of some freedom. Knowing what he wanted to achieve in his project made navigating these trade-offs much easier. In the end, he reached his goal because he managed to purposefully and fairly integrate contributions and opportunities through collaboration. In a way, his project already started benefiting parts of his audience while he was working on it.

Devil's advocate

Taking ownership of your project does not mean that you positively have to shut everyone out of your project. It does mean that you should be able to decide how collaboratively and integrated you want to work. There is a specific case to be made for collaborating with supervisors engaged in your field and open to collaboration—in that case, it might even be very useful to closely and openly integrate your project with other projects as far as regulations at your university allow. Especially if you have a supervisor who follows a more engaged supervision style, don't reject collaboration and co-creation (to a sensible degree) just based on principle. Make a careful decision—but this decision should be yours.

How to tackle

This chapter is not (only) intended to underscore your responsibility for your project—something that might be perfectly clear by now—but rather to encourage and empower you to finalize your project as you see fit.

We'd never recommend you to go against the recommendations of any expert or even your supervisor or one of their representatives. But we want to strengthen your conviction in following those conclusions you draw from your data, your insight, your reflections on the matter. You are the researcher behind your project. It is for no one else to shift, shape, or change your conclusions if, even after careful and close consideration, you do not see the logic or value in their suggestions. Of course, you will benefit greatly from most recommendations along your path, but you cannot follow perspectives that you find it impossible to stand behind.

That said, be careful to pick your battles. Identify what's substance and what's coating. Be more resolute on patiently and courteously rejecting proposed changes to the substance of your work that you cannot get behind. Consider being less rigid on adopting proposals that rather deal with your project's coating: if your supervisor suggests no substantive changes but the adjustment of your project's title, that might be more readily acceptable than to rework entire sections.

Always try to remain open to and grateful for suggestions. They indicate that someone has most likely invested time and effort into considering your project, weighing the options, and making that suggestion. Avoid shooing off helpful and generous minds who try to provide you with options and choices. But be sure to always respectfully treat suggestions made on your project to be just that: options and choices. Grant these options and choices the attention they deserve, and then pick and chose the path you see most fitting to your project.

Experienced peers' two cents

'I encourage the supervisor to provide suggestions for topics, but not be too descriptive about them. It's not so helpful, if it becomes too descriptive and utilitarian. Rather, it is good to say that these are examples of topics. The student, then, can come up with his own ideas and suggestions and I help him to refine this. This is a more enriching experience. It may need more flexibility on the part of the supervisor, but it is less utilitarian and at the end of the day, the better approach for both.' (Ansgar Richter)

'I think we have to acknowledge that supervisors are often the only touch-point for somebody doing a thesis at that institution. That means that whatever that person is saying is magnified 10 times, and it just becomes so much more significant in the student's world. The power but also the importance of this person in the context is really significant. On the flip-side, supervisors are having to take on more and more research students. Mentoring half a dozen students is simply a gigantic workload. It's just a lot of reading and countless meetings and a lot of time that you have to spend on top of all the other commitments that you have. So, the traditional student–supervisor model seems broken. Universities are no longer navel-gazing institutions. And yet, we're still using the same models of research practice that we were using 50 years ago. Something needs to give. Providing that student with more mechanisms of support than what is currently available would be valuable. We know this from social work: the more social supports people have, the more likely they are to be resilient and get through any kind of mental health issues that they have. So, you know, there's a whole body of research that kind of supports this notion from another angle, which we really should be tapping into in a research space.' (Kim Beasy)

'In the context of thesis work, students, and supervisors are quite alike. Both are, in fact, students. It's important to break down the status difference. A supervisor is not a passive recipient. He should be a partial co-author. A poor result to some extent also falls back on the supervisor. To have a debate along the process together with the student and the co-supervisor is indispensable, e.g. for an MA supervisor. This is helpful and also part of the process. I like the thesis defences, when two supervisors discuss with each other and have a real conversation.' (Ansgar Richter)

Throwing off a weight

It may seem strange there could be any other sensation than relief after submitting. There are several of them. Take your time to adjust.

Metaphorically speaking

Any journey comes to an end. In part, reaching your destination after so much hardship is perfectly sweet. But it's probably also the end of an important passage to you. You can only explore any place once, and that one time has passed on this occasion. No wonder that you might feel slightly beside yourself and not just over the moon.

Take a bit of time off to adjust to your new status quo. Having completed a big project will likely leave you slightly hollowed out—tasks that filled your to-do list have disappeared, thoughts that occupied your mind might still be around, but they can no longer become productive. The opportunity to make adjustments has, for better or worse, come and gone. Ideally, you feel it was about time for the project to be finally submitted. Time to calm down for a bit.

Research, to a degree, also means completing and letting go of projects. These more intense and apparently more important multi-month or multi-year projects in particular may leave you with just as many mixed feelings as a long and challenging journey. Take your time to realize what you have accomplished.

Rough coordinates

Relief—'Alleviation of or deliverance from distress, anxiety, or some other emotional burden; the feeling accompanying this; mental relaxation, release, or reassurance. Also: an instance or cause of this; an occasion which provides such release.'

Doubt—'The (subjective) state of uncertainty with regard to the truth or reality of anything; undecidedness of belief or opinion. With plural: A feeling of

The Student's Research Companion. Omid Aschari and Benjamin Berghaus, Oxford University Press.
© Omid Aschari and Benjamin Berghaus (2023). DOI: 10.1093/oso/9780192855312.003.0043

uncertainty as to something. The condition of being (objectively) uncertain; a state of affairs such as to give occasion for hesitation or uncertainty.'

Worry—'A troubled state of mind arising from the frets and cares of life; harassing anxiety or solicitude.'

Emptiness—'Futility, pointlessness; lack of purpose or satisfaction; a feeling of sadness or depression that arises from this.'

Train of thought

Once you get close to handing in your thesis, you may have the most wonderful expectations about the time thereafter: relaxation, maybe a holiday, just finally doing something else. However, there is a peculiar experience that quite a few authors share after having worked on such a substantial product, and it's not always pure bliss.

Reaching the end of your journey can make you feel happy, satisfied, proud, and many more positive sensations. However, it can also fill you with a sense of sadness that the journey is over. Some experience it as a sense of hollowness—something that determined a large part of their thinking, their work, their hopes, and fears, is over. No matter how much you may have felt your thesis to be a tiring and exhausting experience, being done with it does not always release the sense of freedom and relief that we hope for. Instead, some might feel closer to having burned a lot of energy lately. Quite a few quickly catch a cold or some other mild sickness and need to recover for a bit. More reflective responses include worrying about whether 'everything is all right' with the thesis: Did I quote this correctly? Did I do enough? Surely, my efforts in this or that segment should have been more, better, or smarter! When handing in your thesis, you don't automatically hand in the stress as well.

The reality for most highly engaged authors is that they will have invested enormous amounts of energy and focus. This energy needs to regenerate over time. Regeneration does not always and automatically feel good. Partly because you don't immediately regain your old strength, but some of your strength is being redirected towards replenishing your resources before you can spend them again. It is quite common that after a particularly stressful passage, you are lacking energy both to attack and sometimes even to defend—that's where catching a cold comes in.

This is not to predict that you will positively experience a downturn of your energy and engagement after you hand in a particularly stressful project like your thesis—but it is quite common. Simply rest assured that it's not a bad sign to be thrown off for a couple of weeks or even months. Maybe don't plan the most challenging of vacations or even an immediate start to your job. You will likely not be on your A-game right after handing in. Take a bit of time to allow your engine to spin and cool down. You would not immediately go for a sprint right after a marathon, either.

In essence

- Even though you may expect the wonderful sense of relief after having handed in your thesis, you might instead encounter a strange void.
- If you chose to thoroughly immerse yourself in your project, you will probably miss your project to a certain degree—no matter how much it seemed to hold you hostage during the past months.
- Allow yourself to arrive at your new status, and take a bit of time off to adjust. Likely, you will want to recover some energy you could not replenish along the way.

To reflect

- You are done! How do you feel?
- How do you cope with handing in a project that has been on your mind 24/7 for several months?
- Can you find some weeks to unwind and process your advancement?

Two travellers' tales

Damian worked long and hard on his thesis. A few weeks back, the day of submission finally came. Now, in the long-awaited 'weeks after submission', he encounters the strangest experience: he does not finally feel thoroughly relaxed. At times, his mind is still racing, reconsidering the options he chose to design his project. Somehow, even though he has submitted the thesis, his mind is still occupied with it. He finds it hard to concentrate, and also to understand why relief at having completed the project does not finally set in. Instead, he turns to worrying and worrying about details in his experimental set-up and how this might affect his grades. Those were some strange months until he finally completed the defence with his supervisors, and where he learned that his thesis had impressed his two supervisors.

Quinn worked long and hard on her thesis. A few weeks back, the day to submit finally came. Since then, she's taken a few weeks of holiday to get her mind off the project and also celebrate a little. She feels slightly off—as if something that had occupied her for a long time has being removed. Not a uniformly positive feeling. Occasionally it feels more like getting up on a leg that had fallen asleep. But gradually, the senses return and the tingling subsides. She notices how many resources and capacities the project must have occupied over that long time. Well, there will be enough to celebrate once everything is done and over and her graduation swings by. She avoided getting into the worrying-spiral by simply being aware that the time after submission can feel strange. Her supervisors were pretty happy with her thesis, and congratulated her on successfully completing her programme.

Devil's advocate

While having handed in your thesis might leave you feeling a little empty, don't dwell on what you could have done differently or should have added. Try not to over- or under-evaluate your work just now. It is unlikely that you are in a position to arrive at a plausible evaluation, anyhow. Just try to appreciate the new status of having submitted your work. That is an achievement in and by itself—let that sink in.

How to tackle

The most effective way to tackle this unique experience is to know that whenever you unload a large obligation, the emotional response to the release can lead in many directions. Merely being aware of the impact that the project had on you can help you with processing your accomplishment and coming to grips with the new reality of having completed the project.

If you seem to enter a worry-spiral of second-guessing some of your design decisions, rest assured that there have not yet been any perfect final academic projects submitted. It is not about perfection. It is about subjecting yourself to challenge and growing your way out of it. Because you submitted, you have managed to achieve the most important part of it. If you know that you did not commit any of the academic cardinal sins (plagiarism, forging data, etc.), you are very likely worrying far too much.

Experienced peers' two cents

'There is a point where you have to let your baby go. This happens with journal articles, too. You polish, and polish, and polish, and polish and there comes a time when you just have to say: I am done. Every so often an experienced supervisor can be a great help with that. They can tell you if and when you are done.' (Timo Korkeamäki)

'I think the people most subject to the problem of not finding the end point of their thesis, of overdoing, are those who think that the thesis is their life's work, that it must be perfect. They tend to be the most committed, intelligent students. The key then is to recognize that this is not your life's work. This is a particular project, a particular goal. You don't need to give your whole life over to it. You need to work on it, but to keep it within the boundaries of the bigger picture. That is made much simpler by focusing in on what you're trying to actually accomplish with your project.

'In my own PhD program, I witnessed a student who was probably the brightest person in the group. He never finished. His book got thicker and thicker and thicker and thicker and thicker, but he did not give up. He was convinced that he hadn't made a contribution and that he had to keep pushing. He drove himself and everybody else crazy. Including his chair.' (Steven Floyd)

CONTINUE AFTERWARDS

You have reached your destination! While this particular journey is over, the many ways in which it may have changed you may only become apparent gradually. Given your travel experience and the newly earned degree, there are a few hopes and two handfuls of useful suggestions linked to your success.

Take in your accomplishment

Realizing what you accomplished by completing your studies takes time and reflection. It's a more complex achievement than meets the eye.

Metaphorically speaking

It goes without saying that any great exploration warrants celebrations at the end. You took upon yourself hardship and risk, and things might not have turned out as you hoped. But they did turn out well: you succeeded. Time to count your lucky stars and pat yourself on the back for a while. Sure, the journey is the reward. But then, success in completing a journey at least suggest the celebration of receiving that reward in full.

Consequently, try not to rush on to the next commitment, job, programme, or problem to solve. Attend the graduation party, celebrate with your friends and family. Consider that it's not only your accomplishment, but also a source of pride for your family and friends. While you should not celebrate for making anyone happy apart from yourself, it might be helpful to consider the impression your family and friends have about your success, as an indicator to what you achieved. You might not yet fully realize what you have accomplished here—let them help you appreciate the moment.

Research, to a degree, also means mastering consecutive levels of challenge. Since these levels of challenge are difficult from the start and only get more difficult, there is not just a sense of celebration but also a moment of reflection useful after mastering each level. What does it mean to have achieved a Bachelor's degree, a Master's degree, a doctorate?

Rough coordinates

Impressive—'Characterized by making a deep impression on the mind or senses; able to excite deep feeling. Said usually of language or scenes; rarely of persons.'

The Student's Research Companion. Omid Aschari and Benjamin Berghaus, Oxford University Press.
© Omid Aschari and Benjamin Berghaus (2023). DOI: 10.1093/oso/9780192855312.003.0044

Accomplishment—'The action or fact of accomplishing something; fulfilment, completion; achievement, success.'

Realize—'To conceive of as being real; to apprehend with the clearness or detail of reality; (in later use also) to become aware of or come to understand (a fact, situation, etc.). To understand clearly, be fully aware.'

Celebrate—'To mark one's happiness or satisfaction with (a significant event or circumstance, esp. a milestone reached or success achieved), typically with a social gathering or enjoyable activity. In early use spec.: to mark with communal rejoicing.'

Train of thought

When you have reached your destination after a long journey, you'd expect to be thrilled, excited, over the moon. For many who complete their thesis, this is surprisingly not the case. For starters, completing your thesis commonly does not build towards the end in suspense. Usually, the most exciting phase is somewhere after two thirds of the project, when you see that your data has turned out to be plausible or when you complete a substantial subproject that, for the first time, lets you see that your project will, one day in the near future, come to an end. This most exciting day is when you first see your destination from afar.

Between this excitement and actually getting there lies plenty of work, some red tape, and some rather unceremonious procedures like handing in your document. None of that is particularly exciting, so your mind is already thinking and planning ahead: what comes after? Which employer should you pursue? Should you take some time off? So many questions and ideas occupy your mind that it can be easy to discount the festivities of completing your programme. You might have travelled around the world and then completely forget about enjoying the destination for a moment.

While there is palpable truth in the advice to undertake a journey for travelling and not for arriving, each stage has its role. Travelling—or doing the work—is the essential experience you sign up for, no doubt. But arriving—or completing a thesis or programme—is the moment of rest at which you ought to try to relax your muscles and your ambitious mind. There is very little meaningful about working if nothing ever gets achieved. Consequently, achievements do matter. If you don't assign your achievements at least some value by celebrating, relaxing, thinking back and forth, the constant act of working will become its own goal, and consequently will deteriorate in meaning. There is very little point in hiking across the Alps if you don't, for a moment, celebrate your arrival at the destination but instead immediately plan the next excursion.

Chances are that you will find it difficult to slow down to appreciate and celebrate what you just accomplished. If that's the case, allow your family and friends to help you realize your achievement. Your parents will likely be proud to a degree that will feel uncomfortable to you. Even if they (for whatever reason) behave as if they were unimpressed, you can be certain that they are happy to see you have taken a big step. The same goes for siblings. Much more so, your close friends from school or previous academic programmes will be happy for you and will share their positive thoughts. Not to mention your colleagues from your programme: some will be more celebratory, others more dismissive. Try to let yourself take in all this good mood around you, and enjoy slowly realizing that nothing really matters if you don't take time out every once in a while to celebrate what you accomplished. Trust those close and dear to you if they say that—regardless of what grade you earned— you did very well. Indeed, you did. Completing an academic programme is an achievement simply on account of the numerous stressors you endured. No matter your grade, someone will almost always have performed better than you—but you made it through.

There is one clear recommendation for this phase: don't miss the celebration on graduation day. No matter whether you already have a job or feel that there's something more intriguing to do—join the celebration. You cannot buy such a day for money. It comes only because you invested years of your life into a programme and completed it successfully. Don't mistake my recommendation: the food might be mediocre, the music might be debatable, you might feel that your parents are not behaving as you see fit, the speeches will be too long—but that's thoroughly beside the point. This is your and your classmates' day. It's what you've worked toward. Don't miss this. Celebrate.

In essence

- You made it!
- Take a moment to calm down and reflect on what you achieved.
- Successes do not come every day—celebrate them!

To reflect

- What does having completed your thesis and your programme mean to you?
- Do you begin to feel how your investment in your advancement may have shifted your outlook on things? What changed? On what do you think differently than before you started?
- How can you celebrate this occasion in a meaningful way? How can you enjoy your moment in the sun for a bit?

Two travellers' tales

Rachel has always been driven. Before she completed high school, she participated as a guest in a few lectures at university. Before completing her Bachelor's degree, her mind was already occupied with how to succeed in grad school. Now, in the middle of her Master's thesis, it is no big surprise that Rachel is already mostly thinking about which job she needs and where she wants to get. Her thesis seems like something she does to keep her hands busy. But her mind is already far ahead, figuring out the next challenge. Of course, she manages to complete her project on time and in full, but she is not sure whether she actually notices it. Had it not been for the regulations of the university, she would not even have attended the graduation ceremony—that's dealing too much with the past, for her. Rachel lives in the future.

Eddy considers himself an epicurean—he loves to get lost in the moment, in the experience, in the now. He dislikes to linger in the past, which helps with less than stellar exams and awkward exchanges with the odd professor, and he does not count a great sense of anticipation among his strengths. To him, the present could also be called Eddy-time. He works through his thesis, focuses on each facet. He feels both the lows and the highs of progress or lack thereof. And at the end of it, he celebrates, since he feels that he has accomplished something. And accomplishments go best with celebrations. After his graduation, he plans to take a few weeks off, get his head into the new place that he travelled to in the past months, and take some time to figure out where his path continues.

Devil's advocate

There is very little to be said against the idea of acknowledging and celebrating your successes. The only aspect to be wary of might be to rest on your laurels for too long. Even the most excited soul will, sooner or later, realize that their past successes are pleasant memories, but that the next challenge stands squarely before them.

How to tackle

Besides attending your graduation and not passing over the opportunity to celebrate your achievement, there is not much to do. Possibly, take a bit of speed out of your step for a few weeks, enjoy where you are slightly more consciously, and notice how nice it can feel not to want to achieve, solve, or master something for the proverbial five minutes. Just be.

Experienced peers' two cents

'I don't know anybody who would say: "my thesis process was completely painless, and I loved every day of it." There is some pain and suffering baked into this whole process. What people should feel afterwards, when they look at their thesis again a year later, is that they should be proud of themselves. After all, they have passed through a filter that not many people have passed through. It is a good reason to pat yourself on the back.

'When you are working on your thesis, you have to be tough on yourself, you have to self-discipline, you have plenty of other people who are tough on you—your supervisor, your external evaluators. You receive a lot of criticism, and it takes a very thick skin to take on this criticism with kindness and get done even with the last lady who measures your margins. Once you have passed that stage, you're entitled to look back and see that you did something pretty spectacular.' (Timo Korkeamäki)

'Leaving a mark would require the student to rethink and draw new connections within a particular theory or phenomenon with their thesis. This would be how to get other researchers to read your thesis. It would make them rethink or re-examine something that they maybe thought they knew. That's the direct way to make a mark, to change how practitioners or researchers think about a phenomenon and, indeed, part of the world.

'Indirectly, the thesis can also help the student themselves or their advisor. It can change how they think about or approach the problem. This can lead to other research projects or give them a unique perspective that they bring with them to a new workplace that can then shape their environments there.

'Both approaches are useful and effective in leaving a mark—be it directly or indirectly. It is unrealistic to expect that every thesis will receive great outside attention, but then, that's not the only way of being successful. If you do something that truly shapes how you yourself and your supervisor look at the world, a mark has been left.' (Matt Farmer)

Feedback eats grades for breakfast

Grades are simplified, imperfect opinions of your work by another person. Take them for what they are worth. When possible, seek feedback.

Metaphorically speaking

Anyone's journey is slightly different. Some catch a ride here or there, others walk every step on their own. Some take a long time and great care to develop something that they can stand behind, and some simply follow others' advice. Whoever is going to critique your travel report in the end will only have that much insight into what you experienced and how much you grew. They will factor in their professional and sometimes even deeply personal opinions—if their schedules even allow them to involve themselves that deeply. Even though it seems a bit egotistical, the only person who can evaluate how well you have done will be yourself.

Consequently, take the evaluation of your thesis as one opinion on your work, but not as the only meaningful opinion. You will very likely develop more use out of reviewing any evaluative text that you might get or can request alongside your grade. This will contain why your examiner evaluated as she or he did, and it should explain how—in their eyes—your performance could have been better or worse. If you are interested in experiencing your evaluation not only as a pat on the back (or a knock to the head) but as an opportunity to become better, reviewing the expertise on your performance will become key.

Research, to a degree, means enduring evaluation by others. Grades are just the most condensed form of feedback, and they are rarely particularly informative. Look beyond the grade, for actual feedback that helps you to identify what you could have done better.

The Student's Research Companion. Omid Aschari and Benjamin Berghaus, Oxford University Press.
© Omid Aschari and Benjamin Berghaus (2023). DOI: 10.1093/oso/9780192855312.003.0045

Rough coordinates

Grade—'A degree or position in the scale of rank, dignity, social station, eminence, proficiency, etc. A class of things, constituted by having the same quality or value. A mark (usually alphabetical) indicating an assessment of the year's work, examination papers, etc., of a student.'

Feedback—'The modification, adjustment, or control of a process or system (as a social situation or a biological mechanism) by a result or effect of the process, esp. by a difference between a desired and an actual result; information about the result of a process, experiment, etc.; a response.'

Institution—'An establishment, organization, or association, instituted for the promotion of some object, esp. one of public or general utility, religious, charitable, educational, etc.'

Evaluation—'The action of appraising or valuing (goods, etc.); a calculation or statement of value.'

Train of thought

At the end of any academic programme, there is an evaluation. Don't ask why—we did not come up with the idea. The institutionalization of education did. Granted, there is a point to evaluating work for feedback. Since more and more people are studying, the only more or less feasible means of providing core feedback appears to be an evaluation on one scale of arbitrary quality, a grade. Many educators don't like the system either: we recognize that your experience and your personal advancement is commonly not reflected in the grade you receive. It's not unheard of for some grades you receive not to come with the impression of fairness. The number of skewed evaluations is so large because evaluation can go off on so many levels: you, individually, can be mis-evaluated; your class might be the first to receive preferential or discriminatory treatment because of a change in policy; your school might pride itself on particularly tough grading or offer great grades at a discount; the region your school is located in might be known for tough academic requirements. It is hard to overlook that grading is a necessary evil. Consequently, there is still something to be done about it:

Try to emancipate yourself from grading. Your first impulse will be to reject that proposal because you fear for your first job. You cannot ignore grading because you might not get the job you want. That's where the next advice follows: ignore employers that focus on grading and are not interested in you, personally. Easy to say, you might respond. Indeed, it is easy to recommend simply because this recommendation might keep you from a thoroughly pointless hamster wheel geared at shaping your performance within social systems that reward not excellence but conformity. All we can do here is to invite you to think along the path of what happens if you tone down your attention towards linear and mono-dimensional patterns of evaluation and, instead, shift your attention towards generating your own concept of quality in your work and follow that concept ruthlessly. This recommendation would be irresponsible if it were made to an elementary, middle school, or even high school student. But there's where advanced education differs from its fundamental version: you need to demonstrate a greater sense of self-discipline and commitment than simply sitting in a classroom for another three to ten years (if you pursue Bachelor's, Master's, and doctoral degrees). Here, the drive that determines the quality of work should not originate from a desire for good grades—at least not exclusively. Certainly, it can originate from great positioning, from an inspired project, and rock-solid methodology, from the beauty of her project, but not predominantly from the pursuit of good grades as a result of these factors. Either you are driven by what you do, generate quality from that, and view grades as a result of minor importance, or you might be risking to shoot for questionable aims. University should not be a place of transactions, evaluation for performance, but a place of transformation, maturing through learning.

Of course, some see the thesis as a piece of work, and the grade as the reward—we'd like to encourage you to see the thesis as a challenge, the learning during the process as your reward, and the evaluation as one external voice mandated and paid for by the university in order that some numeral or letter should be written on a piece of paper that institutionalizes learning. The evaluation, the numeral or letter, and the piece of paper are not the point of your going to university. The point of your going to university is for you to learn. According to UNESCO, societies invest on average around 4% of their GDP into education. Let's jointly make this generous investment worth more than shooting for some favourable letter or number on a piece of paper.

Instead of thinking about grades, consider your judges or board of evaluators as another stakeholder, and—especially during the design of your project—try to adjust your work to suit and exceed your evaluators' expectations. Consider optimizing for grades merely as a safeguard for quality and as a training for your skills in reading not only requirements but also sources for a great impression on your audience. If you consider your supervisor and your board of evaluators your peers, the grade will merely reflect the degree of acclaim your work can generate from those who are also interested in the field. This is to ascribe to a grade a purely functional role of trying to align your research design with your evaluators' standards.

In essence

- Learning has little to do with evaluation by numbers and letters. Evaluation comes from institutionalism and efficiency.
- If you can, try to do what you can to distance your mind from the idea that a grade can provide a complete, detailed, and unbiased sense of your performance. That goes for good grades, bad grades, and mediocre grades. This gets increasingly pronounced the further you advance through your academic and, later, professional career.
- The feedback you need to heed is the involved, generously invested, detailed, and complete feedback on what you did well and how you can improve. This is much more instructive than where you are a mark on someone's yardstick.

To reflect

- Why do grades matter to people?
- Do grades matter to me? Why?
- What's the point of feedback to performance?

Two travellers' tales

James has always been a good student. He has taken pride in his good grades, in receiving honours, and in leading class rankings. To James, grades are the currency of the academic process—perform well, get reimbursed with good grades. Even though he is aware that grades mean most in the academic world and less outside, he has always found it hard to cope with a mediocre or even bad grade on a performance that he deemed good or—in most cases—better than that of others. James delivers a good effort on his thesis and reaches most of what he wanted to achieve. He receives a good grade. Still, he feels slightly at odds with the assessment: this project was worth much more and cost much more effort than simply a good grade. And he's right: the grade alone cannot really pay off what he invested.

Wilma has always been a good student. Good grades mixed with passable performances and some stellar successes—but Wilma was always slightly suspicious of teachers' evaluations. Often, she found that her performance was either better or worse than what she received as a grade. Not a systematic discounting or raving, just pure inaccuracies. Teachers, it seems to her, are not the last word in precision when it comes to evaluating students—at least since she left undergraduate programmes behind her, where the grading may still largely depend on a score from a multiple choice test. But now, in her PhD programme? She's simply used to teachers only having that much capacity and insight to judge her work. By herself, she knows that the only person she needs to convince that she performed impressively is herself. More often than not, professors are merely precise enough to tell a train wreck from a home run.

Devil's advocate

Even though grades are of limited informative value, they are convenient: they allow employers to rank from best to worst, make an arbitrary cut somewhere, and enable or disable specific paths of your future development. Thus, grades can, sadly, become important when it comes to advancing into programmes or on paths that are limited in attendance in the most simplistic of ways—by only allowing in those who clear a particular bar.

How to tackle

When you complete examinations, try to seek feedback rather than generating too much of an emotional or rational response to the number or letter someone assigned to your work. Whatever the grade, your work always consists of good passages (and you might not know it yet or understand why) and bad passages (and you might not know it yet or understand why).

The biggest reward for having completed work is to learn perspectives from which you might improve your performance the next time around. This is the most substantial benefit you can generate from an examination: learning what to do better.

Truthful, honest, well-founded, and detailed feedback is difficult to come by, since it requires another person to invest ample amounts of time to work thoroughly through your material, understand it, compare it with their own perspective, formulate (often numerous) criticisms, and put effort into phrasing these criticisms constructively so that you don't get bruised by them but learn from then. Even then, feedback from one person will always be the reasoned but subjective opinion of that one person. What one other person can tell you does not amount to much more than what you could have done differently that would seem valuable from their perspective. Ask another person, and you get a slightly different evaluation. Consolidating feedback from multiple sources and finding the common denominator gets you closer and closer to a reliable take on what others think you should change. That, still, does not include your perspective. Did your audience of feedbackers and critics understand what you tried to convey? Do you need to be clearer?

All of these challenges with generating valuable feedback point to the recommendation to start asking for feedback earlier in the process rather than later. At the end of your journey, seeking feedback is a recommended minimum. For your next journey, seeking feedback early, from multiple sources, and integrating it with your intent should become part of your working routine.

Experienced peers' two cents

'There are two aspects here to emphasize. First, my expectation as supervisor is that I am not confronted with the student as a typical researcher. My expectation is that the student has interest in the topic of research (and the topic to be researched). Second, I have the expectation that the student is willing to provide high quality. The drive to provide quality is a mindset that I expect. But the gap between what I can expect and what the result will be is massive.

'This has consequences for how I will evaluate the thesis. As a supervisor, I have two options. First, I delegate the thesis to some extent. Or, second, I reframe my proposition and view the student by taking the approach a typical consultant would take. A consultant is a connector between scientific methods and the practice. If the student manages to reach the level of a consultant, he or she is already performing very well. If the student can go a bit beyond that level and show that they can apply scientific methods as per the current academic practice in research, so much the better.' (Urs Jäger)

'When considering what a thesis can accomplish, I think of this really on three levels of accomplishments. At the most basic, minimum level, the thesis should demonstrate an ability to do a research project that formulates questions, does a literature review, designs a study, and executes it. It should demonstrate mastery of a topic and of at least basic abilities. I think the minimum goal is to write a review article. That's where the conceptual framework comes in. It's a way to organize the literature. Then, of course, to demonstrate writing skills, language skills, as it is part of the minimum requirement.

'As the achievement becomes a more advanced accomplishment, then I would expect the document to identify a relevant problem of some significance in the world, one which is troubling or novel, which can be in the form of a research question. In this middle ground, there is also the requirement to demonstrate the ability to carry out a rigorous methodology.

'And then the skill that's really difficult, and that therefore indicates a more advanced kind of accomplishment, would be to articulate and justify a research model or set of hypotheses. Another way to think about the highest level is to be able to say something of interest, both to academics and practitioners.' (Steven Floyd)

Your degree is a trusted symbol

A degree won from a university is a symbol of trust in you. Be aware of that, and allow this idea to help steer your choices for your next steps.

Metaphorically speaking

If you have been to a region and have become a certified traveller for that trip, people will trust you to tell them what to watch out for and what not to miss. Especially if the journey has been a demanding and risky one, others will depend on your open and reliable account.

Consequently, with every degree you earn, you do not only get a ticket to move to your next challenge, but also a much less discussed obligation to act according to the degree you earned. With each piece of accreditation, people will increase their attention to what you have to say. Not only will they increasingly depend on your judgement, but those institutions who certified your work trust you to a certain degree to at least be able to act in accordance with the standards of their degree.

Research, to a degree, also means building a track record. This track record of past projects, publications, and programmes helps you grow, but it also endows you with credibility. Keep this credibility in mind when you plan your next steps. Nothing stands in the way of making your credibility as focused and specialized or diverse and broad as you would like. But consciously using your credibility to lead people astray is inadvisable, for many more reasons than just leaving your credibility in tatters eventually.

Rough coordinates

Graduation—'The action of receiving or conferring a university degree, or a certificate of qualification from some recognized authority. Also, the ceremony of conferring degrees. The action or process of dividing into degrees or other proportionate divisions on a graduated scale.'

The Student's Research Companion. Omid Aschari and Benjamin Berghaus, Oxford University Press.
© Omid Aschari and Benjamin Berghaus (2023). DOI: 10.1093/oso/9780192855312.003.0046

Trust—'Firm belief in the reliability, truth, or ability of someone or something; confidence or faith in a person or thing, or in an attribute of a person or thing.'

Degree—'A stage or position in the scale of dignity or rank; relative social or official rank, grade, order, estate, or station. A stage of proficiency in an art, craft, or course of study: An academical rank or distinction conferred by a university or college as a mark of proficiency in scholarship.'

Values—'Worth based on esteem; quality viewed in terms of importance, usefulness, desirability, etc. The principles or moral standards held by a person or social group; the generally accepted or personally held judgement of what is valuable and important in life.'

Train of thought

While 'to complete an academic programme' is easy to say, it is less well understood. In most cases, you will not have completed a vocational education that now enables you to carry out a job. Instead, you will have accumulated a combination of topical and methodological insight, personal development, some preparation for the job market, and potentially some motivation for social engagement. Looking back on what it is that you achieved, it might feel difficult to define—beyond merely saying that you 'graduated' from your 'programme'. We'd like to offer you a couple of perspectives on looking at what you just accomplished, from the perspective of the faculty.

The first perspective is that once you have graduated, we trust you to carry the title of our educational institution. You have proved capable in the field of your programme to the degree that we could test that. It is likely that you will make a successful contribution to any group you join which works in the same field or at least operates with compatible methodology (in the broadest sense). We believe that you can be trusted by any future employer to work in your field with no more supervision than is appropriate for your seniority. We've done this journey together (you, other students, and our faculty), and we believe that you will not need much further guidance when travelling in the same neck of the woods. If you do, you will be capable of training yourself to expand your knowledge in the field.

With this trust comes two things: first, something you can build on. Due to your title and your education, employers will take our trust in you as an indication of the degree to which they can place trust in you (and not get disappointed). The more reputable the institution from which you can generate evidence of trust, the more trust will be placed in you. That's the whole concept of reputation in educational institutions—with its many dark sides. There is a second element to our trust in you, however. Trust comes both as a distinction and as a burden. The burdensome element of trust is that you should not allow yourself to fall below the standard that you have been taught. Ideally, those standards were painstakingly high. In addition, carrying an academic title also means that if you went to a good university, you should not deviate from great practice. While the concept of honour is not widely acclaimed in all areas of the world, particularly the West, it should be when it comes to the work ethics and set of values related to your academic upbringing. In that sense, your graduation also means that you subscribe to the standards you learned. While most programmes do not require you to take an oath, consider it great practice to anchor your future decisions in these standards. Most detrimental developments in careers emerge from gradual divergence from those values that other people thought valuable enough to teach. If you consider your graduation a balance of a distinction and a burden, you combine the short-term benefit with the sustainable nature of adopting these values to guide your decisions later on.

Reflect for a moment how this system of trust works that you enter into when graduating. You will experience this as effortless, since your first impression will reflect the unmistakable updraft you experience on the job market. When you enter your professional field, however, we trust you to make sound decisions on what you collaborate on and how you go about doing that. If you feel that the environment you (apply to) work in does not seem to meet the standards, goals, and values that you considered important during your programme, consider making a change. It is all too easy to dismiss doubts about ethical standards, the sense of the mission, or the internal or external conduct of your employer. We do not want you to submit to helplessly and harmfully overworking yourself to serve horrible bosses on projects that mean nothing to you. Burn-out is a real problem, and it comes sooner rather than later in environments in which you grind yourself down for dubious reasons.

Especially when you are a young, bright, and eager entry-level colleague, you will be a magnetic for many, many, many tasks. You will work long and hard—and you can expect to be treated in a friendly manner, to find development opportunities, and to follow missions that you can stand behind. We want (and trust) you to seek those places to work in where you feel you can flourish. Leave those places that drag and wear you down just for some shiny CV line or title. You can do little good if you are thoroughly worn down and burnt out. We count on having you around, somewhere in practice or academia, and doing great things for a very long time. That's why we wanted to teach you in the first place.

In essence

- Being awarded a degree from an educational institution means that people of this institution trust you to be able to act according to academic standards relative to the level of your degree.
- Others, e.g. employers but also project partners or less advanced academics, will build on this trust in you when they work with you or ask you for your guidance.
- At a pinch or when in doubt, you can always consider your degree as a sign of encouragement from your teachers that they trust you to leave toxic workplaces, teams, and companies and seek those environments in which you can flourish.

To reflect

- What does your university trust you with now?
- Does your degree suggest certain behavioural traits to you?
- How can this trust in you shape your choices when building a career?

Two travellers' tales

Frank is a smart guy. He knows what credentials are worth. When applying for his entry-level position, he leans confidently on the prestige of the degree from his leading university. In interviews, he finds it difficult not to show the pride involved in his academic pedigree. This does not come off too well with the interviewers. Many people have degrees from good schools, one who is also an alumna of his university reminds him.

Sandra is a smart woman. She knows that degrees come with the expectation of a certain conduct. She builds on that and tries to ramp up her entry into the job market through recommendations from those lecturers she worked well with. Finally, it's these people who can give the most accurate account of her working ethics and capabilities. Those people trust her to perform, and the relevant contacts in the job market are confident that they will deliver a trustworthy recommendation.

Devil's advocate

While every degree should come with a sense of obligation to work by its standards, there are limits to what you, your university, or anyone can ask of you. This specifically goes for the implied expectation that you should only consider continuing on the path and in the field you already selected. Any type of education should increase your freedom to choose and design your next steps. No type of education ought to provide you with the sense of factually limiting your options in the future.

How to tackle

There is no specific concept or procedure that appears particularly fitting to this mindset. It is, however, a good idea to keep this thought in your mind when navigating through the joints of your career—when you have the opportunity to adjust your course. Allow what brought you here and what bestows trust in you to also guide your decisions for future advancement. You do not need to let this thought burden you too heavily—merely to provide you with another sense of direction that might shape your decision. Especially in modern societies where there are commonly countless ways of interpreting your professional and personal life, considering what your teachers trust you to do might provide some useful orientation.

Do good for yourself and others

Your education may have come with no strings attached. However, it is useful to consider the expectation that you will apply what you have learned.

Metaphorically speaking

Chances are that your expedition was not financed by yourself in its entirety—maybe only to a minimal degree. Possibly, you were on a publicly funded expedition project, most expenses paid for by taxes. What a godsend! Other explorers return home afterwards with their backpacks full of debts.

Consequently, if your education was sponsored to any degree by someone else than yourself, try to keep in mind the benefit you were dealt to the degree that seems appropriate to you. If you feel this notion speaks to you, consider letting it sit for a while and maybe generate thoughts about how to contribute, give back, or enable others in kind. There's no need to feel a burden of needing to repay a debt that you never incurred, there is just an opportunity to try to pass on some of the good fortune you were granted with others when you see the chance to do so.

Research, to a degree, also means being both being in need of funding but also being able to provide and share insight in return. Wherever a system enables you to grow by investing in you, it can only survive if enough of those invested into are able and willing to contribute, share, or sensibly employ what they have learned when the opportunity arises.

Rough coordinates

Apply—'To put a thing into practical contact with another. To bring (a rule, a test, a principle, etc.) into contact with facts; to bring to bear practically; to put into practical operation. To put to use, employ; to spend, dispose of.'

The Student's Research Companion. Omid Aschari and Benjamin Berghaus, Oxford University Press.
© Omid Aschari and Benjamin Berghaus (2023). DOI: 10.1093/oso/9780192855312.003.0047

Contribution—'The action of contributing or giving as one's part to a common fund or stock; the action of lending aid or agency to bring about a result.'

Sensible—'Aware of and responsive to one's surroundings; fully conscious; not unconscious or delirious. Having, showing, or characterized by good sense. Having or showing good sense and sound judgement; judicious, reasonable, practical, prudent.'

Society—'The state or condition of living in company with other people; the system of customs and organization adopted by a group of people for harmonious coexistence or mutual benefit. Senses relating to the state or condition of living or associating with others. Association or friendly interaction with other people; the company of others.'

Train of thought

Your education is the product of many people coming together and setting up an environment in which you and your colleagues were taught and encouraged to grow. Depending on the choice of institutions and your location, this education may have cost you tens of thousands of dollars in tuition fees, only a few hundred Swiss francs each semester in financial contribution, or possibly not even a single euro. In none of those cases would the finance you invested have granted you access to the value of the institutions in which you were taught. In every case, there was some degree of funding from third parties—be it your family, generous alumni, wealthy patrons of research and education, or public funding. In every case, you were fortunate enough to benefit from an environment that those who went before you built for your generation (granted, saddled with considerable student loans, feel free to put quotes around 'fortunate enough'—but you get our idea).

Your education comes with no strings attached. And still, there is only sense in seeing universities as places that emerge from societal involvement and engagement if they succeed in instilling their graduates with the inclination to contribute likewise to societal involvement and engagement. Even if your education does not come with strings attached, we encourage you to stop for a moment, to count your blessings, to consider what countless and nameless others have enabled you to do what you have done, and to plan your next steps based on the results of that reflection. The idea is not to suggest paying back the support you received—the idea is to get inspired by what can be achieved when people come together to build opportunities for advancements of others, and to see what this might tell you about the options that present themselves for you on the job market.

While all of this may seem very demanding, our expectation regarding your next steps is purposefully vague. What you do with your educational good fortune is almost entirely up to you—except for being aware that you are where you are today because other people helped you. This expectation may be vague, but its resulting implications may sound a little more tangible.

A first implication of this vague sense of having been supported is the conclusion that those many people who enabled you want you to do well for yourself. We want you to succeed in the broadest and the most humane sense of the word. Success is for you to define; it may come in many shapes and sizes, and largely depends on attitude and perspective. We want you to be able to adopt attitudes and perspectives in which you can see and appreciate your success and draw energy from that.

A second implication of the idea of having had many people back you and lift you up is that you internalize the feeling to the extent that you pass on the favour to others in your life. Try to enable others. If not individually, join a crowd to help another person. If your success should translate into powerful positions, find ways to use that power to enable and not hinder others in discovering and reaching their potential.

A third implication emerges from whatever we taught you: we believe in the value and benefit of our disciplines. Every tool can be used for detrimental and for beneficial purposes. Consider, with some critical distance, which perspective on your field you can adopt, and how you would like to apply the potential that rests in your field to a beneficial purpose. This reflection might be a great place to dig for a job or a position—where can you apply the potential of your field for good? Become creative. There are plenty of environments in dire need of transformation towards the better, and there are plenty of contexts in which those who are already trying to make a sensible contribution can be strengthened through your contribution. Join those who seem to you to be on the right side of things.

All implications of the expectations linked to your graduation seem related to our with our wish for you to do something you consider worthwhile with your educational fortune, and to think about how you might be able to pass it on to others through enabling them. It may be a vague expectation, but it should not be one that ties you down. At the same time, it seems to be the only reasonable, foundational expectation to be held by people who professionally try to enable others.

In essence

- In many societies, your education was financially covered, to a large degree, by other people—be it family, wealthy donors, successful alumni, or in numerous instances taxpayers.
- Make this investment in you count by applying what you have learned in a way that allows you to make a useful contribution to the society that helped you learn.
- There are countless options to make such a contribution, and no single one is more important than the others. But even considering that whatever you do with your education can generate a positive impact will help you see your education in a context that is more responsible than if this aspect is left unconsidered.

To reflect

- How are you going to interpret your education in your career?
- How is 'making a contribution' going to change when moving from your academic training to your professional life?
- In which way could you make a contribution through applying your education?

Two travellers' tales

Ticia has completed her programme efficiently and successfully. She has always considered university as one of those stages you simply need to get through to finally enter the job market and make some money—and possible a difference, somewhere? Ticia never truly thought that, had she grown up in other areas of the world, she might not be able to afford a university education. 'It's just a thing you do' has been her understanding until now. Off to her first real job!

Gilbert has completed his programme efficiently and successfully. Since there have been some political debates about raising university tuition fees, he has become aware of how attainable a solid education is in his region. To some degree, this provides him a gentle nudge to consider what he will do in future. He notices how attending university and working with his student colleagues has broadened his horizon and filled in many gaps of his previously all too incomplete view of the world. Given the fact that he was only able to get here due to the help of countless others, he wonders which job would allow him to do something similar for those who would benefit like he did.

Devil's advocate

This mindset requires much goodwill and positive intent to hit just the right chord within your mind. Think a little too far, and you might mistake our thought as a requirement that you turn thoroughly altruistic through education. A little too short, and you might reach the slippery slope of sarcasm and towards cynicism: 'I've spent and invested enough years—time for society to pay me back!'

However, there is little useful alternative to seeing teaching and learning as activities directed towards collectively creating something worthwhile. To be open towards this idea is most of what we encourage you to do.

How to tackle

There is not much more to do here than to reflect and keep in mind the general idea of this mindset. See where it brings you.

Keep in touch

While graduating from a programme entails farewells, do not disregard the value of keeping in touch with people of some of your best years.

Metaphorically speaking

One of the most fun incentives of having travelled is that you can share your experiences with those who are just about to go on their own journeys. Enabling others not to fall into the same pitfalls as you did, or empowering them by sharing hints on how to replenish energy, are thoroughly satisfying ways of sharing what you learned. You can only do this if you retain at least some connection to those who are about to start their journeys.

Consequently, try to keep at least in rudimentary touch with your university, the institute you wrote your thesis at, your professors, maybe. There are plenty of opportunities to enable others by mentoring, joining studies, or perhaps even teaching. However, keeping in touch is not only about giving back; it can also just be about keeping in touch with those with whom you shared several years of your life. These shared experiences seem valuable to many people. Disconnecting and discontinuing relationships is always possible, but it also entails building up other relationships from zero, somewhere else.

Research, to a degree, also means long-term relationships. Contacts you have built, people you have grown accustomed to, stories you share. You should always feel free to disconnect from relationships that do not seem good for you, but there's a noteworthy argument to be had for maintaining relationships that link you back to some of your best years.

Rough coordinates

Leaving—'To go away or out, to depart. To stop engaging in or adhering to (a habit, practice, belief, relationship, etc.). To go away from or give up permanently; to stop residing at (a place), belonging to (a society, etc.), working for (an employer), or attending (a school, college, etc.).'

The Student's Research Companion. Omid Aschari and Benjamin Berghaus, Oxford University Press.
© Omid Aschari and Benjamin Berghaus (2023). DOI: 10.1093/oso/9780192855312.003.0048

Staying—'To cease going forward; to stop, halt; to arrest one's course and stand still. To remain in a place or in others' company (as opposed to going on or going away).'

Alumni—'A former pupil or student (typically male) of a particular school, university, etc.; a graduate of a particular seat of learning.'

Community—'A body of people or things viewed collectively. A group of people who share the same interests, pursuits, or occupation, esp. when distinct from those of the society in which they live.'

Train of thought

Especially if your education was more of a painful experience, leaving your school as far behind as possible will be a plausible response. However, for many it still might be a sensible thought not to consider your school as a place in your past, but as an environment akin to an academic home, the alma mater.

Chances are that some of your best journeys will not have been experienced alone but with a group of friends, with your family, or with your spouse. Journeys are great, but the right company makes them excellent. Even though you may have just completed your last trip with your clique of explorers, you will be bound by shared experiences, stories, and a sense of community. Of course, that's a romantic view of the world, but then again, experiences quickly relate to emotions. Even on a trip from hell, having just the right team around you—paired with a great sense of humour—will make most people's days that much brighter. Especially after a project like an educational programme that took a few years to complete, these shared experiences represent a considerable amount of the return that you receive from all the efforts you invested. Keeping in touch with your travel companions will allow you to rekindle these experiences and 'cash in' this return.

Beyond this more emotional perspective on keeping in touch, there are some perfectly pragmatic and opportunistic reasons too. Your fellow students will advance in their careers. You will form a more or less loose-knit network of experts in your field. Even keeping in distant touch can be very helpful when trying to reach your own goals. By extension, keeping in touch or signing up to alumni organizations with your school will help you build a broader network of professional peers beyond your immediate friends during your programme. While some are more and others are less involved in networking, merely being open to the idea of seeing your school not as a place of the past but as a place of reconnecting and collaborating will help you derive potential from this particular association.

Finally, your school will remain a place which you can help support and further—be it by providing mentoring services for younger students, by offering guest lectures from your expert position in the job, or by collaborating in scientific projects with research chairs. Universities are not commercial, but societal institutions. They thrive on contributions. Contributions do not need to be monetary, but are commonly just as welcome in form of collaboration.

In essence

- No matter your core learning experience at university, remember that this is the place where you will likely have made many friendships, explored experiences, dived into thought. And in the end, you came through.
- Try to help your school to knit a helpful network of experts and alumni who are in a position and willing to help students to take their first steps after their academic education.
- There are plenty of opportunities to give back to your academic community—besides financial generosity. Maybe help out as a mentor or facilitate a collaboration with your employer?

To reflect

- What helped you get through university? Who helped you get through university?
- What can you bring to your school's alumni network? What can you derive from it?
- What's a way of supporting your academic community that would feel fun and appropriate to you?

Two travellers' tales

Henry had quite a tough time in university. It took him a lot of time to get settled into his subject; he had to repeat several classes and examinations early on. His final academic project was challenging and did not fully work out in the end, and he also never really felt supported by his professors or their staff.

A rather mediocre experience, he feels. After the graduation party, he vows not to return for some time: now, it's time for something entirely different. Good riddance, university!

Ulrike had quite a tough time in university. She changed subjects twice and finally started the programme that she now finished, a couple of years older than everyone else. It's been quite the marathon for her. However, what made her pull through this marathon were the people around her. She made several close friends who helped her pull through the thick and thin of it. Ulrike is convinced that she wouldn't have made it if it were not for her crew. She starts working in the field, but makes sure to keep in touch with many of her friends. She did not immediately sign up for her university's alumni club—not much use immediately after having graduated—but considers and finally joins the club a couple of years later to reconnect with more distant friends, and even meets the occasional older professor with whom she considers collaborating with on one of her employer's company projects. When she is ready to make a move from her first employer, she got a good tip through the alumni network about what turned out to be her next position.

Devil's advocate

Of course, you are always free to sever any connection you don't feel comfortable with. There is no mandate to keep in touch. For some, simply getting some distance between themselves and their university helps them settle down and get back in touch to see how things developed.

How to tackle

Whether you take the more institutional road—signing up with your alumni club—or prefer to keep things slightly more personal and individual—merely keeping in touch with your former colleagues—is not relevant. What matters most is that you do not sever all links with those people who you enjoyed being around during your university days.

Professionally run alumni clubs can, however, provide you with ample resources and options to exchange with many graduates that you may have never encountered in person during your time at university. Consider how many graduates your university produces each year. Many of them will be fun, might follow exciting careers, might have good ideas on challenges that you work on, or be in other ways great to be in touch with.

Career serendipity

Your university had you on its rails, and your job will soon do the same. Use the flexible joint between two rigid commitments to steer your trajectory.

Metaphorically speaking

Picking your next journey sometimes merely depends on which ships are in harbour today and setting sail tomorrow. They might be looking for exactly your profile, and you might be looking for exactly the position they seek to fill. Or you pick by destination and accept the role as potato peeler for the first leg of the journey—life is tough occasionally. Making a sound choice can take some time and nerves.

Consequently, once you have reached your destination, take some time to appreciate the sense of freedom to choose your next project. It's only in these few phases between projects and commitments that you are not bound by your designated destination so that you can make a turn, pick a different path, and see where that may lead you. Many of us are more or less used to think of our actions as free—but if we don't appreciate the instances in which we truly are, that freedom is not really worth much.

Not only research but also practical work consists of projects, roles, and positions. These projects commonly require dedication to a certain structure, procedure, and idea of completion. This dedication is what allows you to advance and grow your capabilities. But projects are not the home of freedom or choice—many decisions must be derived carefully from context. Freedom of choice is what happens between projects. Don't overlook the value of these gaps between programmes, projects, jobs, and other commitments. Ideally, don't fear these gaps of structure, either. They are those joints that turn your biography into a flexible, living being and not just a stiff and brittle scaffolding. Luck, good timing, and serendipity plays a noticeable role.

The Student's Research Companion. Omid Aschari and Benjamin Berghaus, Oxford University Press.
© Omid Aschari and Benjamin Berghaus (2023). DOI: 10.1093/oso/9780192855312.003.0049

Rough coordinates

Agility—'The ability to move (esp. to climb or manoeuvre) readily and quickly; nimbleness, dexterity; (also) an instance of this. The ability to change rapidly in response to customer needs and market forces; adaptability, flexibility, responsiveness.'

Career—'A person's course or progress through life (or a distinct portion of life), esp. when publicly conspicuous, or abounding in remarkable incidents: similarly with reference to a nation, a political party, etc. A course of professional life or employment, which affords opportunity for progress or advancement in the world.'

Position—'The place in which a person, thing, etc., is located or has been put; situation, site, station. A relation in which a person stands with respect to another or others; a person's circumstances, condition, or situation, esp. as affecting his or her influence, role, or power to act. A post as an employee; a paid office, a job.'

Entry level—'The level at which a given activity, employment, etc., may be entered; spec. the level of attainment necessary for employment, admission to an academic course, etc. Of a person: entering employment, etc., at the lowest level of a scale or hierarchy; having a job available to or suitable for those with relatively little relevant experience.'

Train of thought

Now that your academic programme is complete, making 'the next step' will become centre stage. This is quite a radical change: you are coming out of a programme that more or less predetermined your path for years, and now you are thrown to the opposite extreme of the graduate's freedom: you are thoroughly free to decide where to go next. Of course, the decision feels daunting: the options are beyond numerous and the competition seems stiff.

The time after your last journey is the one before your next. However, while you will see plenty of friends and colleagues scramble to win the rat race for pole position in the career competition, don't be afraid to take a measured approach to your next trip. You already know that carefully selecting your destinations makes a world of a difference between meaningful travelling and a trip from hell.

Finding a job often equates too readily to a somewhat bloodless competition. Who lands the best position with the most prestigious place? Who makes the most money, who negotiated for the nicest perks? Especially for university graduates, this competition is somewhat moot: you will not have the position to negotiate for much. You will likely be applying for jobs that are on the employment mass market. Of course, more and more companies feel the pressure to pick the best of you—but most of them do not have the capabilities to systematically and meaningfully identify talent beyond the most rudimentary signals for future performance (grades, recommendations, experience). In most cases, your luck will depend to a considerable degree on a spreadsheet that will simplify and quantify your talent. This is not meant to be disheartening—quite the opposite: realizing the realities of getting a first job can help shape your attitudes so that you can make the most of the situation.

One useful attitude to emerge from the realities of finding the first job is that you will likely not get exactly what you want. That's not a bad thing. Usually, you don't. Given that in many industries, young employees make their career steps inside or outside their first employer within the first two years, you will have plenty of opportunities to learn the ropes and navigate your way towards the position you will enjoy. Don't be put off by the fact that the position you get appears like an ugly duckling at first sight, if you managed to get into a company and sector that seems to suit you.

A second useful attitude to adopt is to avoid anticipatory defeat: don't tell yourself that you won't get the position and should not even bother. Many excellent people discourage themselves and don't apply. That's the foundation of your opportunity. Allow others to decline to apply—don't do that yourself.

Third, there is a considerable bit of luck involved. Of course, the conventional idea of luck deals with actually getting a good position—but the luck that we are referring to can also capture the opposite: fingers crossed that you will be declined for a position that would have been hell for you. Rejections hurt if you consider them the loss of a dream coming true. However, especially for rejections late in the application process, trust the people you speak to with your potential employer to have a good judgement about whether you'd be happy and high-performing in the position that they have to staff. Some environments you want to avoid submitting to. Here's to having the luck of being spared a nightmare of a position.

Whichever position you begin your career with, it will likely only last for a few years. Turnover rates in many industries are rapid enough to make less than perfectly fitting positions among interesting employers a reasonable trade-off for you to build a foothold and grow further based on your inside knowledge rather than on external estimates.

In essence

- Entering the job market and starting a career requires you to reinterpret yourself once more and find a place in a new environment.
- While you will have ideas about what you want, it is a good idea to remain flexible about how happy you will be about what you might get.
- Starting a career often means finding an entry point and working towards where you want to be.

To reflect

- How do you imagine the change from the academic context to the work context to manifest itself beyond the obvious?
- How can you make the most of the brief moment of increased freedom between two engagements?
- How much are you willing to trade off your understanding of the perfect job?

Two travellers' tales

Veronica was pretty proud when she managed to sign the contract to her first job while still in the middle of her thesis project. In her eyes, this was not only a reward for her hard work during the programme, but also provided a sense of security that she did not have to fear not knowing where to continue after university. She had always liked knowing where things were going in the future. Being faced with no or multiple opportunities to choose from was always less desirable than having exactly one opportunity —it just made life a little easier. And everything ran according to plan—Veronica completed her programme, moved to the city of her employer, and started her job just a few weeks later. A perfectly seamless transition.

Iliad focused on his thesis and made a pact with himself that—come what may—he would first take a bit of time off after completing his study programme. Even though studying came relatively easy to him, he felt that he wanted to take some time off, not only to recharge his energy but also to get his bearings on where he wanted to go next. He is still undecided about whether to continue with a postgraduate programme, collect some experience in a job, or to maybe explore adjacent fields to what he studied. In a sense, he expects the time after his academic programme and before launching into the next commitment to free him from what seem pre-programmed rails where he simply is expected to perform. For a bit, he wants to weigh his options and see whether he can surprise himself by discovering a road less travelled.

Devil's advocate

A pragmatist will likely argue that a sense of freedom between projects is just that: a sense. There still will be an optimal path to take, the one that generates most return. Thus, when trying to optimize, the sense of freedom will crumble to one choice that is mandated through logic. In a sense, it might be more useful to think of freedom as a sense of emancipation—between projects, you're even free to follow the less-than-optimal path, just because of your preference.

How to tackle

Finding your entry-level position, the first stepping-stone of your professional career, depends to a large degree on timing within the market, the company, and the team you apply to. This 'right place at the right time' determinant, sufficient luck, can sometimes be helped with more initiative, a greater network, more exchanges with contacts, but never fully turns into a certainty. Of course, you can further increase your chances and the number of your opportunities by integrating your experiences during your programme, for instance through internships or your final academic project.

Once you have made a successful move into the field, industry, and employer you have chosen, consider a plausible rhythm of two to three years to try to make your steps upwards or to the side. Establishing experience in one industry and with one employer will provide ample pragmatic information on where interesting positions are and when they open up. If there is no alternative way of reaching the bull's-eye position from outside, try to move in, then navigate the organization from the inside.

Experienced peers' two cents

'You have to ask yourself for the path you would like to take. What kind of purpose do you see in your path? What is the achievement that you are trying to fulfil?

'Do you want to enter an academic career or not? As soon as you can answer that with a clear "Yes!", then tactical elements enter your considerations. But that is usually not the case for Bachelor's thesis; the question usually comes up when you are writing your doctoral dissertation. I would not recommend to any junior researcher to try to adopt the logic of academic journals.

'But of course you have to take these considerations into account nowadays. This is the field of tension that you are subjected to if you aim for an academic career.

'There is also always an opportunity to find a third way—your own. This does not automatically mean that you turn an entirely blind eye to the tactical path.' (Günter Müller-Stewens)

'I don't think the substance of the project is as important as the process of skilled thinking that the thesis demonstrates. I think that's where the practitioner community tends to be speaking out of both sides of their mouth. They say they really want critical thinking, but they doubt that the scientific approach develops that. They don't make that connection because the substance of the document may not appeal to them as being something of interest from a practical perspective. If the student really went on an academic track—meaning more development of theory or empirical methods—it may or may not be seen as interesting or relevant.' (Steven Floyd)

Never consider yourself unfree

Education frequently means specialization. This may suggest fewer future options. However, education shall always provide you with more freedom, not less.

Metaphorically speaking

Research tends to turn you into a true expert in one very particular neck of the woods. Certainly, now you know your way around that particular area. While it can be satisfying to become, remain, and profit from being an expert in one area, do not feel surprised if you want to explore a different region. Since curiosity was what got you where you are now—why would you try to lock it down now?

Consequently, there is another balance to be found and another decision to be made between deepening your established expertise in a field you know and branching out from where you are to a related field. Of course, you can stay, reap the rewards of your established insight and maybe even reputation, but also get the sense of slight boredom associated with intensifying rather than broadening your expertise. Or you can go on exploring, apply the self-leadership skills you've taken away from your last projects to find your own path, and enjoy a more diverse learning curve, bearing in mind that positioning on a subject takes longer than you might be willing to invest. Keep in mind also that, of course, there are not only these two extreme paths to choose from, but you can find your bearing between both. Why not, for now, decide generally to stick with your field and gradually branch out into promising new fields? Why not, for now, decide to look for something new to explore, but always keeping the generated insight as a useful support to interpret what you find and maybe even make connections between your old and your new field of interest?

Research both means exploration and building expertise. Some are more interested in the expertise, others in the sense of exploration. Both extremes come with distinct advantages and disadvantages, based on your priorities.

The Student's Research Companion. Omid Aschari and Benjamin Berghaus, Oxford University Press.
© Omid Aschari and Benjamin Berghaus (2023). DOI: 10.1093/oso/9780192855312.003.0050

Depending on what drives you today (this will likely change with time), feel free to pick your path between both perspectives for the foreseeable future.

Rough coordinates

Road—'A path or way between different places, or leading to some place. Originally: a way wide enough to allow horses, travellers on foot, or horse-drawn vehicles or the like, to pass; (later) a wide way which motor vehicles, cyclists, etc., can use, typically having a specially prepared surface. A way, direction, or route taken by a particular person or thing; a course followed in a journey.'

Rail—'A bar or continuous line of bars (originally of wood, now usually of metal) laid on or near the ground, typically in pairs, to support and guide the wheels of a vehicle, as a train, tram, wagon, etc.; the bars which form a railway.'

Freedom—'The state or fact of being free from servitude, constraint, inhibition, etc.; liberty. Exemption or release from the obligations of a contractual agreement. The state of being able to act without hindrance or restraint; liberty of action.'

Specialization—'The process by which organisms, anatomical features, etc., take on a particular form or function in the course of evolutionary change or individual development, typically with the result that there is increased competence in one function at the expense of other functions.'

Train of thought

So, you have travelled to a place and returned to tell the tale—excellent! You may well have grown into the sense of feeling at home in the region. You know the ins and outs and how to get around there. This might make you feel like an expert in this area. And people will consider you as one, too, now that your educational travel agency has certified that you carried out your trip successfully. All of that focuses on where you went and what you found. It focuses less on your becoming an apt traveller. And apt travellers can reach many destinations, not just one.

In essence, we overly tend to focus on our topical expertise and to disregard the experience we have gained in designing and implementing a scientific project. In a way, this extends the old saying: 'Give a person a fish, and they will have something to eat for a day. Teach a person to fish, and they will be fed for the rest of their life', with the additional thought 'Make a person think about accessing all various kinds of food sources, and they will be able to secure a whole town's balanced nutrition.' So: you're not only a person who can fish, intellectually. Consider yourself to be a person who can access all types of food, intellectually.

If you consider on an abstract level what you learned to apply—systematically working with literature, critically reviewing theories, building propositions and hypotheses, gathering, analysing, and presenting data, developing a synthesis, and integrating all of the above into a research report—you should try to see yourself as at least as proficient in your specific field as you are in applying the central techniques of scientific advancement.

Any educational certificate should come with the sense of feeling more free and having more options available than before. Curiously—and maybe sadly—the contrary experience is much more common: since you were taught in a programme that is associated with a certain field, that field is where you are going to 'end up' in. If you are excited to continue in a straight path, that's excellent. This will be very efficient to you. If you have a more diverse curiosity, this can feel more challenging to you: how are you going to explain to a recruiter that you did not continue on your path to dig deeper, deeper, and deeper into your original field?

If you are in the second camp, we'd like to encourage you to put a greater emphasis on the idea that you have just completed a programme that enabled you to think and act more scientifically. The field was the field of application; you might have liked it at the time of choosing your field, a couple of years earlier, but it is not something that you'd like to pursue any further. You would rather not eat fish for the rest of your life, you would rather not become a one-trick-pony, and you'd like to realize your own personal freedom—thank you very much!

It is a rare stroke of luck if people, in their late teens and early twenties, have a clear and reliable premonition of what they want to become ten or twenty years down the road. Most people do not have that kind of predictive certainty—not in their late teens, early twenties, or at any other time in their lives. But it's not only your lack of ability to predict at the beginning of a programme whether that subject will matter to you greatly after you have completed it. Based on your initial experience in your first programme, you will be better equipped to decide on your next programme or your opportunities to enter the job market. Yes, you can do something different. Indeed, applying to jobs or entering new programmes that differ from your original trajectory can help you build a stronger uniqueness among other applicants. You may, if you position yourself suitably, generate considerable advantage compared to other applicants, since you are less comparable. You stand out. That can be an advantageous position—and it can be a problem.

However, if you are of a more diverse curiosity, you will likely thrive around people who welcome and mirror this attitude. Those employers will seek more characteristic, interdisciplinary, and broad-minded candidates, and less streamlined ones. So don't worry too much about how anything less than a straight path might hurt your chances to progress. Your training in working systematically provides you the ability to contribute in many fields—not just the one you already know. If you are curious, it would be a shame to lose this curiosity to the walls of a straight career path.

In essence

- While you do now have some expertise in a field, do not feel overly constrained to stick to this field. An education should provide you with more freedom, not less.
- Chances are that now, several years after you first applied for your academic career, you are a different person with different perspectives because you have access to a greatly extended set of experiences and insights. Don't expect your decisions of years ago still to hold true today.
- When planning to use your freedom to make course corrections, always keep in mind the opportunities to make your experiences and insights converge with where you want to go next. Even though it might not be obvious at first sight, there are almost always opportunities to integrate experiences beneficially into future plans.

To reflect

- Where to next?
- Where are the opportunities to use what you have aggregated in terms of capabilities, experiences, and insights, in the setting you want to head towards?
- What helps you sustain the confidence needed to actually make use of your freedom to choose a professional life path?

Two travellers' tales

Louis loves his field. He has completed his Bachelor's, his Master's, and now his PhD in the same field, and even in more or less the same specialization of that field. Louis loves the sense of expertise, a growing reputation, and to finally get rid of the feeling of need to 'fake it until you make it'—he has made it, in this field. There is not much that would convince him to move to another field. There is just so much still to do, explore, and find out about his subject. A subject he thoroughly stands behind. Maybe, that is one of the biggest drivers of his commitment to the field: even though he has spent years exploring the subject, he has hardly ever discovered perspectives on the topic that he could not sympathize with. A great place to stick around and build a career. It's quick and easy for him to explain what he works on.

Yvonne enjoyed her Bachelor's programme, but got a distinct sense of needing a change of scenery for her Master's. So, she picked a programme that benefited from her undergraduate experience, but added enough new impulses and perspectives. When her Master's thesis came around, the same experience struck again. She started working, and after a few years returned to university to add a PhD. She found a programme in which she could apply both her previous academic and practical experiences, but in yet another field. Yvonne feels like a fish in water when she thinks about her academic career—it's not the individual field that fuels her enthusiasm, but her ability to connect the dots across fields and disciplines. For her, positioning has more to do with an attitude of advancement than with an occupied position. Of course, you should bring some time if you ask her what she does.

Devil's advocate

Going to extremes is hardly ever a good idea. Thus, even though we err on the side of keeping an open mind and giving exploration the upper hand rather than stagnating in one field, it can become impossible to build a reputation among more orthodox disciplines if you start working in an inter-disciplinary fashion. Thus, it is important to consider your decision with the field you are in and the fields you would be interested in advancing towards in mind. Satisfying the urge to explore is lovely, but building a sustain-able positioning in which you can support yourself is not only sensible, but critical.

How to tackle

This mindset predominantly deals with avoiding anything that suggests rules you ought to adhere to. Providing a conceptual approach for that would be besides the point. Go forth, be free. Do what you like. Interpret yourself.

We are aware this encouragement can feel particularly difficult. But everyone around you is constantly faced by that very challenge. Following an established career path can make this much easier. But is this being free? It certainly might if you want it to be.

Fortify your academic skills

You invested greatly in an intellectual cultivation. It will begin to erode in your next job on day one. Protect what you invested so patiently in.

Metaphorically speaking

While research may look like an intellectual travel agency from the outside, with all those people planning and undertaking mental and methodological trips to places they find interesting, it may be more difficult to appreciate that it's not mere tourism. Research trains a sense of how to prepare for a journey, how to keep motivating yourself to put one foot in front of the other, and how to scale sheer cliffs of methodology and not fall off. All of these individual capabilities come together in a way of thinking, experiencing, and steering journeys. Therein lies the subtle fabric of what is to be learned when doing research.

Consequently, try to get a sense of what lies beneath all the careful phrasing of research questions, prior research, methodology, analysis, writing, and so on. What does it mean to you? Since you may continue by leaving the academic context, the chances are high that you will be confronted by many ways of approaching challenges that are rather foreign to this sense of insightfully, objectively, and carefully exploring questions to generate answers. In a way, you have been trained as a professional, appreciative, and responsible mountain guide, but you are now entering the job market in the tourism industry. The sense instilled by your training is likely to come under pressure.

Research cultivates a way of thinking and self-leadership that is distinct from the impressions other activities leave you with. It is a highly critical, highly differentiating, sensitive, and precise way of appreciating the complexities and implications of subjects and methodologies. To a degree, your mind has turned into a finely tuned and highly specialized mechanism that can produce reliable and valid insight. That is the value of an academic education. Keeping this machine tuned and as sharp as possible will determine how much and for how long you will generate benefit from your education.

The Student's Research Companion. Omid Aschari and Benjamin Berghaus, Oxford University Press.
© Omid Aschari and Benjamin Berghaus (2023). DOI: 10.1093/oso/9780192855312.003.0051

Rough coordinates

Sustain—'To keep in existence, maintain; spec. to cause to continue in a certain state for an extended period or without interruption; to keep or maintain at the proper level, standard, or rate; to preserve the status of.'

Versatile—'Marked or characterized by changeability or inconstancy; subject to change or fluctuation; variable, changeable. Of persons: turning easily or readily from one subject or occupation to another; having an aptitude or faculty for fresh pursuits or tasks; showing facility in varied subjects; many-sided.'

Skill—'Capability of accomplishing something with precision and certainty; practical knowledge in combination with ability; cleverness, expertness. Also, an ability to perform a function, acquired or learnt with practice.'

Protect—'To defend or guard from danger or injury; to support or assist against hostile or inimical action; to preserve from attack, persecution, harassment, etc.; to keep safe, take care of; to extend patronage to; to shield from attack or damage.'

Train of thought

If your journey has gained you one particular advantage over everyone who has not made a comparable experience, it is that you are, by now, quite well versed in how to travel. You might, indeed, consider your ability to pack lightly, to plan out your itinerary, to find your stride, a certain type of superpower. In the end, you can endure long treks, you can cross mountain ranges, and you will likely reach the other side—wherever that other side might be.

In other words, you have picked up a mighty, versatile, and useful skill set that will remain yours to benefit from: the ability to apply scientific methodology in solving challenges that come your way. Don't forget that this methodology is not limited to the handful of specific methods you applied in class or in your thesis. If you look beyond these few specific approaches, you will find that your abilities to work with existing literature are considerably strengthened. Now you can stand on the shoulders of giants you did not even know before. Your abilities to critically question insights and tell the more from the less solid findings have developed with time. Now you can tell the bridges you can cross safely from those which you should avoid. Finally, your mental skills to endure an intellectually demanding, complex, and long-term project have strengthened. Now, you can be more certain that you will be able to weather most of what your career might throw at you. In short: you have trained and developed abilities that will help you outlast many others who did not have the fortune of a well-used academic education.

After you leave university, however, you will notice several alternative routes to take from observing other people considering how they might face and overcome a challenge. Picking a scientific approach to solving a challenge is just one of many solution strategies. Chances are that, in your first job, one of the more senior people around you will suggest that whatever you learned in university is invalid 'in the real world', and that they are not going to explain 'how the real world works'. This is commonly the introduction to a more or less sophisticated alternative problem-solution approach which they feel more comfortable with. It might be acting particularly as politically intelligent, financially keen, disruptive, innovative, particularly risk-taking or risk-averse, or just plain lazy. Those who want to share their insight into 'how the real world works' may present an interesting perspective, but we'd encourage you to consider it carefully and critically, and not take it at face value. Often, these views are of limited inspiration, seemingly shared to cement their sponsors' position and current conditions.

Be this as it may, you have invested several years of your life to adopt the sense of scientific problem-solving. Do not be afraid (or maybe just too unaware of it) to use it. You can steer your mind to apply a methodologically reasonable approach to solve challenges that you, your team, or your company face. In a way, your training might even make it feel difficult to accept alternative approaches to problems. This does not imply that you would know better what to do—in most instances, you lack one of the most valuable resources: experience. But you have a sense of which approach will yield more robust and reliable insights, and how you need to handle yourself when implementing your approach. You have been through the desert of a thesis before, you know your way around.

Try not to discount, disregard, or lose your scientific mind along the way. You (and, likely, many taxpayers) invested dearly in your specific type of superpower.

In essence

- Having followed and completed your academic programme, you will be imprinted to a certain degree by thinking scientifically. Consider this the main benefit of your training, your academic superpower.

- Many people at the beginning of your career will try to discount your academically trained insight and way of thinking. This seems to be a bad habit of many experienced practitioners—maybe just a way to underscore their own importance.
- Try not to abandon your scientific mind in favour of the alternative problem-solving approaches offered to you.

To reflect

- Can you tell how your training has transformed your way of thinking about problems and solving challenges?
- Have you already experienced a practitioner trying to tell you that you're just book-smart and that they are going to tell you how the real world works? What did you answer?
- How can you best protect your investment into learning how to think scientifically about a challenge?

Two travellers' tales

Xiana is happy to have finally crossed the threshold between the academic and the real world, as she puts it. Not that she disliked studying and enjoy her time at university. It's just that she is thoroughly excited to finally put what she learned to good use. In her new job, she has found new ideas, new problems, and new techniques to solve these problems. Every once in a while, she wonders in which regard, exactly, her academic programme helped prepare her for this job—except for providing her with the certificate necessary to apply. Somehow, her new environment seems to have swiped away most of what she spent years on at university. As if it never happened.

Karl is glad to finally start into his career as well. He seeks positions that bear some resemblance to the activities he enjoyed at university. His goal is to try to apply and further cultivate what he learned in university—finally, with 'real' data and working on 'real' challenges instead of exercises. He notices the difference in cultures between his workplace and his university, and realizes that he will probably need to learn some new tricks. But Karl does not really want to lose what he invested in as a student. It's been four years of his life, altogether. It would be a waste to let what he learned go to waste.

Devil's advocate

While it may be true that an academic education can develop talented minds to produce excellent contributions, there is a well-known phenomenon whereby people with high expertise can not communicate their insights to those audiences that might generate practical benefit from it. Retaining a scientific mind determines how long you will generate benefit from your education, but developing and maintaining a sense of how to explain your thoughts to those more practically inclined is the other, critical component of making a contribution. Part of that means training your patience while explaining, consciously appreciating that different people bring different talents, and that no amount of expertise can replace friendly, courteous, and helpful conduct. One traditional and noteworthy occupational habit of academics to be kept in mind—and ideally in check—is the tendency to think and work yourself into isolated topical silos rather than branching out into a connected and integrated understanding of the world.

How to tackle

Given the option to choose your solution strategy, consider approaching challenges with the tools and strategies you learned in your academic programme. This might mean insights as pragmatic as concepts you have picked up and found useful, or skills as abstract as staying critical in your assessment, systematic in your analysis, following the facets of academic rigour, using curiosity and discipline when they are needed, and so on.

There will not always be the option to select your solution strategy—especially if your task includes a briefed-solution strategy. This might relate to politics in your work environment, power struggles, procedural guidelines, and many more tactics that are common in modern-day office work. In a way, you can adopt your academic skills in any of these scenarios, but many of them do not synchronize well with your academic mind in terms of the desired result. In practice, the overarching goal will often be to get things done on time (ASAP), within budget (low), and at desired quality (good enough)—not necessarily a carefully developed and more reliable insight into a subject. They are not mutually exclusive, but the goal systems typically are conceptually different.

In some instances, you may need to cut sharper corners on quality and analytical depth than you would ideally like. This will wear on your understanding of which level of quality truly 'does the job', since eventually, more or less any level of quality work 'will do'. While there are certainly many highly professional work environments out there—there must be—you will find more that you will come to understand as 'cooking with water', if that. This does not mean being over-critical of practical work, merely a difference in goal systems: practice tends to optimize for getting things done for keeping the system productive and synchronized, while academia optimizes for careful and robust development to provide grounds that others may build upon. In this trade-off, try whenever you get the opportunity to protect, train, and apply the skills you have developed.

Experienced peers' two cents

'Students can show and educate themselves on why we are doing things in the business world. So that we are not only focusing on how, but also why. Learning the theoretical underpinnings of the business world. Their education becomes more future-proof this way. Students don't only educate themselves on the problems of today, but they understand why they have to solve challenges today, and that will allow them to tackle challenges of the future.

'In the business disciplines, everybody is speaking about artificial intelligence, machine learning, robots, but the value of being able to think and argue is not going to decrease. The repetitive tasks that we do will be done by robots in the future. To teach how to hold the hammer when you're trying to hammer a nail—that will be less valuable in the future because, for all those simple things that everyone can understand, there will be another solution. Rather, being creative, also being able to apply theoretical knowledge—I doubt that this will go out of fashion.' (Timo Korkeamäki)

'Einstein once said that imagination is more important than knowledge. It was not his general theory of relativity, but rather that he saw metaphysics. He enjoined using his imagination.

'For students to adopt this mindset, they need to understand why it is critical to think like heroes in science. Einstein, Curie, and Darwin are good examples. I would start with asking the students: what made these heroes what they were? They were thinking the world. They were exploring Whyquestions. Ask what the problem is they are trying to solve (or contribute towards solutions). Why is something as it is? Why is the sunset coloured the way it is? These are the big questions that makes one think differently.

'Soon one becomes aware that one lacks the skill set to overcome these hurdles. We don't need to get discouraged by that. Usually, it means I have to develop a certain skill set, acquire a specific knowledge, read, collaborate. Who do I need to work with to do that? This allows people to focus on the skills that are necessary to solving those problems. It is a more goal-oriented approach, that requires putting yourself more into the background. In other words, it is not so much an environment for "ego's". You need to always enjoy the perspectives that other people can bring. The "how" involves doing good science and research on the way to the discovery.' (Gundula Bosch)

Grow forward

Remember how your thesis meant bringing the will to grow? This ability to consciously grow is one of the most useful lessons of a final academic project.

Metaphorically speaking

While research can lead you to many places, it does predominantly train a specific set of muscles. Occasionally, you feel as though you want to continue and continue training these muscles, and at others, you get that distinct sense of training something else for a while—maybe to return later. Both your sense of curiosity and your capability to investigate things you are interested in are, luckily, very portable and broadly applicable skills.

Consequently, try to get a sense of the way you want to grow next and follow that sense. You do not need to stick to what you have done before— even though there are some advantages to building up a distinct track record. Growing is more about understanding in how many ways you can grow (plenty), and making conscious decisions how to grow next and how much growth you're up to shouldering in the following months and years.

Research, to a degree, trains your motivation and ability to grow. Try to get a sense of how many ways you can interpret growth for you personally. Even though academic programmes which serve hundreds of people at once may suggest otherwise, your sense and experience of growth is individual. You may choose to join others on their trajectory, but you are also free to find your own path.

Rough coordinates

Sustain—'To keep in existence, maintain; spec. to cause to continue in a certain state for an extended period or without interruption; to keep or maintain at the proper level, standard, or rate; to preserve the status of.'

The Student's Research Companion. Omid Aschari and Benjamin Berghaus, Oxford University Press.
© Omid Aschari and Benjamin Berghaus (2023). DOI: 10.1093/oso/9780192855312.003.0052

Growth—'The action, process or manner of growing; both in material and immaterial senses; vegetative development; increase. The process of causing or assisting to grow; production by cultivation.'

Path—'A course of action; a way of proceeding; a mode of behaviour or conduct; esp. a way of life leading to a spiritual goal. Also: a sequence of events or operations; the course of a person's life; (occasionally) a line of thought, argument, etc.'

Encouragement—'To inspire with courage sufficient for any undertaking; to embolden, make confident. To stimulate (persons or personal efforts) by assistance, reward, or expressions of favour or approval; to countenance, patronize; also, in bad sense, to abet. To allow or promote the continuance or development of (a natural growth, an industry, a sentiment, etc.); to cherish, foster.'

Train of thought

Since you've travelled, you might feel like sitting down for a bit. Maybe stay where you are and reap the rewards of your advancement. If you enjoyed 'being on the road', however, you will likely only be able to endure remaining stationary for a limited time. As soon as a few weeks have passed, you'll think about new destinations. A month or two later, you'll consider first plans for your next excursion. And before you know it, you're in the middle of your next adventure—however different this may look.

Even though graduation from your programme will suggest to you that you have arrived, that you have grown, and that you have reached the level of capabilities that can rightfully be certified, this will likely only satisfy you in the long term if you really did not enjoy your individual experience of facing that particular challenge. Especially if you had a positive overall experience with growing through learning and challenging yourself, you'll add the mode of being challenged as one of the sources by which you can and like to be excited.

In most cases, however, it's impractical to study one programme right after another because you want to grow in so many directions. Even though you are free to do so, you will find that while the subject and even the methodologies change, the higher-order capabilities that you adopt—working according to scientific principles—will remain roughly comparable. Thus, you'd find that you'd learn and relearn the same capabilities.

Consequently, the proposal to keep growing is instead directed at finding your own path, along which you'd like to grow next. Often, it will mean that you will try to look at your capabilities from a different angle. Maybe you will grow into a leadership role. Perhaps you will grow more thoroughly into your subject as an expert. Maybe you will grow into a more holistic role as an entrepreneur in your subject. All these options offer the opportunity to apply your key skill set of being able to coordinate yourself while growing, maintaining your motivation and energy levels, working through rough patches, and in the end succeeding.

Any recommendation to keep growing comes with the encouragement to purposefully reflect, reinterpret, and recreate your own path based on what you have achieved so far. The tripling of the prefix 're-' already suggests that 'to keep growing' is a recursive challenge that will never be fully achieved and will demand a curiously large degree of introspection—perhaps more introspection than your sense of what might be *en vogue* with other people. Growth is a constant development that builds on what you have today. Think of it as interest that continuously accrues on the sum of your aggregated advances. However, since you're in the position to determine and define the amount of interest, you are allowing your own maturing to materialize.

There is another critical piece of encouragement that is required here: do not be afraid to trust in your own ability to assess your situation, draft a plan of your next steps, and then continue on your path. There is no blueprint for your growth process. There may be plenty of exemplary cases around you on how to grow and what to reach, but there are no guarantees that you can simply follow another person's path and reach the same destination. It all comes down to whether you trust your judgment, your capabilities to synthesize your own plans and make them come to life. The good news here is that this is precisely what you trained for in your final academic project, on the most meta level: your objective judgment, your careful planning, and your determined implementation. You can do that. Trust that you can be successful. Not (only) because you've been encouraged, but because smart people have taught you well and trust you enough to carry their academic degree. They would not have graduated you if there was considerable doubt in your abilities. So, why should you doubt them?

In essence

- Try to keep growing. Not because that always sounds like a good idea, but because your successful training suggests that you might be good at it. So, why not continue doing that?

- Interpreting what 'growth' may mean to you personally requires a sizeable or increasing sense of respect towards your slowly emerging and recognizable personal preferences. To grow, you need to first understand what kind of person you would like to grow into.
- Finally, growth requires a constant effort of self-assessment, planning, and implementation. This takes more confidence, courage, and energy than the alternative, stagnation.

To reflect

- What kind of person do you want to grow into, next?
- How could you go about periodically and purposefully reviewing your status quo, reinterpreting your trajectory, and setting a new heading?
- What helps you feel confident enough to follow or create your own path instead of feeling obliged to follow others?

Two travellers' tales

Zuzanna has completed her Bachelor's degree last year, and continues by doing her Master's in the same field without thinking much about alternatives. Most of her colleagues are taking this route, and it seems like a plan that is not often questioned—so it seems to be the right way to go. While it does feel a little like more of the same, she is optimistic that the university has carefully designed a great learning experience for her that sensibly builds on top of what she did in her Bachelor's. During her new programme, she got the sense that the most likely experience came true: it was a bit more of the same, but she also took away some new experiences. Now she is really looking forward to the job market—this was a lot of studying!

Michael is happy to have completed his Bachelor's degree last year. He has a distinct feeling that he will start to work for one of the employers in his field for a while. It seems to him that he's done nothing but exercising the theoretical and methodological side of his brain for a few years, with no exercise at all for his practical mind or his hands. He simply does not want to grow further in that direction, for a while. So: regular job market it is. Even though many of his colleagues continue on to do their Master's, he simply feels more balanced and happier not sticking to that one particular set of skills. Three years later, he continues with his Master's degree. Now, he has the added advantage of actually having seen in the wild what many of his fellow students have merely read about in books.

Devil's advocate

Growth costs energy. Thus, growth is something that must be afforded. In that sense, growth occurs when you are in the privileged position of being able to afford it. If your personal, health, financial, family, or any other context draws energy from you—and this is a reality for the majority of people—have mercy concerning how much growth you ask from yourself. There is no sense in setting yourself up for continuous exhaustion. Grow with care for yourself and others.

How to tackle

One way of implementing the idea of 'keeping growing' is to think about future employment, commitments, engagements, and associations, not only in terms of how much they pay and which titles and potential they might come with, but whether they will be great opportunities for you to develop into a direction that you would like.

There are plenty of environments in which you may generate much income, climb the career ladder, and acquire shiny roles and titles—but they simply do not allow you to branch out into areas that seem particularly fulfilling to you. Of course, you may bear in mind the level of remuneration, but our experience and observations suggest that going and growing against the grain of your personality and abilities comes at a high toll for the energy that you will have available.

'Compensation schemes' have their name for a reason. Consider what a seemingly great opportunity aims to compensate you for. Are you willing to be compensated for that? Do you have a sufficient understanding of what it is you will be paid to do and are you willing to do that – removing the compensation from the picture, for a moment? Be attentive to the sensation of growing in a suitable or unsuitable direction, of learning something you will want to build upon or being taught something you wish you had never learned.

Experienced peers' two cents

'Another skill comes into play here: independent study skills. Students need to select their topic, their area of focus, the resources that will be useful. Even if they will be getting support from their supervisor, there are many things to do on their own which develops their independent study skills. That will be a lifelong asset for everyone who goes through this process—not only completing their thesis but picking up skills that will be useful in any field, wherever they go—even if they do not pursue research degrees or further education.' (Madhu Neupane Bastola)

Share the fire

Once you have discovered your way of facing and overcoming an intellectual challenge, consider helping others to discover and find their way.

Metaphorically speaking

No matter how you cut it: research means taking a very long hike towards your destination. This hike is exhausting. Many people take this hike simply because others say they need to do it to have their hiking skills judged, to get a hiking certificate. And then there are those who found their love for hiking, for exploring, for becoming more athletic, for being out in the fresh air, for experiencing nature. To those people, hiking tends to be less strenuous. And they are usually good at inspiring others, explaining why hiking makes more sense than just being judged for hiking skills.

There is no obligation to share with others how you access the fun and purpose in research. But there is great reward connected to it. Inspiration shared is inspiration doubled—especially if you inspire a young and energetic mind with an attitude that will help their curiosity paired with their skills go a long way. Multiply that potential by roughly 50 million graduates around the world, each year, and the advantage of sharing inspiration for research becomes even more palpable.

Research, to a degree, also means sharing an impression of what curiosity and skills can accomplish, of why research matters. Since it has nothing to do with methodology, theory, or practical implications, this aspect is all too often overlooked or brushed off as a subjective bit of sense-making that is pure motivational nectar to anyone who is trying to understand why they should get thoroughly engaged in a research project.

The Student's Research Companion. Omid Aschari and Benjamin Berghaus, Oxford University Press.
© Omid Aschari and Benjamin Berghaus (2023). DOI: 10.1093/oso/9780192855312.003.0053

Rough coordinates

Inspire—'To infuse some thought or feeling into (a person, etc.), as if by breathing; to animate or actuate by some mental or spiritual influence. To influence, animate, or actuate (a person) with a feeling, idea, impulse, etc.'

Lonely—'Having no companionship or society; unaccompanied, solitary, lone.'

Transaction—'That which is or has been transacted; an affair in course of settlement or already settled; a piece of business; in plural doings, proceedings, dealings.'

Transformation—'The action of changing in form, shape, or appearance; metamorphosis.'

Train of thought

Once you've travelled this far, we'd like to encourage you to try to inspire others to travel more as well. Given that you've crossed deserts, navigated the seas, and overcome challenging peaks and gorges, it would be a loss not to have you share your insights to help others find their motivation and their confidence, and maybe renew their strength to complete their next journey. Remember how lonely exploration can feel? How utterly segregated it seems to be working through mountains of material and wondering whether you will ever reach your destination?

The central reason behind this request of ours is that we have found many modern academic and work environments to be less than inspiring to most people enrolled or employed there. Many settings offer mostly transactional experiences—get task, perform task, get grade/get paid. While transformational experiences are on the rise in professional settings, they often seem to be motivated by capturing and retaining the workforce rather than by truly and thoroughly reviewing the reasons and incentives we work for.

Realism suggests that transactional relationships are likely here to stay. The advertising of a more transformational outlook on the opportunities that life presents to you tend to sound more idealistic. But there is a useful bridge to be built between the two perspectives: except for the bleakest projects, there is more than a single reason to engage a project. Meaningful projects commonly include a number of payoffs. Many of these pay-offs even interact with each other. Making the effort to try to identify in how many ways a project can generate benefits is the bridgehead from a strictly transactional to a more transformative look at why we do what we do. In fact, keeping in mind all the reasons why pursuing a project makes sense is much more complex than the much more easily perceived sense of 'because it feels like the right thing to do for me'. And we are half-way to a transformational perspective. A key component here: the versatile pay-off of investing yourself in a project is subjective. While research and its methodology may be as objective, the reason you pursue a project greatly depends on what you as a researcher value. The reason we pursue our individual projects is subjective. Keeping this apparent juxtaposition of appropriate mental states in mind and knowing where to draw the line between what you are encouraged to decide for yourself and where you need to adhere to other researcher's recommendations is not always easy.

When it comes to inspiring others to make as much as they can out of their research opportunities, it might just take reminding people of how many ways their project can generate value for them—if they engage it more thoroughly than merely trying to get it over with. While the combination of motives will be thoroughly individual, what matters is the diversity, interconnectedness, and perceived relevance of motives in the individual researcher. Conversely, there is not much to be won from a project that is merely done for credit and certification. Several months of lifetime and work are simply too high a price for merely participating in an administrative act.

While much about modern universities may suggest that their key contribution is to generate a certified workforce, we hope that this book has supported your convictions that an academic education can and should do more. It ought to inspire young people to develop and maintain their curiosity, and put it to good use in projects that help us all to learn about the world.

In essence

- Once you've come as far as you have—in your research process and in this book—we would like to encourage you to share your insights and energy with others still undecided about whether the research experience can be useful for them.
- Realism suggests that people do research for some sort of transactional profit—grades, certifications, points. We suggest that the bridge between a transactional mindset (I do this because I get X for doing it) and a transformational mindset (e.g. I do this because I want to grow) is simply to broaden the horizon of possible benefits until individual benefit dissolves in a sense of broader purpose.

- The years of an academic programme and months of a thesis cannot only be justified by a certification process for the later career. They need to come with a notable sense of maintaining curiosity and putting it to good use.

To reflect

- What are good ways of inspiring students to take on opportunities such as the final academic project in a thorough and engaged way, instead of merely getting it done?
- What can help tilt the scales in favour of more involved and motivated individual projects at university?
- Who is already on board with this mindset? Who is on the fence? Whom will this never reach?

Two travellers' tales

Nick is happy that he has completed his academic programme. He is thoroughly looking forward to the beginning of his career, and does not shed too many tears about leaving university. After leaving the university, he rarely looks back and instead considers his new environment to be 'the real world'. Even though he receives invitations from his alumni club every once in a while, he hardly ever considers actually connecting with current or former students of his programme. Work is for him: university is in his past.

Andrea is happy she has completed her academic programme. She looks back onto her time at university with mixed feelings: many friends she met; many late hours worked; many pointless exercises; but also several instances of feeling that she learned, grew, and could apply her curiosity. It seems to her that university meant most to her when she found the opportunity to make projects count. When she found the perspective that enabled her to fully engage herself, rather than just following instructions. She wants to help other students to find the perspectives that help them get more engaged and generate insightful and purposeful moments for themselves. She engages herself in mentoring programmes, and when there's an opportunity to share perspectives or inspiration on how to make university a purposeful place, she's game.

Devil's advocate

Inspiring others means just that—not to sugar-coating, selling, or advertising what we do. Those who we try to win over and persuade to immerse and engage themselves in research are smart enough to build strong defences to anything that is being actively marketed. Here, 'inspiring' might simply mean sharing what purposeful research looks like to us, and how holistically satisfying it is to see it come together. If enough researchers would share more often what inspires them about their work, many diversely motivated populations of students will find those narratives they can identify with.

How to tackle

Efficient ways of inspiring others usually does not come with a predefined structure or concept, a programme to sign up for or a group to join. Even mentoring programmes with your university are not always designed for that one specific function, rather than many functions.

To try to inspire others to make more of the opportunities that they are presented with takes rather basic requirements and skills. First, try to be available to those who seek your opinion or guidance. When you get the chance to hear someone's thoughts about how to tackle their next step, use the opportunity to formulate your perspective and share your experience.

Second, role modelling goes a long way: not only does it provide a palpable example for how trying to implement transformational self-leadership and career building, but it also provides you with the need and the guidelines to walk your own talk as much as pragmatically possible. Role modelling also entails that you possibly never fully embody the concept of immersing yourself in the work itself, and not just be driven by the reward, but that you try to adjust your perspective towards what you believe in and not towards what might seem the most established in your given environment.

Third, keep seeking. As an extension to the idea of attempting to role-model your way and inspire others, set out to keep an open mind about what your destination might finally look like. Exactly because you are on your journey because you like to travel, it is perfectly fitting to consider your destination always a bit ahead of you, around the next bend, and over the next hill. In the end, reaching it is secondary—travelling there is most of the fun.

Experienced peers' two cents

'We cannot give what we do not have. If we do not know how to improve their research, how can we guide students? Supervisors need to be continuous learners. Difficulties will be there—there are many students. But only if we take the responsibility of supervision sincerely can we make a difference. One of our goals is to become better supervisors every year.' (Madhu Neupane Bastola)

Index